Egypt's Beer

# Egypt's Beer

*Stella, Identity, and the Modern State*

Omar D. Foda

University of Texas Press ⌇ Austin

Requests for permission to reproduce material from this work should be sent to:

Permissions

University of Texas Press

P.O. Box 7819

Austin, TX 78713-7819

utpress.utexas.edu/rp-form

♾ The paper used in this book meets the minimum requirements of
ANSI/NISO Z39.48–1992 (R1997) (Permanence of Paper).

Library of Congress Cataloging-in-Publication Data

Names: Foda, Omar D., author.
Title: Egypt's beer : Stella, identity, and the modern state / Omar D. Foda.
Description: First edition. | Austin : University of Texas Press, 2019. |
Includes bibliographical references and index.
Identifiers: LCCN 2018057426
    ISBN 978-1-4773-1954-3 (cloth : alk. paper)
    ISBN 978-1-4773-1955-0 (pbk. : alk. paper)
    ISBN 978-1-4773-1956-7 (library ebook)
    ISBN 978-1-4773-1957-4 (non-library ebook)
Subjects: LCSH: Beer—Egypt—History. | Beer industry—Egypt—History. |
Beer industry—Government policy—Egypt. | Beer industry—Political aspects—
Egypt. | Drinking of alcoholic beverages—Egypt—Religious aspects—Islam. |
Stella (Beer)—History.
Classification: LCC HD9397.E32 F63 2019 | DDC 338.4/7663420962—dc23
LC record available at https://lccn.loc.gov/2018057426

doi:10.7560/319543

# CONTENTS

All translations are my own unless noted otherwise. For transliterations, I have used the simplified *International Journal of Middle East Studies* system. Diacritical marks have been omitted for proper names, which have, when possible, been rendered in the accepted English form—e.g., Gamal Abdel Nasser instead of Jamal ʿabd al-Nasir. Citations for the Egyptian National Archives use the new system classifications in lieu of the old folder numbers.

# ABBREVIATIONS

| | |
|---|---|
| AH | Archives of Heineken NV |
| CB | Crown Brewery |
| Cobra | N. V. Koloniale Brouwerijn |
| DD | Diwan al-Dakhiliyya (Department of the Interior) |
| DWQ | Dar al-Wathaʾiq al-Qaymiyya (Egyptian National Archives) |
| EK | Erick Carl Kettner |
| HBM | Heineken Bierbrouwerij Maatschappij N. V. |
| IOF | Ismail Omar Foda Personal Collection |
| MS | Maslahat al-Sharikat (Department of Companies Archives) |
| OTOC | Office des Territoires Occupés et Contrôles (Maktab al-Bilad al-Muhtala wa al-Khadiʿ li-l-Riqaba; Office of Occupied and Controlled Territories) |
| PB | Pyramid Brewery, Société Anonyme de Bière "Les Pyramides" SAE |
| SAA | Stadsarchief Amsterdam |
| WvH | Oscar Adrian Eduard Egbert Lewe Wittert van Hoogland |

# The Egyptian Beer Industry

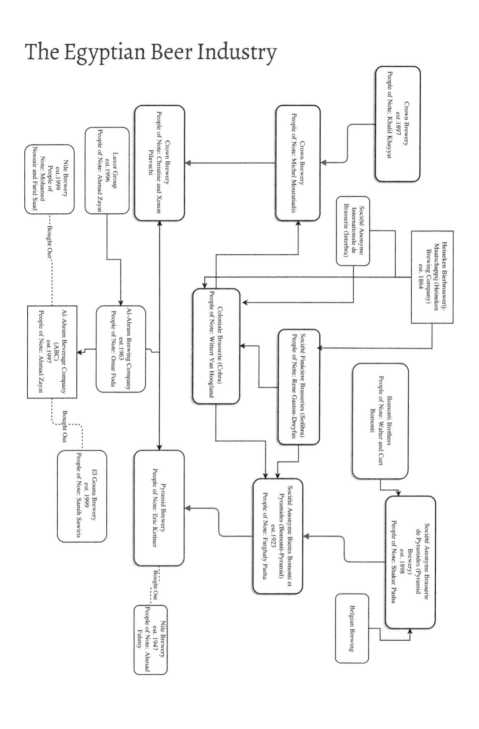

You know, without doubt, every group of people needs a distraction.
For example, there's arak in Turkey and Lebanon. We wish for beer to
become the popular drink in Egypt. It is my pleasure to inform you
that it was the ancient Egyptians who first manufactured beer.
—Isma'il Hafiz to Gamal Abdel Nasser, January 3, 1960

When I read the above words, said by an employee of the Cairo-based Pyramid Brewery to the president of the republic of Egypt in 1960, I was shocked.
Not because I thought the quest to make beer the distraction of the Muslim-
majority country of Egypt was quixotic, if not downright delusional. I was
shocked because these words, which I came upon in the middle of my research for this book, confirmed something I, but very few others, believed:
that beer, specifically Stella beer, was an inseparable part of Egyptian culture.

A Western audience may strain to understand how this fact is anything
more than frivolous trivia. Are there not more important things to talk about
when thinking about Egypt? Its post-1960 economic struggles and uncertain
political future? Where it fits in the "Islamization" of the region overall? No,
finding an Egyptian beer cannot provide tidy answers to policy questions.
But as this book shows, finding an Egyptian beer, and understanding its history, can help us grapple with the major economic, political, and cultural
issues that face the country today.

Beyond grounding some of the most critical contemporary issues for
an outsider, how Egyptians remember this beer is vital to Egyptians themselves. It taps into a still unresolved battle about the very nature of Egyptian identity that, since the 1970s, has cleaved the country into two. There
are Egyptians who would say that of course there is an Egyptian beer; it is
called Stella beer. They remember fondly the days when flashing, neon-lit
Stella-beer advertisements were common sights on buildings in downtown
Cairo. There are others who would answer no. They recognize the existence
of Stella but group it with the rest of the foreign alcoholic beverages that signified the moral corruption of Egypt brought by foreign regimes, Western-
looking elites, and deluded and failed governments. Between the 1950s and
1980s, it was the first answer—"Yes, Egypt has a beer!"—that shaped Egyptian government policy and popular culture. However, from the 1990s on-

ward, it has been the second answer, "no," that has come to predominate. All public traces (advertisements, signs, commercials, etc.) of Stella, and other alcoholic beverages, have disappeared as ostensible affronts to Egypt's sensibilities and Islamic culture.

This study argues, in short, that there was unquestionably an Egyptian beer called Stella. Stella, and beer making in general, was a consistently popular and profitable enterprise in the Muslim-majority context of Egypt. Despite political, social, and economic changes—and changes in its public visibility—it won a large popular following among middle-class men and women. Its story illuminates vital issues in modern Egypt's historical trajectory.

However, Stella did not appear fully formed as the Egyptian beer par excellence. It, like many who have come to the country, was Egyptianized. Using American, Dutch, and Egyptian archival sources, as well as Arabic literary, audio, and visual sources, this book tells three interlinked stories about Stella's Egyptianization: the transformation of two companies, Crown and Pyramid Breweries, the sellers of Stella, from transnational beer ventures into unequivocally Egyptian companies; the transformation of the product itself from a foreign and vaguely illicit product to an unquestionably Egyptian one; and the transformation of brewing technology from foreign importations to accepted methods of Egyptian beer making. These transformations happened during an exciting period, from 1882 until 1980, spanning Egypt's move from a quasi-colonial state under British Occupation to an independent country within a highly competitive global economy.

However, Stella's Egyptianization was not the end of its story. This book also examines the struggle of Stella to thrive in post-1980 Egypt. In the 1980s and 1990s, Stella began to fade into the background as the pillars of its success—its popularity among the middle class, its government support, and its high quality—collapsed. Its middle-class audience diminished as the very definition of what it meant to be Egyptian changed. Due to a mix of begrudging government support, growing cultural contact with conservative Gulf regimes, and the power of the message of political Islam, more middle-class Egyptians came to believe that Islam was the essential feature of Egyptian identity. This change was matched with growing public religiosity, which made Stella's presence in Egyptian culture uncomfortable.

As the market dwindled, so did the support of the government. In their desire to fix Egypt's fundamental economic problems, the government pushed for the liberalization of the economy. While the wholesale privatization of the economy was slow going, their policies did open Egypt up to foreign capital and companies. Likewise, the government was doing its own work to equate Egyptian identity with public religiosity.

But these issues may have been easily overcome if the quality of the beer had remained. However, with the loss of their director of twenty years, Ismail Omar Foda, in 1985, Stella lost one of its greatest advocates. From that point on, its decline was noticeable. Stella went from Egypt's choice of beer to the butt of jokes.

This was not the end of Stella and the company that sold it, al-Ahram Brewing Company, which had formed out of the conglomerated Pyramid and Crown Breweries. As part of President Hosni Mubarak's push for privatization, al-Ahram came under the control of an Egyptian American business group led by Ahmed Zayat. Their takeover in 1996 was a return to the roots of the company. Zayat and his group were transnational, multiethnic, and multireligious, and they used their foreign business connections to bring new technology, new distribution methods, and new marketing campaigns. They even facilitated the reentry of Heineken into the Egyptian beer market, selling the company to them in 2003. Nevertheless, beer's place in Egypt remained ambiguous. And so it remains today, where the memories of its history are slowly disappearing.

To tell the story of Stella's rise as Egypt's beer and its struggle for continued relevance in contemporary Egypt, we must rely on a hybrid history. Instead of cordoning economic and cultural affairs apart from one another, this book shows that the two spheres make sense only when they are considered together. The need to connect the economic to the cultural is particularly pressing in the field of consumer goods, where a company's success or failure hinges upon its ability to embrace, reject, or even change cultural norms and practices. As such, this study looks at both macroeconomic matters (e.g., global economic integration and economic imperialism) and microeconomic matters (e.g., prices, consumption, and distribution) together with social and cultural issues, including the development of a middle class, the emergence of youth culture, the politicization of religion, and changing notions of entertainment in daily life.

In addition, this book adds to the growing literature on the history of technology. Specifically, it examines how technological advances—such as new techniques for brewing, refrigeration, and transport—not only undergirded trends and developments in Stella sales, but also shaped consumption patterns and altered cultural conceptions of food, drink, and nourishment. This study also illustrates how Stella beer, and the companies that sold it, succeeded because it used new technologies, like refrigeration, to exploit the inherent advantages of the Egyptian context, including an abundant water supply, a cheap labor force, and a large population. Thus, the history of technology will serve as another medium through which this study integrates the economic and cultural.

## How to Study Beer in Egypt

This monograph ties the history of Stella to larger conversations happening in the study of the intersection of society and economy in the Middle East. Most notably, Robert Vitalis, Relli Shechter, and Nancy Y. Reynolds provide fresh perspectives on Egyptian economic history by shifting the focus of study away from the traditional production-based outlook. In *When Capitalists Collide: Business Conflict and the End of Empire in Egypt*, Vitalis examines the composition and maneuverings of the executive sphere in the Egyptian private sector and shows how its foreign and native dimensions overlapped during the years from 1920 to 1955, a time when European and Egyptian businessmen shared common interests and capital ventures. In *Smoking Culture and Economy in the Middle East: The Egyptian Tobacco Market, 1850–2000*, Shechter conducts a microanalysis of the tobacco industry to provide insights into the social, cultural, and economic development of Egypt.

In *A City Consumed: Urban Commerce, the Cairo Fire, and the Politics of Decolonization in Egypt*, Reynolds examines the consumption habits of Egyptians in colonial and semicolonial Egypt—especially regarding apparel—during the period from 1882 to 1952 to assess larger cultural changes that were occurring in Egypt. Like the work of Shechter and Reynolds, my book draws from literature, film, and advertisements to craft an integrative socioeconomic history of Egypt. Unlike these two works, however, this study folds in technological history while examining, again, a truly unique product in Muslim-majority Egypt, locally produced beer.

This study also adds nuance to the field of the history of alcohol and other bottled beverages. For example, Iain Gately's *Drink: A Cultural History of Alcohol* considers alcohol's evolution across a vast expanse of time and space. While this type of work can no doubt provide interesting cross-cultural comparisons, its massive span limits the amount of meaningful conclusions that one can draw about Egypt or even the Middle East more broadly. Another example is John W. Alexander's *Brewed in Japan: The Evolution of the Japanese Beer Industry*, which narrows the focus to a certain time frame (1800–present), area (Japan), and beverage (beer) to produce more specific conclusions.

Likewise, Marie Sarita Gaytán's *Tequila! The Spirit of Mexico* uses a narrow scope to tell the history of an alcohol and its industry.

Scholars have begun to conduct these types of study on the history of the Middle East. Published in 2002, François Georgeon's article "Ottomans and Drinkers: The Consumption of Alcohol in Istanbul in the Nineteenth Century" was groundbreaking in its confirmation of the link between alcohol consumption and identity in the Middle East. Among the few works that delve into the history of alcohol in the nineteenth-century Ottoman world, it argues that starting in 1800, there was a change in attitudes among residents of Istanbul toward the consumption of alcohol. Alcohol was no longer a private habit, to drink in shady taverns on the edge of town, but became a way to "affirm [one's] adherence to the values of the modern world" by drinking in public places located in the heart of the city.[1] Malte Fuhrmann's 2014 article, "Beer, the Drink of a Changing World: Beer Consumption and Production on the Shores of the Aegean in the 19th Century," follows in the footsteps of Georgeon by studying the consumption and production of a specific alcoholic beverage, beer, in the Ottoman domains. Finally, Nathan Fonder's dissertation, "Pleasure, Leisure, or Vice? Public Morality in Imperial Cairo, 1882–1949," discusses how the morality of intoxicant consumption and gambling in Cairo was defined at the nexus of popular culture, the weak Egyptian state, and the British colonial presence.

This book engages with the issues raised in each of these works but provides a broader yet more focused view. Chronologically, it covers more than a hundred years of Egyptian history, starting from its colonization in 1882 and ending in the last decade of Hosni Mubarak's reign. However, its narrative is anchored to the story of one beer, Stella, and its connection to the major historical events transpiring in its more than century of existence. As I show, Stella's story offers a new and different understanding of Egypt's modern history.

My analysis is based heavily on archival records found in three countries: Egypt, the Netherlands, and the United States. In Egypt I focused on the Egyptian National Archives (Dar al-Wathaʾiq al-Qawmiyya) in Cairo and its Department of Companies Archives (Maslahat al-Sharikat), which, as its name suggests, preserves the histories of most of the major companies in Egypt from the 1920s to the 1950s. I also closely consulted the archive of Egyptian periodicals housed at the National Library (Dar al-Kutub) adjacent to the Egyptian National Archives. This archive was a fertile source for a wide variety of beer advertisements, which significantly shaped my understanding of how these companies aimed to sell beer to Egyptians. Unfortunately, due to the exigencies of publishing and the quality of the source material, I have been able to include only a small sampling. What has been included is the product of balancing the often countervailing purposes of maintaining the fidelity of the images and allowing them to be legible to the reader.

This book also uses the City Archives of Amsterdam to study the Heineken Brewing Company, which played a significant role in the Egyptian beverage industry. From the 1930s to the 1950s, Heineken was a major stockholder in Crown and Pyramid Breweries. It was only when the Nasser government nationalized these companies in 1963 that the relationship ended. However, nearly four decades after this nationalization, Heineken reentered the Egyptian beverage market when, in 2003, it bought al-Ahram Beverage Company (ABC), the successor to Pyramid and Crown Breweries, which by then had expanded to become Egypt's leading alcohol producer.

While Egypt and the Netherlands provide information on the internal workings of the beer industry and its international reach, the United States, specifically the Presbyterian Historical Society in Philadelphia, provides information on the cultural impact of the beer industry. Its records on the Presbyterian mission in Egypt underlie my discussion of the pitched cultural battle surrounding beer in Egypt that occurred in the period under study.

## The Outline of the Story

This book begins by considering the origins of beer manufacturing in Egypt in the period from 1880 to 1920. The first chapter observes the technological transition of beer production into an industrial concern in the nineteenth and twentieth centuries. I look at not only the technological innovations that initiated the industrialization of the beer industry (advances in the study of yeast, in refrigeration, in bottling, and in transportation infrastructure), but also how this history of advancement differed from traditional narratives of the East being "enlightened" by the West. The Egyptian beer industry flourished as a hybrid entity, one that was neither exclusively foreign nor Egyptian. This hybridity gave the industry both the foreign capital and the expertise to compete with the international brands and the local business connections and market familiarity to guard against the errors that a foreign venture would likely face. However, this powerful combination of foreign and local would not have worked were it not for the concomitant cultural changes that were taking place in Egypt. This period witnessed the rise of a new middle class of Egyptians, the effendis, who, in an attempt to meld both East and West, created their own distinctly Egyptian "modernity," signaled through the use of new social spaces and through the consumption of new products, including modes of dress. Because of beer's social value as a modern and secular product, many Egyptians found it to be a powerful tool for communicating identity.

Having sketched the general outlines of beer's entry and early development in Egypt, the rest of the book is dedicated to telling the story of one beer, Stella, and the companies that sold it, Crown and Pyramid Breweries. Chapter 2 details the origin of the product that sits at the center of this work, Stella beer. Stella grew out of the competition between Crown and Pyramid Breweries. Each dominated one of Egypt's major markets. Crown controlled Alexandria, Pyramid controlled Cairo, and they were both constantly looking to expand into the other. When it became apparent that neither had the money or technical ability to take full control of the country, they decided to work together. The child of this partnership was their premium offering, Stella. Although they did not know it at the time, this beer, bearing the Italian name and housing Egyptian ingredients, had found the market sweet spot. Its quality put it on par with the imported beers, but its low price made it a more attractive option for the growing number of beer consumers in the country.

Although the beer that would come to dominate Egypt, Stella, would start its ascent in the 1920s and 1930s, it was only during the World War II era when the companies that sold it, Crown and Pyramid Breweries, would find their formula for success. Looking at the period from 1940 to 1952, chapter 3 shows how these two companies became integral parts of the Heineken Brewing Company's international empire. During this time, Heineken became the lead investor in both breweries and set about not only increasing their say in all decisions the beer companies made, but also in streamlining the operations of both companies by consolidating them. This provided numerous positive effects on both the product and the company management. With a crisper and more consistent Stella, and the power of a multinational backing them, these two companies could weather the growing demands of the Egyptian government. This war-torn era provided the government a greater chance to monitor companies within its borders than ever before. This newfound opportunity, coupled with the rising tide of Egyptian economic nationalism, emboldened the Egyptian government to be more assertive in its relationship with limited liability companies, especially those with foreign ties.

As chapter 4 shows, the period from 1952 to 1958 marked both the cultural ascendency of Stella beer and the ever-increasing pressure of an activist Nasser-led government. In this period, Stella became a national product, with a standardized recipe and brand. Stella carved out its role as the refreshing drink of the summertime and as the drink immediately associated with youth, relaxation, and having a good time. Paradoxically, this occurred as Nasser's regime slowly worked to gain greater control of the private sector. To Nasser's way of thinking, the private sector was troublingly subject to the control of foreign capitalists and feudalists who were stifling the economic progress of Egypt. The most remarkable aspect of this period was the government's push for the "Egyptianization" of the financial sector, which entailed identifying "foreign" workers, executives, and sources of capital and finding native replacements for them. This process culminated with the Nasser government's nationalization of the Suez Canal in 1956.

After this point, as chapter 5 shows, it was a battle between the management of the Egyptian breweries and the Nasser government over what constituted a "model company" in the period from 1958 to 1961. For the management of the breweries, a model company was a profitable one that had the autonomy and the efficient, disciplined, and obedient workforce to implement Heineken's methods of brewing. For the Nasser-led government, a model company was one that would make large profits autonomously but was willing and able to mobilize in support of Nasser's grand projects, such as the United Arab Republic (UAR) and his vision for the Egyptian economy. It was Nasser's vision that won out when he nationalized and conglomerated Crown and Pyramid in 1963.

The transition, as detailed in chapter 6, from private companies to a public conglomerate brought radical changes for the makers of Stella in the period from 1961 to 1972. The new conglomeration, dubbed al-Ahram Brewing Company, became part of the Egyptian government's General Corporation of Food Industries. As a part of the government, it faced new advantages and challenges. The most significant advantage was that it now had a monopoly on beer sales in the country. It truly was *the* beer of Egypt, and due to the closed borders of the Nasser government it faced no outside competition. However, nationalization also brought numerous problematic issues, including the flight of both capital and expertise, the inability to use imports to fill production gaps, and most of all administrative and bureaucratic bloat. Despite these issues, the company remained extremely profitable. Thanks to the work of both the Dutchmen and the Egyptian entrepreneurs that the Nasser-led regime would rally against, Stella beer had become the beverage of choice for young Egyptians looking for fun. It was in this period that Stella became the unquestioned cultural artifact that is so fondly remembered by a certain generation of Egyptians.

Stella would maintain its cultural and economic importance in the 1970s and 1980s. As chapter 7 shows, this success was in spite of Anwar Sadat's al-Infitah (Opening), which started in 1974. The Sadat and later Mubarak governments' push to "de-Nasserize" Egypt, which meant courting foreign and Arab investment, could have hurt Stella and the company that sold it. Rather, the stability of the company, aided by a government loath to undermine the ballooning public sector, inaugurated its most successful period. Nevertheless, the signs of decline were starting to accumulate. The first was the loss of one of Stella's greatest allies in 1985, Ismail Omar Foda, to retirement. He had led the company since nationalization and was committed to producing a high-quality product. Likewise, Egypt, in this period, was undergoing fundamental cultural change. Spurred by begrudging government support, the growing cultural contact with conservative regimes like the Saudi government, and the power of the message of political Islam, Egypt experienced an Islamic revival. This revival made displays of religiosity more important to Egyptian public life and in turn made Stella, which could no longer escape its alcoholic qualities, a less welcomed part of Egyptian society. By 1997 Stella faced an uncertain future.

As chapter 8 shows, in 1997, Stella, and the company that sold it, was a "distressed" asset. Sales were flat or declining, its reputation was tarnished among beer drinkers, and its cultural presence in Egypt was shrinking. It is appropriate to conceptualize the fate of Stella in the terms of neoliberal capitalism, because that is how it was viewed by the government and the group, led by Ahmed Zayat, who would privatize it. The government saw its privatization as a way to push forward other privatizations, while Zayat saw it as a profitable venture, though Zayat, operating with the buzzwords of neo-capitalism, instituted some significant changes. This period, in many ways, was a return to Stella's roots. Zayat and his group were transnational, multiethnic, and multireligious. They used their foreign business connections to bring new technology, new distribution methods, and new marketing campaigns. They even facilitated the reentry of Heineken into the Egyptian beer market in 2003. This return to form showed once again that beer making in Egypt could be a profitable venture. Nevertheless, their pivot to nonalcoholic beverages buried the long and proud history of Stella beer.

In sum, this study seeks to tell the history of Egypt from 1880 to 2003 through the study of the culture, economics, and technology that surrounded the production and consumption of Stella beer in Egypt. The history of Stella not only provides an excellent entry point for the study of Egyptian economics of this period, but also provides an unparalleled case study of economic success in the period from 1880 to 2003, a rare quantity considering the massive economic change the country witnessed during that time. Stella beer, the flagship brand of Pyramid and Crown Breweries, achieved a powerful presence in all popular forms of art and media, ranging from Arabic novels, songs, and films to newspapers and magazines. Its success was built on a fascinating mix of technological innovation, efficient use of local resources, world economic developments, executive excellence, and shifting cultural dynamics, making it a story about far more than merely profits on the balance sheet.

# Grand Plans in Glass Bottles
## Importing the Modern Beer Industry into Egypt

The dates are steeped in the water for forty days in winter, and for ten to
fifteen in the summer. They are then mixed with yensoun or anise, and the
mixture is boiled for a half day. This mixture is then put into the still where
distillation occurs. . . . The liquor is very white and smells strongly
of anise. Its quality is less than liquor made from wine.
—Commission des sciences et arts d' Égypte, *Description de l'Égypte;*
  *ou, Recueil des observations et des recherches qui ont été faites en Égypte*
  *pendant l'expédition de l'armée française*

The above description of arak from the *Description de l'Égypte*, a collection
of the work of the savants who accompanied Napoleon on his expedition in
Egypt between 1798 and 1801, attests to the presence and nature of alcohol
production in Egypt prior to 1882. In this period, the arak business—as well
as the *būza* and wine business—was overwhelmingly local, artisanal, and a
do-it-yourself operation. This chapter will show that the beer businesses that
appeared in the period that followed, 1882 to 1920, were entirely different in
scale, methods, goals, and technology. Those that appeared after 1882, aided
by the colonial apparatus in Egypt, were industrialized ventures that aimed
to use imported and cutting-edge technology to reach the Egyptian market.
To label the businesses as an "import" is not to deem them "foreign" or "un-
wanted," but rather to recognize that they grew out of complex motives on
the part of Europeans to bring an industrialized alcoholic beverage industry
to the country and to spur a growth in demand for the beverage among the
Egyptian population.

## Beginnings

While it is possible to overstate the impact on Egypt of the British Occupation of 1882, in the case of Egypt's beer industry, the occupation was truly
a seminal moment. The massive impact of this invasion can be understood
only within the context of the events that led up to it. The British invasion of

1882 grew out of Khedive Isma'il's (1830–1895) push to transform Egypt into a "modern" state.[1] For Isma'il, a modern state was one with greater control of its population. Building on the reforms of his grandfather Mehmet Ali (1769–1849), Isma'il expanded Egypt's police force, army, and bureaucracy. In addition, believing that a modern state was one that adopted the latest European cultural and technological advances, Isma'il invested in cultural landmarks (the Cairo Opera House, theaters, palaces), infrastructure (railways, telegraphs, etc.), and education, aiming to make Egypt the equal of the countries of Europe, with Cairo as his "Paris along the Nile."[2] These programs were funded primarily by loans from British and French banks, which were willing to offer easy credit because of the boom in Egyptian cotton prices in the 1860s. However, the revenue the government was able to generate could not keep up with its loan payments, so in 1875 Egypt defaulted on its debt. In response to the debt crisis, the foreign creditors forced Isma'il to create the Caisse de la Dette, or the Debt Commission, which, through the heavy taxation of the Egyptian populace, aimed to pay off Egypt's interest payments and amortize its debts.[3] The harsh measures provoked Egyptian unrest, which was partially stemmed by the removal of Isma'il in favor of Tawfiq (1879–1892). Nevertheless, a powerful movement soon coalesced around a charismatic colonel, Ahmad 'Urabi, who led an open rebellion that engulfed the country between 1881 and 1882. The sustained success of the 'Urabi revolution, with its antiforeign message, raised the specter of nonrepayment to such a level that in 1882 the British came to occupy Egypt.[4]

The economic pretext of this invasion emboldened Evelyn Baring (later Lord Cromer [1841–1917]), the controller-general of Egypt and the head of the British Commission there from 1883 to 1907, to enact a set of economic reforms that opened the Egyptian market up to global trends and forces.[5] These policies brought some stability to the Egyptian market and, together with Cromer's courting of foreign investors, brought a boom of foreign investment in Egypt after 1893.[6] Between the years 1897 and 1903, the amount of foreign money invested in Egyptian companies doubled from 12 million Egyptian pounds (livre égyptienne [LE]) to 24 million.[7] It is within this boom of foreign investment that the Egyptian alcoholic beverage industry developed.

Yet it was not only Cromer's economic policies that drew the eye of foreign investors. Around the same time that Cromer was restructuring the Egyptian economy to be more outward looking, a series of technological developments were taking place both within Egypt and abroad that had made the country an appealing market for investment. Perhaps the most significant internal development was the expansion of the Egyptian infrastructure. Although the beginnings of Egyptian infrastructural development lay in the regimes of Mehmet Ali (ruled 1805–1848), who, among other things, instituted an Egyptian postal system, and Saʿid (1822–1863), under whom a 209-kilometer railway line was installed between Cairo and Alexandria, it was under the reign of Khedive Ismaʿil that the great Egyptian infrastructural expansion truly began. In Ismaʿil's quest to place Egypt on par with European countries, he invested heavily in Egypt's infrastructure. Arthur E. Crouchley estimates that during Ismaʿil's reign, he spent around LE 40 million on infrastructure, much of it borrowed on cotton credit.[8] This investment proved fruitful; by 1877, "[t]here were 1,519 kilometers of standard-gauge railways and 13,500 kilometers of irrigation canals, many of them navigable throughout the year."[9] Ismaʿil was also Egypt's greatest proponent of telegraphy. Under his rule, Egypt became a telegraphic hub connecting Europe and India through the Malta–Alexandria cable and connecting the Suez and Karachi through the Red Sea cable.[10] In 1865, Ismaʿil even expanded on the work of his grandfather Mehmet Ali when he bought the Poste Européenne, a postal service established by Europeans that connected Cairo, Alexandria, the Delta, and Upper Egypt.[11]

Together with the Suez Canal, which had opened to traffic in 1869, these developments meant that Egypt now had an infrastructure that could not only handle the transport of humans and goods both within and abroad, but also keep operations in Egypt connected to Europe. When the British arrived in 1882, they continued to work on this infrastructure. This work served a dual purpose: it was both a way to strengthen British control of the country by increasing Egypt's connectivity to the British Empire and a way to implement the technoscientific ideals that lay at the heart of their conceptions of a "modern" state.[12] This infrastructure development meant that established companies such as Johnnie Walker (whiskey, Scottish), Guinness (beer, Irish), and Otard (cognac, French) could not only bring their products to Egypt but also distribute them.

## Scientification of Brewing

The economically friendly policies of Cromer and the development of an Egyptian infrastructure may have incentivized investment from foreign beverage companies, but technological developments in the beer industry itself also made expanding into foreign markets desirable.[13] The most important of the technological developments were the advances in microbiology and the study of yeast. European brewers who came to Egypt in the late nineteenth and early twentieth centuries would have deemed the recipe for *būza*, the slightly alcoholic, farina-like beverage native to Egypt, at best "traditional" and at worst "backward." The recipe relied on the permeability of process, meaning that due to the nature of the machinery (earthenware containers, reed pipes, palm-leave filters, etc.) and techniques (handcrafting, lack of sterilization and refrigeration, etc.) used in *būza* production, foreign organisms and materials were bound to enter somewhere in the transition from raw materials to final product, just as materials essential to production were bound to exit. The resulting product was inconsistent and uneven in quality. The permeability of the production process was no longer inevitable once European scientists of the mid- to late nineteenth century came to truly understand the process of fermentation and yeast's role in it.[14]

Scientific discoveries concerning fermentation and germs as the cause of spoilage changed the production of beer from a process filled with guesswork to one of the century's most significant displays of the human ability to control nature.[15] With this new sense of control, brewers of beer sought to improve other parts of the process, which had for so long relied on ideas passed from master craftsmen to apprentices. Thus, discoveries in zymology (the study of fermentation) and microbiology inaugurated the scientification and mechanization of brewing.[16]

The scientification and mechanization of brewing allowed for the technological buildup of the industries and in the process removed the artisan brewer as the main beer producer. Previously, to make a large amount of beer, a company required numerous brewers who had spent their lives learning the craft; now, however, one could produce a great deal of beer with just a few people who had mastered its science, supported by a host of interchangeable unskilled laborers. Likewise, for one to master the processes of brewing, one no longer had to work his way up the apprentice and artisan chain; instead, one went to schools that taught brewing sciences, whose curriculum included not only descriptions of how to make a product but also discussion of the science that underlay it. The de-emphasizing of the artisan brewer encouraged a growth in scale among beer both domestically and abroad. The late nineteenth century saw the rise of major world beer producers such as Bass, Guinness, and Heineken.[17] As we will see later in this work, for a company like Heineken to start producing beer abroad, all it needed to do was select a few well-trained representatives who could be sent to a country to implement the processes of the home factory and ensure quality control of the product.

The scientification and mechanization of brewing not only made the industry more scalable and transferable, but also instilled order and predictability into the brewing process, while making it more efficient and standardizable. The developments also eliminated the permeability of process that was a distinct feature of *būza* production but was anathema to technoscientific ideals.[18] Brewers' decision to start pasteurizing their beer was significant: while pasteurization eliminated all possible microorganisms, it could also cause the beer to become stale and flat.[19] The sacrifice of flavor for preservation was the ultimate rejection of the permeability of process in favor of order and control.

The scientification and mechanization of the beer industry were tantamount to its modernization. Thus, the expansion of the industry into Egypt was heavily tied to its own modernization. The relationship between modernization and expansion was only natural, because the sense of control that modernization gave to its brewers led them to believe they could transfer everything they knew about brewing to an entirely different geographic and cultural setting and still turn a profit. As I will show in the next section, a different aspect of "modernity" reinforced this thinking by producing a large demand for "modern" beverages among the Egyptian population.

### Changing Tastes

Although the technological advances described above made possible the importation of a beer industry into Egypt, this importation would have been fruitless were it not for a crucial cultural change in the population: a growing demand for alcoholic beverages. The origins of the sustained and durable growth of the alcoholic beverage industry in Egypt lay in the emergence of a new class, the *effendiyya*, during the Mehmet Ali dynasty's (of which Isma'il was a prominent member) quest to create a "modern" Egypt. The effendis were a small group of "new men," set apart from other Egyptians by their education, their Western manners and dress, and their worldviews. By the end of the nineteenth century, the effendis came to represent a "new urban society, new social institutions, and new ways of life," serving as engineers, doctors, lawyers, journalists, and political activists. They included in their ranks the sons of the provincial elite who were on their path to the honorific title of pasha or bey, as well as to full inclusion in the national hierarchy.[20]

Members of this new secular elite, which subsumed much of the old elite through "effendification," associated themselves with "modernity," which to them was synonymous with their self-identification as secular, Western, and elite, as distinct from both the nonelite masses and the traditional al-Azhar-trained hierarchy. The *effendiyya*'s modernity, like that of other middle classes of the region, was a performative act that involved the use of new media, new social spaces, and especially new consumer goods.[21] Consumer goods were an important way for Egyptians to craft their identity through participation in "commodity communities."[22]

In this context, alcohol served as an ideal commodity for the effendis to perform modernity because its consumption achieved a double effect: while linking its Egyptian drinker to the "modern" European, who drank on social occasions, alcohol also separated him from both nonelite and religious Egyptians, who viewed alcohol as socially suspect at best or as religious anathema at worst. In the case of colonial Egypt, alcohol consumption represented the rejection of the traditionally trained al-Azhar shaykh in favor of the effendis.[23] In any case, in the late nineteenth and early twentieth centuries, *effendiyya's* consumption of alcohol distanced them from most other Egyptians.

Another group of drinkers whose consumption was shaped by the policies of the Mehmet Ali regime were the urban subalterns. Unlike the *effendiyya*, they were not the desired product of a push for modernity but rather were an unforeseen outgrowth of the Mehmet Ali regime's push for Egyptian urbanization. Between 1820 and 1882, the populations of most of the major cities in Egypt saw significant growth due primarily to migration from the rural areas of Egypt.[24] For example, Alexandria saw a 10 percent growth rate from 1820 to 1846, as compared to the .04 percent growth rate of the total population. Mansura and Suez each grew at a rate double the rate of total population growth in the period from 1846 to 1882.[25] Urbanization was thus slowly beginning in the period 1840 to 1882, with nearly one and a half million people living in cities by 1882. While some of these migrants were wealthy landowners, the great majority were *fellahin* looking to escape a hard, rural life. For these new migrants, the consumption of alcohol was a potent signifier of "modern," elite life.[26]

The processes that formed these two groups of drinkers, urbanization and "effendification," only accelerated after the arrival of the British in 1882. As Mohammad A. Chaichian has pointed out, "One of the dominant and common features of colonial domination is the concentration of commercial, administrative, and political institutions in a few localities for the purpose of reducing the costs of running the colony."[27] Egypt was no exception; fourteen cities saw growth greater than the total growth of the population in the first fifteen years of British rule in Egypt. Cairo, the imperial nerve center, saw the greatest growth in the period, with a growth rate of 12 percent compared to the 1.4 percent of the general population.[28] Overall, between 1882 and 1907, the urban population of Egypt increased by 50 percent. Not only was there a significant population of British soldiers and officers in Cairo, but many local Egyptians also moved to the city to fill service jobs in the new imperial administration.[29] Thus, thousands left the countryside for cities in the North, with Cairo and Alexandria being the premier destinations.[30]

Colonial rule aided the process of effendification. Under the British, an influx of foreign-born residents, who had few religious qualms about drinking, flooded the urban spaces of Egypt.[31] Between 1897 and 1917, the foreign population grew at a significant rate, with the largest increase coming from Greeks, Italians, North Africans, Maltese, and Ottoman subjects.[32] For example, in Cairo, between the years 1897 and 1907, the number of foreign residents nearly doubled, from 31,543 to 62,000.[33] Cairo and Alexandria, because of their economic and political importance, proved to be the primary destinations of immigrants from southern Europe and Greater Syria. By 1907, "11.5 percent (75,000) of Cairo's population and 17.6 percent of Alexandria's population" were foreign born.[34] Demographically, these immigrants were overwhelmingly from the lower middle classes.[35] These foreign-born residents normalized the consumption of alcohol in the cities and also drove the alcohol business itself.

Because of the demographic shifts, there was a proliferation of spaces in which one could drink. While the exact number of places is unknown, by 1899 the British consul estimated that there were more than four thousand establishments in Egypt that sold alcohol.[36] The alcohol licenses issued in Cairo from 1891 to 1896 give a sense of the dynamics of the business. The records show that foreign protégés—residents protected by foreign governments—especially Greeks and Italians, played a significant role in the proliferation of drinking spaces. For example, in the year 1893, Greeks and Italians constituted 75 percent of those receiving licenses to sell alcohol.[37] The predominance of Greeks and Italians was typical of the Egyptian economy in this era.[38] For example, the tobacco industry was a major employer of Greeks.[39]

With the preponderance of Greeks and Italians in the distribution of alcohol in Egypt, it would be easy to dismiss the burgeoning Egyptian alcohol industry as a foreign imperial imposition. However, on closer inspection, the picture appears to be far more nuanced. When we shift our gaze from the managers of these establishments, who tended to receive the licenses, to their owners, there appears to have been a significant Egyptian contingent among the latter. For example, the British consul reported that of the 4,015 alcohol distributors in 1904, 2,257 were foreign and 1,758 were local subjects.[40] One of the most prominent owners of bars was the elite Jewish businessman Yusuf Qattawi Bey. The Qattawi family, alongside the Mosseris, led the Jewish community in Egypt from the 1880s to the 1920s.[41] Yusuf Qattawi Bey played a significant role in the sugar industry, land reclamation, and Bank Misr.[42] In the late 1890s, he also owned eight separate establishments that sold spirits. These places, dispersed primarily in the Muski and Azbakiyya districts of Cairo, included bars (e.g., Crini Bar), cafés, restaurants, and even an ice cream shop.[43]

Economic involvement in the alcohol industry was not strictly the domain of non-Muslims. The British consul also reported that, in 1904, 385 of the alcohol distributors in Egypt were Muslim owned. The records bear this out, with many of the Cairo licenses featuring Muslim names, some with honorifics like *pasha* and *bey* attached to them. One noteworthy example of a Muslim alcohol distributor was Mahmud Pasha Falaki, who owned three bars in the ʿAbdin district in Cairo. Even more noteworthy were three princes who held alcohol licenses: Ibrahim Pasha, Halim Pasha, and Husayn Pasha. While these princes may not have been personally involved in the sale of alcohol, there is no denying that the properties of each of these royals housed a café or bar. One particularly illustrative example of such an establishment was the bar Bodega Nouvelle Avenue. Established in 1894, it sat on the property of Prince Halim Pasha, on Gamal Street in Azbakiyya, and was run by an Italian, Riccardo Belloni.[44] As shown elsewhere, the royal family was not shy about profiting from the business of bars and taverns.[45]

Who were the denizens of these drinking establishments? The historical record provides few answers. However, we can get a sense from a stinging social critique of turn-of-the-century Egypt, *Hadir al-Misriyyin aw Sirr al-Taʾakhkhurihim* (The present state of the Egyptians, an explanation of their backwardness), written by Muhammad ʿUmar, a writer known only by this work and by his employment in the postal service. In this work, ʿUmar divides Egypt into three classes—the rich, the middle, and the poor—and then criticizes each for what he perceives as its failures.[46] ʿUmar uses alcohol consumption as a key part of his critique. The houses of the rich, he asserts, are filled with "bottles of liquors" and stacks of wine barrels, which are proof of the group's indolence, profligacy, and self-indulgence. In the middle group, the youth spend all night drinking in the ever-increasing number of bars, cafés, and dance clubs in Egypt, which represent the insidious penetration of Western habits throughout the country. As for the poor, despite their indigence, they drink even more than the rich, especially at religious festivals like *mawlids* (saints' birthday celebrations). The poor people's consumption is attributable to their ignorance and their prioritization of enjoyment and pleasure over all other values.[47]

While Muhammad ʿUmar crafts a neat taxonomy of Egyptian drinkers,

Ibrahim al-Muwaylihi's (1846–1906) turn-of-the-century novel and social critique, *Hadith ʿIsa ibn Hisham*, presents a far more nuanced picture.[48] The sections most pertinent to this study are those in which the two protagonists, ʿIsa ibn Hisham and the pasha, visit drinking establishments. Their first stop is the "club" (*klūb*), where the grandees of the Egyptian state drink, bet, and gamble in a palatial multiroom house. From there, they travel to four locations (a meeting hall, a restaurant, a tavern, and a dance hall) that fall within close vicinity of ʿAtaba Square, or, as Ibn Hisham calls it, the "square of drunkenness" (*saḥat al-sukr*).[49] Here the protagonists shift from Ibn Hisham and the pasha to the *khaliʿ* (playboy) and the *ʿumda* (village chief), a deliberate indictment of those most susceptible to alcohol. The playboy is a depiction of the new class of tarbush wearers (*mutaṭarbishūn*), the *effendiyya*, whereas the *ʿumda*, who owns a thousand *feddans* (0.42 hectares or 1.038 acres) of land, represents the uncultured rural elite that was slowly integrating into the urban hierarchy and absorbing its cultural mores.[50] In addition, the *ʿumda* stands in for rural migrants to the city, who are ignorant of urban custom and victimized by urban depredations.

However, these domains were strictly a male prerogative. In the only scene of *Hadith ʿIsa ibn Hisham* wherein women make a prolonged appearance, they are portrayed negatively. Ibn Hisham recounts how the most "beautiful" dancer in the club transforms "into the guise of a harpy appearing in a desert mirage, a ghoul grimacing and leaping around, or a bear quivering and crawling."[51] Similar to the Egyptian social evaluation of female dancers and performers that Karin van Nieuwkerk details, Egyptian intellectuals perceived alcohol-consuming women first in terms of their gender and then as alcohol consumers.[52] In al-Muwaylihi's harsh rebuke of women in drinking clubs, we see a redefinition of femininity that helps to constitute a new effendi manhood.[53] Thus, in *Hadith ʿIsa ibn Hisham*, only low-status female dancers and prostitutes frequent drinking clubs.

Despite this exclusion of women, many clubs did list a woman as their manager. For example, an Austrian protégée, Anne Fiedler, oversaw the Steinfeld Bar, founded in 1894 in Darb al-Mahabil in ʿAbdin. Women were not limited to managerial roles; they could also be owners. A good example is Caterina Bakesova, an Austro-Hungarian protégée who opened up the Anglo-American Bar in Harat al-Mudarrisin in Azbakiyya. While many of these owners were European protégées, with Austrian subjects featuring most prominently, Egyptian women, both Christian and Muslim, also served as owners. The lists of owners include names such as Sayyida bint Muhammad al-Zakiyya, Jawhara bint Haslan, and Marie Bittar.[54]

## The Pyramid and the Crown

With the economic, technological, and cultural requirements in place, Egypt would prove to be a fertile ground for early beer investors. On May 15, 1897, a group of Belgian investors, led by Albert Heyndrickx, founded the Crown Brewery of Alexandria in Belgium, with a capitalization of 1 million francs. They built a factory in the Ibrahimiyya district of Alexandria, where the company had instant success. After that, the board decided to open another brewery in Cairo to exploit that city's larger market.[55] In 1898 the board opened Société Anonyme Brasserie des Pyramides (Pyramid Brewery), which had a factory on the outskirts of the city and an initial capitalization of 1.5 million francs. These two breweries, the Crown and Pyramid Breweries, were transnational ventures, with all the capital and some of the leadership coming from abroad, while local protégés and business-minded Egyptians oversaw the daily management and functioning.

The lead investors in the Crown and Pyramid Breweries were part of a larger influx of Belgian investors and industrialists into Egypt; no fewer than thirty Belgian companies were founded in Egypt in the period between 1897 and 1907.[56] This Belgian penetration of the Egyptian economy was emblematic of the massive inflow of foreign capital into Egypt after the arrival of the British. These foreign investors chose to establish a brewery because the beer market in Belgium was too fractured to support a new large-scale brewer; this meant that they had to look abroad for hopes of greater growth.[57] Thus, the two beer companies were the by-product of trends in both Belgian brewing and Belgian economics in the late nineteenth century.

Although the Crown and Pyramid Breweries were in Egypt, they were transnational. The directorate of both companies was split between Alexandria and Brussels, where the head offices were located. Two members of the five-person board for Crown and three members of the seven-person board for Pyramid lived in Brussels, while the rest, who were a mix of Egyptian citizens and foreign protégés, maintained operations in Egypt. The transnational character of the directorate was due to the small size of the Belgian community relative to other foreign communities like the French and the British.[58] To maintain a strong business presence in Egypt, much of the financing and direction had to come from the metropole; many Belgian firms were tied closely to large metropolitan banking and holding companies in Brussels.[59]

The relatively small size of the Belgian community in Egypt also necessitated that Belgian businessmen rely on the business-group model, wherein a group of companies from different sectors and in different countries was under the control of a small unified directorate. Perhaps the most famous group of companies was the Groupe Empain, which was led by Baron Édouard Empain, the man who built the Paris Metro. His group consisted of Andre Bertholet, the French architect and designer of the Paris Metro; Henri Urban, a member of the board of the Chemin de Fer Économique and a director of companies that had established trams in Turin, Odessa, Naples, and Russia; and Jean Jadot, an engineer who specialized in light railways. This group acquired the concession for the Cairo tramway and developed an upscale residential neighborhood in Cairo, called Heliopolis. The Lambert-Rolin group, headed by the prominent Belgian glassmaker Florent Lambert, based in Brussels, was another example of this model. This group included the Pyramid Brewery, as well as the Anglo-Belgian Company Limited of Egypt, the British Tropical Africa Company (which worked in the Congo), a railway company, a tramway company, a cement company, and even a company in charge of maintaining gardens in Cairo.[60]

Although a large portion of both companies' leadership was in Belgium, both utilized Belgians living in Egypt and powerful members of the Egyptian business elite. One board member of the Crown Brewery, Georges Nungovich, a Belgian national and major hotelier, was on the advisory board and board of directors of two other companies and the owner of the Georges Nungovich Egyptian Hotel Company. Another local Belgian member, A. L. Gorra, was on the board of directors of three other companies. As for local Egyptians, the presidents of both companies were Egyptians from the Pasha class: Khalil Khayyat Pasha (Crown Brewery) and J. G. Shakur Pasha (Pyramid Brewery). Each man had important positions in other joint-stock companies as well. Khalil Khayyat Pasha was a director in the Société Égyptienne de Tabacs, the Egyptian Land investment company, the North Egypt Land Company Limited, and the sole director of the limited liability company Tambeki Monopoly Company. J. G. Shakur Pasha, meanwhile, was the managing director of Société Anonyme des Ciments d'Égypte and the chairman of the Manzala Canal and Navigation Company.[61] These two businessmen were early examples of the native oligarchs who would come to dominate the Egyptian economy in the late 1930s and early 1940s.

Despite the Greeks not being heavily involved in the financing and leadership of these two companies, they still played a significant role in their operations in Egypt. Two Greeks, M. M. Miltiade and Henri Klonaridis, used their local connections to help the Belgian entrepreneurs found Crown Brewery in 1897. Their role was so significant that Athanasios Politis incorrectly cited them as the founders of the Crown Brewery, thus crediting them with being the originators of the beer industry in Egypt.[62] As I have shown, it was not the native Greeks but foreign entrepreneurs who, using local intermediaries and transnational business connections, believed they could build a modern beer industry in Egypt.

## Establishment

The men who founded and led the Crown and Pyramid Breweries were insistent on bringing to Egypt the scientification and mechanization that was taking place across Europe in the late nineteenth century. What this meant in practical terms was that these breweries charged their brewing operations to men trained in some of the most important beer-brewing countries in Europe. Crown employed a German brewer, Alfred Weber, and Pyramid employed a Czech brewer, Jan Křeček.[63] These brewers aimed to replace the permeability that was so distinctive to the *būza*-making process with "total control"—the assumption, often misguided and hubristic, that through the assiduous application of the most current technologies, brewers could produce a standardized and sturdy product in a timely and cost-efficient manner. This sense of control was especially important in a market like Egypt, which, in the eyes of these entrepreneurs, had not yet been fully modernized.

So what did completely controlled brewing look like? It started with the malted barley, which was imported to Egypt from Czechoslovakia. Barley was malted by soaking the grain in water about two days; then, the grains were exposed to moist air, at about 15 degrees Celsius (60 degrees Fahrenheit), and allowed to germinate. This germination started to break down the starches and proteins in the barley into fermentable sugars. The barley was then dried or kilned at 40 degrees Celsius (100 degrees Fahrenheit) to arrest the breakdown of its starches and proteins.[64] Because malting is one of the key processes for establishing a beer's flavor, these breweries used only imported barley from the fields of Moravia that had been malted by the best malt makers in Czechoslovakia.[65]

Using the imported malted barley, the Egyptian breweries would start the brewing process proper, which included crushing, mashing, boiling, lautering, cooling, fermenting, and storing. First, crushing the malted barley separated the outside of the barley, the insoluble husk, from the interior of the barley, the germ. Then mashing broke down the starch in the barley into fermentable sugars. Mashing could take two forms, infusion or decoction. Infusion meant soaking the barley in water at 65 degrees Celsius (150 degrees Fahrenheit) in the same way one soaks tea leaves to make tea. Decoction, on the other hand, involved separating out part of the malted barley and water and bringing it to a boil at 100 degrees Celsius (212 degrees Fahrenheit). This boiled mixture was then returned to the rest of the water and barley and allowed to infuse. Regardless of which method the breweries chose, mashing was subject to total control; it occurred in a mash tun, imported from Belgium, that was made of sterile copper. The mashing stage was when the second raw material, water, was introduced. Unsurprisingly, the breweries were particular about their water. The Pyramid Brewery thought that the water of the Nile was unsuitable for any of their products and drew their water from artesian wells that the company owned.[66]

After mashing, lautering removed the husks of the malted barley that had been separated out by crushing. The sugar-filled mixture remaining after lautering, called wort, was then boiled for forty-five to ninety minutes, and hops were then added. The hopping of the wort had a significant impact on the beer's taste (adding the distinctive bitterness), consistency (helping to precipitate any remaining proteins), and shelf life (making it more durable). The breweries imported the hops from the choicest harvests in Bohemia, a place known for its hop making, and stored the hops in a refrigerated room to preserve their taste and aroma until they were ready for use.[67]

While the beer-making process up to this point was quite similar to the būza-making process, the next three steps truly differentiated the two beverages. The breweries had to cool the hot and hopped wort to a temperature of either 7 degrees Celsius (40 degrees Fahrenheit) or 15 degrees Celsius (60 degrees Fahrenheit) and then add the yeast, which was a proprietary strain owned and perfected by the brewery. The strain had a significant impact on the beer, and thus a good strain of yeast was a precious commodity. The choice in temperature also had a significant impact on the product. A lower temperature allowed for bottom fermentation, meaning that the yeast that sank to the bottom of the beer carried out most of the fermentation, while a higher temperature ensured top fermentation, where the yeast at the top did most of the work.[68] These two types of fermentation produced different types of beer: bottom fermentation produced lagers, and top fermentation produced ales.

If the brewery was making a top-fermented beer, it would allow the yeast to ferment the wort for a couple of days (two to seven) at a temperature ranging from 15 to 24 degrees Celsius (60 to 78 degrees Fahrenheit) and then store it for less than a week at 7 degrees Celsius (45 degrees Fahrenheit). It would then have its final product, an ale.[69] If the brewery was making a lager, on the other hand, the beer had to be stored for eight days at 7 to 13 degrees Celsius (45 to 55 degrees Fahrenheit) to allow primary fermentation to occur. After those eight days, bottom fermentation would start, and the brewery would have to store the beer for around three months at 1 degree Celsius (34 degrees Fahrenheit). Fittingly, the name "lager" was derived from the German word meaning "to store."[70]

This entire process, from mashing to storing, could not have been done without the instruments (thermometer, saccharometer) and technologies (Saladin boxes, mechanized sieves, ice machines, cooling vats, copper piping, etc.) that were the tangible results of the scientification and mechanization of the beer industry in late-nineteenth-century Europe. The breweries, on their arrival in Cairo, imported the top-of-the-line varieties of these materials from Belgium and housed them in factories that were kept in impeccable shape.[71]

Despite the breweries' commitment to "modern" brewing, their early days were trying. The Cairo operation, which was still under the control of Crown Brewery, soon ran into financial trouble because of poor management and overexpansion. The company would have dissolved were it not for the intervention of another group of Belgian investors, the Lambert-Rolin group, in 1904, which addressed the brewery's financial problems through the amortization of debts and the selling of assets and stocks.[72] This overexpansion was caused by the fact that beyond the initial successes, the breweries faced a problem: Egyptians who were drinking beer were more likely to choose imported varieties from well-established brewing nations like Germany or Austria rather than Egyptian brands. The fledgling beer industry was also hurt in these early years by the Egyptian government, which did not place significant duties on imported beer and thus eliminated one of the main advantages that local companies might have had.[73]

Soon after the breweries' founding, they would face another major hurdle, the stock market crash of 1907. The crash was a direct result of the influx of foreign capital into the Egyptian stock market between 1898 and 1906. Typical of an economic bubble, a speculative fever overtook Egypt in 1905 and 1906 as "land companies sold land for very little deposits, banks lent liberally on shares . . . [and] second or even third mortgages could be readily obtained." The inevitable "market correction" came when the American market dipped and wreaked havoc in the Egyptian economy. The most visible effect of the crash was that it wiped out many of the firms founded during the boom. The number of cases for bankruptcies in the courts rose from 310 in 1907 to 520 in 1908 and 546 in 1910.[74] Egypt did not truly recover from this market correction until after World War I. Despite the general gloom of the economic scene in Egypt, both beer companies survived. Their survival was due in part to the profitability of the breweries despite, or perhaps because of, the economic downturn. The fact that another set of Belgians founded a beer company in 1909, Société Anonyme de Belge Brasserie d'Égypte (Belgian Brewing Company), is indicative of this counterintuitive profitability.[75]

The Crown and Pyramid Breweries were able to survive and thrive amid the economic downturn by generating revenue streams beyond the sale of domestically produced beer. The sale of malt and ice, two products essential to beer but that also had a market on their own in Egypt, proved to be lucrative enough to keep the businesses afloat. Malt could be used to make vinegar and other food products for animals and humans, while ice was the primary way things were refrigerated in this era, so both remained viable products. Through these alternative revenue sources, the breweries were able to weather the storm and maintain profitability until the beer business truly took off during World War I.[76]

World War I was vital to the establishment of the Egyptian beer industry because it cut Egypt off from the global economy with which Lord Cromer had worked so hard to bring the country in line. Although the temporary isolation of Egypt provided a terrible shock to its economy overall and to those companies that were heavily supported by foreign capital and goods, for local producers the isolation provided the protection from foreign brands that the government would not.[77] Those companies that had survived the prewar economic downturn, including the two beer companies, were able to reinvest in their infrastructure to better adapt to the local market. Adaptation was necessary because despite the industrialists' assumption of the superiority of the modern over the traditional, the establishment of a modern beer industry in Egypt was not a frictionless process.

The most obvious example of breweries' adaptation comes from the refrigeration machinery that the companies used after World War I. Recognizing that the Egyptian environment was harsher than they imagined, the companies invested in and expanded their cellars so that they could house a greater amount of beer. Likewise, they used several methods for cooling or refrigerating their beer: they kept some beer in casks in their cellar, some beer in tanks made of enameled iron also in the cellar, and some in vats armed with a system of internal refrigeration.[78] The juxtaposition of these three methods represented the reality of technologic change in Egypt. While all of these technologies were imported, each represented a different phase of brewing. Casks were a quintessential feature of premechanized brewing, cooling vats were a feature of the introductory phase of mechanized brewing, and the internally refrigerated vat was a hallmark of the latest innovations in brewing. As several scholars have shown, despite the typical assumption that the arrival of new technology or ideas would immediately replace the old ideas, the reality was that technologies tended to agglomerate and exist simultaneously until older technology was slowly phased out, if at all.[79]

The shape of adaptation was slightly different in the case of the raw materials used to make the beer. Although originally the breweries limited themselves to using imported malted barley, locally grown rice eventually became an important part of their beer recipe. Cooked rice was added to the malted barley before mashing and served as a filler to make the breweries' supplies of malted barley last longer.[80] This transition was only logical, as Egypt was a significant producer of rice; its use in lieu of imported malted barely was an easy way to lower overhead without drastically affecting the beer. A similar process occurred with the water that the breweries used. Originally, they deemed Nile water unsatisfactory for their beer production; however, these companies eventually had to face the reality that Nile water was the only consistent source of water in the country and to avoid using it was simply poor business. Nevertheless, the idea of total control persisted as the breweries insisted on analyzing the Nile water before every round of brewing, sending samples to major European laboratories so they could deem it fit for making beer.[81]

The creation of an industrialized beer industry in Egypt was spearheaded by Europeans, yet this industry was not a foreign imposition completely at odds with the culture and people of Egypt. As this chapter has shown, although the pioneers in this industry were European, the arrival and the success of the beer industry were not the capitulation of a nation to the demands of its new colonial masters. Rather, they represented the confluence of revolutionary trends in the beer industry that pushed European brewers to expand into untapped markets, as well as massive social and cultural changes in the Egyptian population that created a demand for new alcoholic beverages. While it would be naive and false to claim that these beer ventures were not aided by the presence of an imperial power in Egypt, much of what attracted the investors were trends and events that were already taking shape before the British invaded Egypt in 1882. In particular, the consumption of alcoholic beverages was becoming a key marker for many Egyptians of their new "modern" identity.

The importation of the technologies that lay at the heart of industrial beer production was not a frictionless process. The companies that arrived in Egypt were not immediately profitable but instead met with early difficulties and had to diversify in order to survive their early days. Their techno-scientific mind-set, one shaped heavily by the sense of "total control," was challenged by the particularities of the Egyptian situation. Only by adapting their methods and leadership structure to Egypt, calling on early business elites, and exploiting the advantages of the country, including plentiful water, grains, and population, did these companies establish an industrialized base in the country. Thus, these early ventures, which would eventually serve as the base of the modern Egyptian beer industry, survived only through the significant investment, persistence, and commitment of the businessmen who led this industry.

# A Star Rises

*Stella and the Egyptian Beer Industry, 1920–1940*

Brilliant yellow, as if it was made of amber (*kahramān*), it beams in
its glass and gladdens anyone who gazes on it, drinks it, or tastes it.
This power makes Dressler beer perfect for those hot days, as it can
refresh and renew your strength.
—Dressler beer advertisement, *al-Ahram*, July 29, 1938

It is not hard to see the angle the above advertisement takes to sell beer to the
readers of the Egyptian daily *al-Ahram*. Published in the heart of the summer, it offers beer as the perfect solution to the weariness caused by working
under the hot Egyptian sun in an air-conditioner-less world. For contemporary readers, it may be a little disorienting to see beer placed as a beverage
of refreshment, but the imagery and claims are surely familiar. Just think of
how brands you know use the heat to sell you their product. Recall the cool
droplets of condensation dripping down the full Coca-Cola glass as bubbles
of effervescence jump from it. The task is not too difficult as you, and most of
the planet, live in a world saturated with advertisements using natural feelings—thirst, hunger, sleepiness, etc.—to sell you products. Yet for Egyptians
of the 1920s and 1930s, this social phenomenon was only beginning. This
chapter looks at this development as Egypt entered the consumer age in the
period from 1920 to 1940. It shows how Stella beer rode on the wave of consumerism to become part of the Egyptian cultural scene.

## Internal Transformations

In post–World War I Egypt, the beer business was a profitable one. This was
especially true for the two largest Egypt-based breweries, Crown and Pyramid. Immediately after World War I, the companies' beer production grew
from the prewar level of around forty thousand hectoliters (hl) per year to
seventy-one thousand hectoliters per year in the period from 1923 to 1929.[1]
These levels of production made the breweries not only economic power-
houses in Egypt but some of the largest bottled beer producers in Africa.

Although Egypt was a Muslim country, its beer industry was well in advance of most other colonies in Africa due to the regulations imposed by colonial powers. Starting with the Brussels Act of 1890, and strengthened with the League of Nation Treaty Series, colonial powers, including Britain, France, Belgium, and Italy, had prohibited "the importation, distribution, sale, and possession of trade spirits of every kind" in the continent of Africa.[2] These ordinances grew out of the infantilizing discourse that was used to justify the colonial presence in Africa. Europeans used the indigenous alcohol cultures present in sub-Saharan Africa to argue that these populations were intemperate and in need of civilization. At the same time, they strictly forbade Africans from importing or consuming alcohol familiar to Europeans (grape wine, spirits, and hopped beer) for fear of its corrupting influence on the uncivilized populations.[3] However, Egypt and the rest of North Africa were spared this paternalism.[4] While this regulation stymied the creation of any large-scale native brewing ventures in other African countries, Egypt remained unencumbered. It would take until the 1920s (Kenya Brewers Limited) and later (Nigerian Brewing Limited, in 1946) for ventures on the scale of Crown and Pyramid to appear in other African countries.[5] In Egypt the beer companies did so well that the capitalization of Pyramid Brewery placed it in the top twelve best-funded companies in Egypt at the time.[6]

Despite their profitability, the companies were undergoing a significant internal reorganization in the period from the 1920s to the 1940s. The first step in this transformation was the entrance of two enterprising Swiss brothers, Walter and Curt Bomonti, who had founded the first brewery on the European side of Istanbul in 1890 and had significantly altered the beer market in Egypt.[7] They had become familiar with the intricacies of the beer industry in Egypt through their work supplying beer to the Navy and Army Canteen Board of the British occupying forces.[8] They made their first foray into the Egyptian market with a brewery/rice mill built in Alexandria under the name "Bomonti Brothers." Their venture was so successful that in 1923 they were able to buy and consolidate Pyramid Brewery, Belgian Brewing (another brewing interest in Egypt), and their own beer company into a new entity named Société Anonyme Bières Bomonti et Pyramides (henceforth Bomonti-Pyramid).[9] Although the brewery came to bear their names, the Bomontis resided in Bern rather than Cairo. Another member of the new board, Jacques Ruch, lived in Zurich. Rudolph Yost, a Swiss citizen who lived in Alexandria, represented the Swiss industrialists at the meetings with the rest of the board, composed of two British protégés, a Greek protégé, and another Swiss citizen living in Alexandria.

While the Bomontis took control of Pyramid, Crown remained locally owned. After its founding in 1897, Crown had gone through several chairmen. After Khalil Khayyat Pasha, a British protégé named Edward Crewe was the head of the company until 1925. After 1925 Charles Cantoni, whose father had been in the retinue of Kaiser Wilhelm II (r. 1888–1918), took over and would chair the company until 1932. Although Cantoni was the chairman of the board and president of the company from 1925 to 1932, it was Max Raybaud who ran the day-to-day operations of the brewery as the managing director. Raybaud would serve in this position until the 1940s.[10]

At first Crown was a direct competitor to the newly formed Bomonti-Pyramid in the Cairo market. Although Pyramid had broken off from Crown after its establishment in 1898, Crown maintained a presence in Cairo to take advantage of Egypt's largest market. However, the breweries quickly realized that a partnership made more sense than an expensive battle to try to conquer the country.[11] Therefore, in 1921, even before Bomonti-Pyramid had taken on its final shape, the two breweries agreed on a plan to exploit the beer markets of all of Egypt. This sales agreement proved very lucrative for both firms. For example, they together sold more than seventy-five thousand hectoliters of beer in Egypt in 1928.[12]

Their success caught the eye of René Gaston-Dreyfus, the son of a wealthy French banker, who had established a brewery in Morocco, Brasserie du Maroc, in the 1920s. In 1928 he started overtures to try to enter the Egyptian beer market. Gaston-Dreyfus initially went to Charles Cantoni, who was serving as the head of Crown Brewery, with grand plans of buying the entire local industry. However, when Cantoni offered Gaston-Dreyfus only three thousand shares, a small noncontrolling stake, he decided to look for other ways to achieve his goals. Gaston-Dreyfus settled on Bomonti-Pyramid when one of his business contacts alerted him that Jacques Ruch, who owned 45 percent of Bomonti-Pyramid stock and was the largest shareholder, was willing to sell. After an initial rebuttal, Gaston-Dreyfus was able to buy not only Ruch's shares in Bomonti-Pyramid but also those in the Istanbul-based brewery Bomonti-Nectar. With these interests now added to his Cairo and Moroccan interests, Gaston-Dreyfus had a small multinational venture, which he incorporated and named Société Finánciere Brasseries (Sofibra) in 1929.

After buying into Bomonti-Pyramid, Gaston-Dreyfus set out to "purify" the board of the company. Although Bomonti-Pyramid had been successful, it appeared to Gaston-Dreyfus that Curt Bomonti, the son of founder Walter, and his cousin Rudolph Yost had placed the company on a dangerous path. Gaston-Dreyfus saw Curt, who was the chairman of the board, as a dimwitted clod who preferred to spend nights out on the town rather than do any work. The only reason he maintained his position was that his family held so many shares. Yost, who was the managing director, in Gaston-Dreyfus's view had enriched himself off the company but had done very little for it. Because of their mismanagement, Bomonti-Pyramid was unable to meet the growing demands of the Egyptian population and thus had to sell inferior beer that would have otherwise been tossed away. By 1932 Gaston-Dreyfus, through some clever maneuvering, was able to excise both Bomonti and Yost and replace them with René Ismalun and Pierre Geisenberger, respectively. Gaston-Dreyfus was familiar with Geisenberger and his work at a brewery in Dakar, while Ismalun, who was part of the Egyptian Jewish community, came highly recommended by one of Gaston-Dreyfus's associates. Gaston-Dreyfus, showing his imperial chauvinism, did not have a high valuation of Ismalun. He believed that he was lazy and "not a genius," but he was, most important, "honest."[13]

After reorganizing Bomonti-Pyramid, Gaston-Dreyfus set about taking control of Crown. He found his way in with a stockholder named Mr. Rollo. After convincing Rollo to sell his four thousand shares, Gaston-Dreyfus was able to manipulate him and raise his stock holding to nine thousand shares. Gaston-Dreyfus would have been able to take a majority over the company by buying the three thousand shares from Cantoni were it not for the intervention of Constantine Mouratiadis, a Greek protégé, lawyer, and major stockholder in Crown Brewery. He was also the tangible link between Crown and Pyramid under the Bomontis, for besides being a major stockholder he ran the sales operations for both breweries in Cairo. Seeing the aggressive maneuvering of Gaston-Dreyfus and fearing for the lucrative life he had carved out for himself, he entrenched himself both within the operations in Cairo and on the Crown Brewery board. Thus, before Gaston-Dreyfus could have the chance, he was able to become the chairman of the board of Crown and its majority shareholder.[14]

Gaston-Dreyfus sought the advice of his men on the ground, like Geisenberger, on how to proceed regarding the first real roadblock to his control of the Egyptian beer industry. They advised Gaston-Dreyfus that if Sofibra engaged in open warfare with Mouratiadis, they would be embroiled in a ruinous war that would fracture the excellent working relationship between Crown and Pyramid and cost Bomonti-Pyramid a great deal of money. They advised Gaston-Dreyfus to instead come to an agreement with Mouratiadis, which granted his desired autonomy in Alexandria, so that he and Sofibra could work together and maintain the profitability of the two breweries. This détente not only avoided a costly conflict but also allowed Bomonti-Pyramid to build up enough reserves so that if Mouratiadis ever proved himself a problem, they could engage in open warfare with him. However, it never came to that. After the initial bit of posturing, they settled into a workable and profitable partnership, renewing the two companies' joint sales agreement in 1923, 1925, and 1931.[15] Gaston-Dreyfus cultivated an excellent relationship with their respective administrations. Although he was based abroad, in Paris, he spearheaded close collaborations between the boards and encouraged unanimity in the breweries' goals. Gaston-Dreyfus had such a positive influence that when Heineken bought him out, members of the Crown Brewery board asked him to stay on as an executive member.[16]

The foreign-backed consolidation of the beer industry in Egypt was typical of the Egyptian joint-stock companies of the time. The Egyptian tobacco industry underwent a similar process of centralization driven by the multinational British-American Tobacco Company. In the period that Bomonti-Pyramid was consolidating the beer market, BAT rapidly expanded in Egypt. By 1927 it owned six tobacco factories in Egypt and had become the second-biggest tobacco company in the country. In that same year, it merged with the largest tobacco company in Egypt, Matossian, and renamed the conglomeration Eastern. At that point, Eastern owned 90 percent of the tobacco market.[17] Likewise, a few "heavily capitalized, vertically integrated, and politically powerful firms" took control of the textile industry in Egypt in the 1920s. The push for consolidation in these industries was spurred by the tariff reforms of 1930. Local leading business magnates saw these reforms, which were meant to limit imports, as their opportunity to dominate their respective sectors. They thus aimed to establish "large and powerful firms in the late 1920s" to make it difficult for new firms to enter.[18]

## External Threats

The desire to consolidate was driven not solely by the entrepreneurs' natural tendency to limit competition, but also by the real local and foreign threats to their survival. On the local level, there were two breweries, Cavafakis and St. Georges, competing with Crown and Bomonti-Pyramid to capitalize on the growing beer market in Egypt. However, these breweries were never serious challengers to Crown and Bomonti-Pyramid. Both were too small and too poorly established to overcome the fact that they sold a low-quality beer. They quickly fizzled out, unable to compete with Crown and Bomonti-Pyramid, which sold affordable and high-quality products. Nor could Cavafakis and St. Georges compete with the host of European beers that were present on the market, which were more expensive than Crown and Bomonti-Pyramid but of a superior quality.[19]

Such foreign beers were the true obstacles to the continued growth and success of Crown and Bomonti-Pyramid. After World War I ended, Egypt was reintegrated into the world market and once again filled with imported alcoholic beverages, including beer. Foreign alcohol mainly entered the Egyptian market through alcohol agents. These agents aimed to maximize profits through the diversification of the brands they sold. Thus, an internationally known brand of beer was an essential part of their business portfolio. For example, Walker and Vallois, who were the sole agents of Johnnie Walker in Egypt, were also the main importers of Amstel and Allsop's beer.[20]

These agents ensured that the Egyptian beer market was a truly global one. There were beers from the major beer-producing countries, including Germany (Dressler, Kupper), England (Allsops, Watneys, Whitbreads), the Netherlands (Amstel, Heineken), and Czechoslovakia (Urquell), but also from smaller beer-producing countries like Denmark (Carlsberg), Greece (Fix), Sweden (Falcon), Japan (Asahi), and Scotland (Tennet's). Agents imported beer in two forms, in cases of bottles and in barrels or kegs, the latter being the most effective way to import beer while maintaining the quality. (Kegs were both sturdier and more likely to keep their seal than bottles, which made them valuable because bottle breakage was a significant source of lost revenue.) The beer imported from these countries was consumed throughout Egypt; Alexandria and Lower Egypt consumed roughly 35 percent of the imported beer, while Cairo and Upper Egypt consumed the rest, 65 percent.[21]

Four of the biggest importers of beer into Egypt were Société McEwans, Slavick & Co., Eredi Albertini, and the Fix Brewery of Greece. Société McEwans made a great deal of profit because they were the sole supplier of beer to the British army stationed in Egypt; this was a huge concession because the army was rather prodigious in its consumption. For example, in 1934, out of the eighty-four thousand hectoliters consumed in Egypt, the British army and their families drank sixteen thousand hectoliters. McEwans was thus able to afford a bottling plant, where they could bottle the beer that they imported in barrels or kegs. They were also able to afford to market and sell their beer to nonarmy personnel. The second importer, Slavick, was the main agent for Heineken in Egypt. They had a strong presence in Cairo and a powerful control of the beer market in Port Said. Very little beer was sold in Port Said without Slavick's approval.[22] The remaining two major importers, Albertini (which sold Urquell Beer, Puntigam, and Bavaria Beer) and Fix (which sold its own brand of beer), had local connections in Alexandria that bottled the beer they imported.

These foreign competitors had a loyal market in Egypt. The rich and affluent beer drinkers of Egypt, among whom were both foreign- and Egyptian-born elites, consumed foreign beers mainly out of "reasons of snobbery, preference, or nationalism."[23] Elites, with their financial wherewithal, were an important group to capture, yet Crown and Bomonti-Pyramid struggled with these consumers because their consumption was not tied heavily to price. Rather, they bought and consumed certain beers based on taste and the desire for the social and cultural benefits of beer.

The foreign breweries, besides carrying the prestige of their foreign brand, also had the financial backing of corporations looking to establish Egypt as a new profitable market. Their financial advantage is most clearly seen in their advertisements, a medium that in the period from 1920 to 1940 was enjoying its own explosion in popularity. Prior to World War I, Egypt had neither a medium with a wide enough circulation nor a population with enough literate members to sustain an effective print advertisement campaign. However, after World War I, an increase in the number and circulation of newspapers and other periodicals enabled the print advertisement business to see sustained growth. By 1928–1929, the "circulation of [the] Arabic press was estimated at 180,000 daily." This expansion reflected both a growth in literacy, especially among the *effendiyya*, and a decrease in the cost of production.[24]

One excellent example of an information-rich advertisement from a foreign beer company is a 1928 ad for Kupper Beer (fig. 02.01). Underwritten by Sander & Sanderkuk, the design features the name "Kupper Beer" in English above a picture of its bottle and a large selection of Arabic text adjacent to the image.

This advertisement, like most of the advertisements for foreign brands, has a distinct collage aesthetic. The Arabic text appears to have been superimposed next to the picture of the bottle and the English title. This bricolage approach was an excellent way to tailor the message to the Egyptian audience while keeping down advertising expenses.

What is immediately apparent in looking at this advertisement, even to the non-Arabic reader, is the prominent placement of the bottle. It is the icon that defines this advertisement. The primacy of the bottle is no doubt attributable to the fact that at the time, the glass bottle was, in addition to refrigeration, another major technical innovation in the modern beer industry. Prior to the 1900s, glass bottles were, like all glass products of the time, handblown by craftsmen. As the beer industry grew, this artisanal production proved to be a major bottleneck for the industry, as the scarcity in bottles limited the volume and quantity that brewers could sell. The demand for glass bottles pushed entrepreneurs to attempt to automate the

Figure 02.01. Kupper beer (*al-Ahram*, August 10, 1928, 3)

glassblowing process, and it was in 1903 that Michael Owens, working for Edward Libbey at the Toledo Glass company, was able to perfect an automated machine that could produce eighteen thousand pint bottles a day.[25] This innovation was soon internationalized, so that by the time these advertisements were being created (1923–1940), the beer bottle had become an integral part of the beer industry. The beer bottle was indeed an extension of "total control" brewing, an approach that was predicated on the (often misguided) belief that using the most current techniques and technologies would enable brewers to control all variables and remove all "foreign" bodies from the brewing process, and thus produce a consistent and standardized product. No wonder, then, that the iconography of this advertisement, and of most other advertisements discussed in this chapter, traded on the fetishization of the beer bottle.

In addition to the primacy of the bottle, what is also immediately apparent, almost jarring, about the advertisement is the mass of Arabic text that sits adjacent to the bottle. This advertisement exemplifies the information-rich advertisements that foreign beer companies produced. The large mass of text displays the arguments that foreign companies used to sell their beer to the Egyptian public. As the advertisement notes:

> There needs to be a reason for residents of tropic (*al-manāṭiq al-ḥārra*) or sub-tropic areas to drink beer. The most important reason to do so is that beer does not upset your natural balance nor cause you to switch from one state to another. Likewise, for one to drink beer it needs to contain the best elements to quench the thirst and refresh its drinker. All of these characteristics come together perfectly in Kupper Beer. As a result, it has, for many years, been the choice of beer for the Egyptian people.[26]

Immediately noticeable is the classification of Egyptians as residents of tropic or subtropic areas. This division of the world into geographical zones based on climate originates with Aristotle, for whom these geographic zones determined not only the flora and fauna that were present in a region, but also the physiognomy and temperament of the people who lived there. This geographic determinism, as with a great deal of Aristotelian thought, was absorbed by classical Arabic thought and then transferred to medieval European thought.[27] By the 1920s, the division of the world into geographical zones had regained prominence with the work of a Russian climatologist and amateur botanist, Wladimir Köppen, who published *Die Klimate der Erde* in 1884 and revised it in 1918 and 1936. Köppen divided the world's climates into five different regions: tropical, dry, temperate, continental, and polar. His classification system was less deterministic than Aristotle's in its evaluations of the people who lived in each region.[28]

In any case, the turn of phrase in the advertisement evokes scientific authority, as it situates Egyptians in a separate group from the Europeans and explains why they should drink beer. The Kupper advertisement appears to draw more from Aristotle's ideas of climatological determinism than Köppen's, as it is followed by a message about upsetting natural balances and temperaments that are inherently different from those of the Europeans. This message clearly appealed to those trying to sell beer to Egyptians, for a similar statement is made in a 1938 advertisement for another German beer, Dressler: "There is nothing better for residents of the tropics like a refreshing (*mun'ish*) drink."[29]

The idea that beer provides refreshment (the Arabic root *nūn-'ayn-shīn*) is another shared feature of the two advertisements. In fact, beer as a refreshing beverage, and the corollary that beer quenches thirst (*taṭfī al-'aṭsh*), is one of the most persistent descriptors of the beverage in these advertisements. Dressler was particularly enamored with this angle. For example, another of their advertisements states, "When the midday sun is at its most intense and the temperature rises, there is no drink that quenches the thirst and refreshes the spirit like the beer with the most beautiful pure color, Dressler beer. It is crafted expertly and without any harmful (*ḍāra*) chemicals."[30] The portrayal of beer as a refreshing drink is premised on two distinct features of the beverage. The first is the effervescence of the beverage, a by-product of the fermentation process. The supposed rejuvenating power of effervescence was widely assumed among Europeans even in the Middle Ages. The drive to produce water that contained effervescence similar to what occurred in nature was the main driving force of beverage technology in the eighteenth and early nineteenth centuries. One of the European beverage industry's first major success stories, Schweppes, was built on this research.[31] Brewers went to great pains to maintain beer's effervescence, filling bottles using a counterpressure device that kept the pressure within the bottle high enough to prevent foaming (loss of $CO_2$) when the beer was poured in.[32] Thus, the glass bottle and its cap were essential in maintaining one of the key components of beer's refreshing nature.

The second distinct feature of beer was its temperature. The linkage between the refrigeration and beer industries was strong, with the beer industry being at once a prime innovator in and consumer of refrigeration technology; beer companies often supplemented their sales of beer with the sale of refrigeration technology. This strong connection meant that if there was any industry that could provide beverages at below room temperature, it was the beer industry.

The ability to control temperature allowed companies to sell beer that was not only cool and refreshing but also limpid and golden. One of the distinct features of industrially produced lager beer is its clear yellow color, which results from both the bottom brewing (yeast tends to collect at the bottom) and the filtering process used on the beer, which removes all the particulates that could make a beer cloudy. Dressler also used this quality to great effect: "Brilliant yellow, as if it was made of amber (*kahramān*), it beams in its glass and gladdens anyone who gazes on it or tastes it. This power makes Dressler beer perfect for those hot days, as it can refresh and renew your strength."[33] In this passage, Dressler beer's brilliant yellow color is equated with refreshment, as the consumer's refreshment begins when he or she looks upon the amber-colored beverage. Like the others discussed above, this advertisement portrays beer as the ideal drink in Egypt's hot climate.

But the pure yellow color was more than a signal of refreshment; it was also a sign of quality. Another advertisement (fig. 02.02) notes, "Dressler beer is carefully crafted from the finest varieties of barley and blended oats to improve its taste and to preserve its limpid color permanently."[34] The emphasis on quality ingredients and quality production was a way to differentiate this product from beer's cheaper cousin, *būza*. Because the consumption patterns of the lower classes were driven by price concerns, relying on the lower classes was a losing proposition for the beer industry.[35] No matter how efficient production and distribution were, beer could not compete with the price of *būza* produced in cafés and homes.[36] Therefore, the beer companies took the strategy of presenting beer as the drink of the modern Egyptian (*effendiyya*).

In one Dressler advertisement (fig. 02.03), the images that accompany the slogan exemplify the beer companies' target audience of *effendiyya* (sing. *effendi*; English, effendi).[37] The *effendiyya*, who have recently received a great deal of scholarly attention, were a group of young Egyptians who were distanced from the average Egyptian by their education; their "culture," i.e., Western manners and dress; and their secular worldview.[38]

The image depicts an effendi couple (the man dressed in a suit and fez, the woman in a hat and an overcoat) enjoying a large bottle of beer that they have just purchased from a uniformed drink seller plying his wares at a mobile drink stand. Beneath that scene are two hands, one holding a glass and the other pouring a bottle of Dressler beer into the glass. Reading together the slogan, "Dressler beer is carefully crafted from the finest varieties of barley and blended oats to improve its taste and to preserve its limpid color permanently," and these two images, the story that emerges is one of the imagined Dressler consumer: an effendi couple who, after enjoying a day out in the hot sun, perhaps at one of Cairo's modern parks, are looking for a drink of sure quality and purity that can quench their thirst. The only option for them, at least in the narrative of the advertisement, is Dressler beer.

Figure 02.02. Dressler (*al-Ahram*, July 29, 1938)

Figure 02.03. Dressler (*al-Ahram*, July 15, 1938, 7)

The targeting of effendi is fully realized in the advertising campaign of another foreign beer company, Amstel, whose advertisements feature only Arabic text and images that evoke the luxury of foreign products while maintaining connection with the local culture. One advertisement (fig. 02.04), for example, shows a pair of dark hands, between lines of Arabic, pouring an Amstel into a glass—label out, of course.

ان صفاء

بيرة أمستل

هو صورة ظاهرة

لمزاياها الحقيقية

النقاوة

والخفة

والترطيب

بيرة العارفون

Figure 02.04. Amstel (*al-Ahram*, February 23, 1931, 10)

The use of dark hands implies luxury because, as Eve Troutt Powell has expertly shown, race and class were strongly linked in Egypt at this time.[39] In this instance, the dark hands depict the hands of either a Nubian or Sudanese servant who would most likely be in the employ of a wealthy Egyptian. This implication is made explicit in two other Amstel advertisements: one portrays a caricatured black servant in traditional dress pouring an oversize bottle of Amstel (not shown), which he carries like a heavy piece of furniture, into an oversize glass;[40] the other (fig. 02.05) depicts a more realistic black servant wearing a table server's (*sufragī*) outfit, holding a tray with an Amstel on it in one hand.[41]

These advertisements traded on the social dynamics of Egypt to evoke the luxuriousness of their product and appeal to their potential customers' sense of modernity. Drinking beer signified one's identity as a member of a certain class. For example, in the first Amstel advertisement above, the image is framed by the slogan that Amstel is "the beer of those in the know." The phrase makes beer exclusionary and aspirational. But what was the secret knowledge that encouraged the modern Egyptian to drink it? A line from the first advertisement, the one with the dark hands pouring, gives a hint: "The purity of Amstel beer reflects its choiceness, freshness, and lightness."[42] The slogan invokes the beer's industrialized and standardized production, which can produce a cool and impurity-free beer, in order to inspire the modern Egyptian to drink it. Brewers took great pains to ensure that their beer was pure, and, again, this purity depended upon the technological innovation of the glass beer bottle. Brewers washed the bottles assiduously, sterilizing them to remove any possible contaminants.[43] Then, after capping the bottles and creating the vital seal, the brewers sent the bottles through a pasteurization process, where the bottles would be heated to 60–65 degrees Celsius (140–151 degrees Fahrenheit) to eliminate any microorganisms that may have survived previous stages of the process.

Companies were not content to portray their beer as merely refreshing and unadulterated, however. They also aimed to invest it with curative powers. In the Amstel advertisement that depicts the *sufragī* holding the beer bottle on the tray, the text states, "Amstel Beer: it cures the sick, and removes the cares and worries of a person's life."[44] A similar allusion to the drink's curative powers is seen in the advertisement of another foreign beer company, Guinness. An advertisement whose title can be translated "Guinness Is Good for You" (fig. 02.06) features an anthropomorphized pint of Guinness smiling, and at the bottom are lines of Arabic arranged in the two-hemstich line form of a *qasīda* (ode):

Figure 02.05. Amstel (*al-Ahram*, February 16, 1931, 12)

Guinness is good for you, Guinness frees you
From worry and weakness, Guinness cures
what ails you
Guinness is good for the celebrating youth
Ask your doctor about how Guinness can set you right

> Drink Guinness in the morning
>    And the night saying:
>    Guinness, the original stout.[45]

This advertisement is an excellent example of the trend, discussed by Relli Shechter, of foreign companies using translated advertisements to keep down overhead and maintain their "winning formula."[46] The highly successful "Guinness Is Good for You" campaign, started in 1928 in Europe,

Figure 02.06. Guinness (*al-Ahram*, April 17, 1939, 4)

was based on advice solicited from doctors and emphasized the healthful benefits of Guinness.[47] While the translation may have been simply a matter of economic expediency, there was precedent in the Arabo-Islamic tradition for using alcohol as a curative. The prioritization of the medicinal properties of Guinness is, in fact, in line with the juridical opinion of many Hanafi scholars who believed that alcohol could be imbibed if medicinal.[48] Indeed, the exhortation to drink beer in the morning echoes a fifteenth-century Cairene theologian, Shams al-Din al-Nawaji, who compiled an anthology of anecdotes and poetry that praised the *sabūḥ* (the morning draft of wine).[49]

The focus on alcohol's curative powers originated early in the history of advertisements. A great deal of advertisement prior to the nineteenth century in the West was focused on selling patent medicines and nostrums that were purported to cure all manner of diseases and health problems. It was only in the late nineteenth century that advertising underwent a major shift, as allopathic medicine gained unprecedented legitimacy and medical crusaders were able to show that these patent medicines and nostrums were composed of questionable ingredients and had questionable effects. With the professionalization of the advertising industry, advertisers tried to distance themselves from these disreputable products, preferring to focus instead on other, less questionable, products. Nevertheless, the regenerative rhetoric that was a mainstay of patent medicine advertisement was merely transferred to new, less disreputable products. As Jackson Lears puts it, "Rather than deriving restored vigor from nerve foods, blood purifies, tonics, and exhilarates, target audiences were urged to turn toward Coca-Cola, Quaker Oats, or Welch's Grape Juice."[50]

## Local Opposition

The medicinal focus served another purpose in a majority-Muslim country like Egypt. It was a way to subvert the vocal opposition to the growing alcohol industry in Egypt. Because of relatively low-alcohol content, beer could slip through certain Islamic reasoning. For example, Shaykh Muhammad Faraj al-Sanhuri, an Egyptian religious scholar, recognized the unique threat posed by beer. As he states in his 1917 tract, *Al-Muskirat* (Intoxicants), in which he documented, described, and ruled on the legality of the alcohol present in Egypt at the time: "Beer (*al-Jiʿa*) contains alcohol, but less than alcohol products, vinegar, perfume extracts, flour, and the bodies of animals and plants. There are varieties of beer that have less than 3 percent alcohol by weight. So one does not need to fear intoxication unless one drinks a great deal."[51] The concession that beer has a low alcohol content and must be consumed in large quantities in order to cause intoxication is very significant in the context of Islamic discussions of temperance. The Qur'an was not iron-clad in its condemnation of all intoxicants. One of the four schools of Islamic legal thought, the Hanafis, took this ambiguity to its logical conclusion, arguing that certain alcoholic beverages were permissible for consumption as long as they did not intoxicate, especially if they had medicinal properties.[52]

A medicinal beer would be a particularly troublesome foe for Islamic temperance advocates, and it's no wonder then that we can find many coming out hard against the beverage. For example, in Ahmad Ghalwash Effendi's treatise on alcohol, *Athar al-Khumur fi al-Hayya al-Ijtima'iyya* (The effect of alcohol on a society), he places beer in a category of beverages that derive from the rotting of intoxicating grains like barley, wheat, and rice and that can carry the name *būza* or, as the pre-Islamic Arabs referred to it, *mizr*.[53] Ghalwash was mainly concerned with debunking the claims that beer could nourish the body and help people to do good work.

Ghalwash argued that the amount of nutrients (sugars and proteins) contained within beer was so small that to get any nutritional value from the beverage, one would have to drink a tremendous amount. This overconsumption would counteract any benefits that beer may have because of the large amount of alcohol that would come along with it. This is not to mention the fact that it cost twenty dirhams to pay for the amount of beer that one would have to consume in order to equal the amount of nourishment contained in one loaf of bread, which cost only one dirham. So, for Ghalwash, a person would be extremely stupid and wasteful to try to subsist on beer.[54]

Ghalwash's argument and treatise came out of a particularly fervent time of temperance in Egypt, which was roughly contemporaneous with the time frame of the alcohol advertisements discussed above. Between 1920 and 1940, there were at least two major organizations in the country dedicated to the eradication of all alcohol, the Woman's Christian Temperance Union and the Egyptian Temperance Association (Jam'iyyat Man' al-Muskirat li-l-Qutr al-Misri [ETA]), which Ghalwash headed.

The WCTU in Egypt was the local chapter of the World Woman's Christian Temperance Union (WWCTU), the international wing of the American temperance organization founded in 1874 to fight for, among other things, a sober world. It "was intimately tied to the American Mission in Egypt (supported by the United Presbyterian Church of North America [UPCNA]); most of its members were either missionaries for the UPCNA or Egyptian converts who were trained in one of the Presbyterian schools." On the whole, it was not a popularly supported movement. It always suffered from a small membership drawn almost exclusively from upper-class European evangelicals and Egyptian Christian women. Nevertheless, it enjoyed access to decision makers in Egypt and a worldwide network of early feminists. It used this powerful network to disseminate the curriculum of Scientific Temperance Instruction (STI). The curriculum used books like William Tyler's *The Physiological Side of Temperance*, which provided a "technoscientific" justification for temperance. They argued that abstemiousness was a key component of "modern," healthy life, as it prevented the mental and physical damage that alcohol could cause to the body.[55] While the actual science could be faulty, STI couched its temperance argument in the unimpeachable rationality of science, while adding the imprimateur of the doctors and scientists who would attach their names to it.

This work proved significant, as it jibed with "an Islamic conception of modernity, which spliced the techno-scientific with a reinterpretation of the Islamic tradition" that was percolating both in the religious establishment and in the developing Islamic Far Right from the 1910s to the 1930s in Egypt. Its impact was bolstered by American Prohibition, built on the Eighteenth Amendment, which legislated Prohibition, and the subsequent Volstead Act, which enforced it in 1920. The net effect was that Islamic thinkers could reappropriate temperance as proof of Islam's transcendental perfection, and thus the teleology of progress was reversed. "Islam and Egypt no longer sat behind, but were placed ahead. Now every step that the West made towards temperance was an example of how it was 'catching-up' to the Islamic world that had always known the benefits of the abstention from alcohol."[56]

Thus, we see anticolonialist movements, like the Muslim Brotherhood and later Young Egypt, a radical nationalist party with fascist leanings formed in 1933 by Ahmad Husayn, adopt scientific temperance as a central part of their reform packages.[57] Likewise, major Islamic thinkers of the era, including Muhammad Rashid Rida, incorporated it into their writings. The ETA, and its leader, Ghalwash Effendi, was the most significant example of this trend.

The work of these temperance fighters in Egypt mainly took the form of lobbying government officials. They had a minor success when the WCTU was able to convince the minister of education to include some aspects of STI in the national curriculum. The ETA was also able to successfully lobby to eliminate new licenses for selling alcohol. However, this concession came with a significant caveat, as it did not apply to any of the European Districts (*al-Akhtat al-Urubiyya*) in five cities—Cairo, Alexandria, Port Said, Ismailia, and the Suez, which were hubs of the alcohol trade.[58] Beyond these results, the on-the-ground impact of both the WCTU and the ETA, which also suffered from membership issues, was rather small. They were hurt further when the experiment of American temperance ended with the repeal of the Eighteenth Amendment in 1933. Although both would continue on after this point, with the ETA surviving to this day, "their moment of international and domestic relevancy had passed."[59]

Nevertheless, these temperance activists, like the advertisers, set the parameters of beer's cultural place in Egypt. The advertisers' focus on its refreshment, its purity, and its curative properties would become the standard by which all beer was sold in Egypt. In particular, these ideas would be fully incorporated into the brand imagery of the beer that would bring Crown and Bomonti-Pyramid to the top of the Egyptian market, Stella. And when Stella became the hegemon of the Egyptian alcohol market, these ideas became inextricably linked to beer itself. However, the sunny image of beer was tempered by the narrative established by the Islamic teetotalers, which highlighted beer's danger as an intoxicant of the mind and body. As we shall see, this multifaceted image of beer would become the Egyptian cultural standard.

## Catching a Star

Although Crown and Bomonti-Pyramid could not match the advertising might of foreign companies, they made their own forays into advertisements. In 1934, for example, the company spent 200,000 piasters on a campaign in Cairo that included newspapers, magazines, calendars, menus, and drink lists, as well as cinema advertising. The company also erected tents at forty-four of their clients' sites, including the Anglo-American Bar, and supplied mirrors, flashing signs, and billboards with the company's name emblazoned on them.[60] This expenditure came after spending nearly a half-million piasters on advertising in the three years beforehand.

Further evidence of their advertising forays is found in a 1928 issue of *al-Ahram*, one of Egypt's oldest and most famous dailies. Titled "Bières Crown Pyramides," the image portrays an old man, a young man, and a woman drinking from an oversize foamy mug. The three people, attired in Western dress, are ethnically ambiguous. At the bottom of the advertisement, an Arabic line reads: "The Beer of Pyramids and Ibrahimia in Egypt." This bilingual advertisement is designed to accomplish a great deal in a small space. By using a French splice of the two recently linked breweries, the advertisement reinforces the connection between the two companies and capitalizes on any brand loyalty among Francophones. The middle image portrays the beer as both delicious (frothy, overflowing) and "modern" (read: suitable for Westernized, secular, and liberal citizens), by having the young and old, male and female, enjoy the delicious beer together. The image trades on the idea that the consumption of a modern product makes the consumer modern. Finally, the script at the bottom appeals to the Egyptian nationalist by using Arabic and uses the names of the major breweries themselves to show that this beer is "Made in Egypt."[61]

Due to Bomonti-Pyramid and Crown's local presence in Egypt, their advertisements could rely primarily on the resonances of images (frothy mugs, men and women drinking together) to sell their beer. People, especially residents of Cairo and Alexandria, could associate the brand with a concrete structure within Egypt. Moreover, with the partnership between Bomonti-Pyramid and Crown, brokered by Gaston-Dreyfus and Mouratiadis, these breweries had, for a time, come to dominate the "local" beer market. In 1934 these two breweries sold 77 percent of the beer purchased from local brewers.[62]

Nevertheless, it was not advertisements that would win the battle for the Egyptian beer market. Rather, it was a high-quality, low-cost, and evocatively branded product supported by a strong and effective sales system. The keystone for the success of the partnership between Crown and Bomonti-Pyramid in the face of foreign competition was the label they launched from it, Stella. This shared brand enabled the breweries to sell a product nationally.

The breweries positioned this new beer as an upscale cousin to the blond beers that both breweries were selling under their own names. Stella was also a blond beer, but it had slightly higher alcohol content and a higher price tag. In Alexandria a large bottle of regular Crown beer cost 2.5 piasters at grocery stores, while a large bottle of Stella cost 3.5 piasters. The difference was even starker at bars, where the regular beer could cost from anywhere from 4 to 6 piasters, while Stella could cost 6 to 10 piasters. Along with a higher price and alcohol content, the breweries also were assiduous in their application of their total-control brewing methods to produce a high-quality beer, meaning better taste, brightness, and foam stability. As a result, Stella compared favorably to beers imported from Europe.[63]

Although Stella's high quality had enabled it to make some inroads among the elite, the breweries ultimately decided not to target the group because it would always have members who would not drink Stella because it was made in Egypt. Instead of pursuing them, the breweries decided to focus on those residents of Egypt for whom beer was a luxury and for whom price was extremely important: the employees (*muwaẓẓafīn*), artisans, and workers of Egypt. By employees, they meant both high-level office workers (those whose made 25 pounds per month or more) and low-level office workers (those who made between 10 and 20 pounds per month). By artisans, the breweries meant those specialized workers who made 5 to 7 pounds per month. And by workers, they were referring to, as they called them, "indigenous" workers who made between 2 and 3 pounds per month.[64] This income-based sketch of the breweries' imagined consumers signals that the breweries had their sights set on a wide swath of Egyptians, from the effendi to the urban worker.

Crown and Bomonti-Pyramid breweries targeted these groups by producing a beer that was high quality, yet cheaper than its competitors. For example, whereas a case of large bottles of imported beer would sell at 248 piasters per case, the breweries could sell a case of Stella beer at 128 piasters per case.[65] The prices could be kept low largely because of their business model, which involved the import of most of the raw materials of beer (malt, hops, and yeast) and the use of cheap and plentiful local resources (labor, rice, and water) to produce a product more affordable than its imported competition.[66]

We also see this market targeting in the name that they chose for their beer. Using the Italian word for "star," *Stella*, was a masterful way to craft the product for the Egyptian market. The Italian language, like the culture itself, was perceived as exclusive, as only the truly "educated" Egyptians would know Italian, yet familiar. Due to the long and prominent presence of Italians in Egypt, the Italian language had seeped into Egyptian colloquialisms, especially vis-à-vis luxury products. For example, *mūbīlīyya* (Arabic colloquial: "furniture") from the Italian *mobilia*, *lūkānda* (Arabic colloquial: "hotel") from the Italian *lokanda*, and even the word for beer itself (*bīra*) had entered from Italian, *birra*. In addition to the Stella name's evocation of familiar Italian culture, it also fitted nicely in an Arabic context. The word was easily transliterated into Arabic (sīn-ta-lam-alif) and contained no difficult sounds for the Arabophone speaker. Even the word written in Arabic was flowing and continuous, containing none of the long vowels that usually break up foreign words written in Arabic.

By aiming at this market, Crown and Bomonti-Pyramid may have been able to circumvent their foreign competitors, but they placed themselves in competition with other, more popular, products. Specifically, they had to compete with Turkish coffee and whiskey. Turkish coffee offered a better price, had none of the religious baggage, and was also typically served with a free glass of water—a strong incentive at the time. Whiskey (as well as brandy and arak), for their parts, offered more alcoholic bang for the buck, as they were only slightly more expensive and offered much higher alcohol by volume. The breweries saw whiskey, in particular, as a direct competitor to beer and believed that, if the public authorities placed sufficiently high tariffs on whiskey and were stricter in their fight against whiskey adulteration, the consumption of beer would increase in line with the decrease in whiskey consumption.[67] Both Turkish coffee and liquors were difficult opponents, and the breweries would struggle with them until the late 1930s, when Heineken bought into both breweries. As I will show in the next several chapters, Heineken figured out a way to tackle these two competitors and make beer a primary leisure-time drink of the effendi. However, even before Heineken took over, the breweries were thinking of how to beat out Turkish coffee and liquors. This fact is evident in one of Heineken's first feasibility reports on the country. The report speaks of two ways that Stella beer could win this battle for the money of the effendi and the worker.

The first strategy identified in the report was to further beer's connection with the Egyptian custom of *mezze*, which, as it was practiced in Egypt, often consisted of spicy dishes and hors d'oeuvres: "ham, salami, meats, cheeses, supplemented with Eastern specialties such as crab, shrimp, cucumber." Heineken's plan was to promote the pairing of *mezze* and beer by promoting a practice whereby *mezze* would come free with an order of a beer.[68] Although this practice would place a burden on the sellers of *mezze*, it was great for the sale of beer. Not only did it add value to beer, tying it closely to an indigenous custom, but it also supplied the customer with dishes that would make them thirsty for another beer. By the same logic that many bars in America offer free pretzels or peanuts, the encouragement of *mezze* in Egypt boosted beer sales.

The second strategy identified in Heineken's report for expanding beer's role in Egypt was that beer could be branded as a key hot-weather alcoholic beverage. In Egypt, the hotter the weather, the more beer people would drink. As evidence of this link, one of the depots in Alexandria was open only for the six months of the year when it was hot enough for people to swim on the beach. As I will show in the following chapters, Heineken would use these associations of beer with *mezze* and with warm weather, especially the latter, to sell beer to effendis and workers in Egypt.

## Selling the Star

The targeted marketing and high quality of Stella would not have meant much if they were not matched with a strong and effective sales system. The most telling example of the joint sales system of the breweries was Egypt's largest market, Cairo. The nerve center of the joint operation in Cairo was the Central Bureau, located at 68 Ibrahim Pasha Street, in the heart of the city. The bureau was in charge of delivering all the beer produced in the Bomonti-Pyramid factory to the markets of Cairo, Suez, and Upper Egypt (which was classified by the companies as anything geographically south of Cairo). The head of the bureau was none other than Constantine Mouratiadis. The choice of a Greek made sense because Greeks ran the majority of the brewery's clients (bars, cafes, pubs, restaurants). The choice of Mouratiadis, specifically, made sense on three levels. First, his father, Michel Mouratiadis, had worked for Crown, so he had a significant familiarity and familial connection with the business. Second, he had all the personal characteristics that companies look for in their leaders: he was outgoing, personable, honest, and loyal, and he enjoyed a good reputation among what one Heineken employee called "Europeans," of which the Greek community was part.[69] Third, as a major stockholder in Crown—he would eventually become the largest shareholder in the company—he embodied a tangible link between the two companies who ensured that the operations in Cairo would suit the needs of both breweries.

Mouratiadis had almost complete control of the Cairo operation. He was the director of the company's storage facilities, its customers' accounts, general statistics, general accounting, commercial services (sales), and advertising. He organized the people below him into three departments: bureau employees, salespeople, and stock workers/deliverymen. Inside the bureau, he employed six people: a head accountant, an accountant, an assistant accountant, a secretary, a cashier, and a debt collector. He paid them between twenty-five Egyptian pounds, the pay of the chief accountant, and sixteen pounds, the pay of the debt collector. Outside of the bureau, he employed two salespeople. His head of sales was a sixty-something Greek man, Mr. Metaxas, who oversaw all the markets to which Bomonti-Pyramid sold product. Mouratiadis employed another salesman whose sole responsibility was Cairo. He had three men charged with running the stock houses and another four who delivered beer to customers.[70]

The sale and delivery of beer in Cairo and Upper Egypt were organized in concentric circles centered on the Central Bureau. The first circle encompassed those retailers, grocers, cafés, bars, and beer halls that were close enough to the Bomonti-Pyramid factory to receive direct deliveries. The next circle contained those locations that were outside the immediate vicinity of the factory but still within Cairo proper. This circle covered establishments in Azbakiyya, Bulaq, 'Abdin, and Bab al-Luq. Instead of delivering directly from the factory, Bomonti-Pyramid used fifteen depots throughout Cairo to deliver their beer. The deliverymen of Bomonti-Pyramid ran these semi-

autonomous depots; they received shipments from the factory and then arranged their delivery schedules with the customers. In the next circle were
those customers who lived in the suburbs of Cairo, which at this time included Giza, Dokki, Zaytun, Heliopolis, Helwan, and Maadi. Six more depots
served these suburbs. Out of the twenty-one depots of Bomonti-Pyramid
(fifteen in Cairo and six in the suburbs), fifteen were run by Greeks, two by
Muslims, one by a Coptic Christian, one by an Italian, and two by people of
unclear identity (they could be either Coptic or Muslim). Beyond the confines
of Cairo and its suburbs, wholesalers, based in Cairo, did most of the work of
the brewery in places like Aswan, Minya, and Fayum. The only customer outside of Bomonti-Pyramid's circles was the British army. They always received
direct deliveries of beer, no matter their location.[71]

The points of connection between these circles and the center were the
brewery's salespeople and the deliverymen. The salesmen went out to the
establishments in each of these circles to find new business and negotiate the contracts between the purchasing parties and the Central Bureau,
which was in charge of all sales. Payment could come in the form of cash
or credit. While the salesmen established the terms of the relationships, it
was the deliverymen who serviced and maintained them. Deliverymen were
charged with delivering beer from the warehouses to both the direct pur-
chasers (bars, cafés, etc.) and the depots in Cairo and the suburbs. The technology of transportation that was at the deliverymen's disposal once again
shows the agglomeration of new and old technologies rather than new technology eliminating the old. They had four to ten motorized trucks depending on the season, five horse-drawn trucks, eight to ten scooters, and thirty
handcarts.[72]

The deliverymen were central to Bomonti-Pyramid's business in Cairo,
enjoying a level of autonomy not typical of our contemporary conception of
deliverymen. Instead of being assigned certain delivery routes and clients,
they cultivated their own client bases and had strong relationships with
those to whom they delivered. The deliverymen received no salary from the
brewery; instead, they made all their money off the one-piaster commission they received on every dozen bottles of beer they delivered successfully. These men determined their own routes for bringing the beer from the
warehouses to the clients, and they were also the ones to receive payment
and look after unpaid debts. The only accountability these deliverymen had
to Bomonti-Pyramid was that their receipts had to match up with the beer
they sold. This system worked only because most of the deliverymen were
former employees of Mouratiadis from his time at Crown before he took
over control of the Cairo office.[73]

The system presented some significant advantages. First, it allowed for widespread publicity for the brewery's products. Each of these deliverymen was an evangelist for the company, and he would use his strong relationships with clients to solicit advice on new potential clients. Second, this system allowed the brewery to efficiently supply its customers with beer. Because these deliverymen knew their clients so well, they could make sure that no one went too long without the proper supply of beer. For example, they would know that a certain beer hall always ran out of beer on a Wednesday and thus would make sure to deliver to them on Thursday. Finally, because the deliverymen had such good relations with the clients, they could keep track of clients' debt situations and help ensure they never owed too much to the brewery.[74]

There were downsides to this system as well. First, because the breweries had no real relationship with customers, it was difficult for the brewery to deal with them directly. In addition, accounting could get confusing, as each deliveryman used his own system. There was also the unfortunate reality that some of these deliverymen could either lose or steal some of the money that was intended to reach the company. But perhaps the most significant difficulty this system presented was that these deliverymen were not very easy to replace.[75]

On balance, the system functioned well for Mouratiadis. He worked hard to keep the clients within these concentric circles connected to the center, especially those within Cairo proper. For the places that could receive direct deliveries, Mouratiadis made sure that they were visited daily and stocked well. Generally, if an order was placed in the morning, it was ready that afternoon. If it was ordered in the afternoon, it was typically delivered by the next morning. Mouratiadis was also very generous with these clients. For example, in 1934 he gave an advance to sixty-seven of these establishments that equaled roughly 2,700 Egyptian pounds. Most of this money was meant to fund these establishments' retrofitting their bars with the mechanisms to serve Bomonti-Pyramid's beer from a keg on tap. This was an important step, as most of the "high-quality" foreign beers were served on tap. Another advantage to serving beer on tap was that delivering barrels or kegs instead of bottles reduced costs; the brewery could ship more beer at one time in a sturdier case because barrels and kegs were much less likely to break than bottles.

Mouratiadis was also generous with the depots in Cairo. His generosity came in three forms. First, the lease for eight of the fifteen Cairene depots was in his name, and he paid the rent for all fifteen. He also paid the phone bill for six of the fifteen. Second, besides paying service fees, he also gave the depots free coolers, scooters, and handcarts to run their businesses, replacing the materials when they wore out. Third, Mouratiadis would give the depots free ice produced by Bomonti-Pyramid. This ice was a significant gift because these depots used ice to refrigerate their beer. Mouratiadis did all of this because depots were concentrated primarily in what were known as the European districts of Cairo. There was, thus, a significant growth potential here if he could establish a fleet of loyal depots. This growth was essential because Cairo was Bomonti-Pyramid's most profitable and successful market. Outside of Cairo and its suburbs, Bomonti-Pyramid did not sell a great deal of beer.

Whereas the Bomonti-Pyramid operation was under the control of a Greek stockholder at Crown, it was an Egyptian citizen, Mr. Gibara, who ran Crown's operations in Alexandria. While the biographical information about him is scant, we do know that he originally came from Syria, was a director on the board of Crown, and spoke fluent Greek, Italian, English, French, and Arabic. Crown paid him 50 pounds per month in salary and bonuses, and he oversaw a staff of ten employees in the Alexandria bureau. Of the ten workers, five were Greeks (a typist, a debt collector, an assistant accountant, a cashier, and the head of the warehouse), four were "Arabs" (all four served as porters), and one was Syrian (the chief accountant). The highest paid, at 19 Egyptian pounds per month, was the cashier. The next-highest paid was the Syrian head accountant, who had a salary of 18 pounds per month. The Greek typist was the only woman employed in the office, and she made only 6 pounds per month. The only employees of the bureau who made less than her were the four "Arab" porters, who were paid 4 pounds per month.[76] Of Mr. Gibara's three salespersons, one was in charge of Alexandria, Mr. Caritato; one would travel to the villages, Mr. Sirakis; and one was in charge of the brewery's relations with the beer depots.

Crown organized the Alexandria and Lower Egypt market similarly to the market in Cairo and Upper Egypt. Again, the Central Bureau sat at the center of five concentric circles. The first circle covered those cafés, brasseries, restaurants, and grocers who were located near enough to the factory to receive direct shipments.[77] The circle just outside this one contained those customers outside of the immediate vicinity of the Crown factory (figs. 02.07 and 02.08), who received beer from the six depots. The third circle covered the customers in the suburbs of Alexandria. The fourth circle encompassed all customers located in the villages and cities above Cairo. The last circle included all the export markets, including Syria, Palestine, and the Dodecanese.

Although Crown organized its markets similarly to Bomonti-Pyramid, the

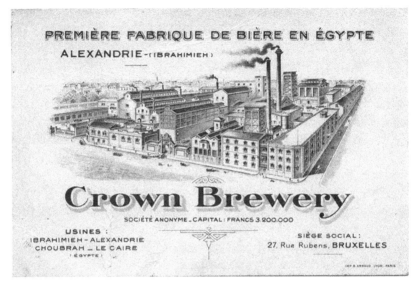

Figure 02.07. Postcard, Crown Brewery (Norbert Schiller)

Figure 02.08. Crown Brewery factory (Norbert Schiller)

way it connected these circles differentiated the Alexandrian brewery from its Cairene partner. All beer produced by the Crown factory was delivered to the Central Bureau. From here, the porters employed by the Central Bureau would deliver to all the establishments within the first circle. The three deliverymen who were in the service of Crown would also pick up their beer from here. These three oversaw the six depots of Alexandria, which operated semiautonomously like the depots of Bomonti-Pyramid. Crown's three deliverymen covered all the expenses of transporting the beer and were paid by commission: they received two milliemes for every bottle sold by them and eight milliemes per dozen bottles they successfully delivered.

However, these deliverymen did not have as much autonomy as those of Bomonti-Pyramid. The salesmen of Crown directly controlled their routes and deliveries, which were all formalized in contracts between clients and the Central Bureau. Moreover, they relied on the largesse of the Central Bureau for the continued functioning of their depots. The Central Bureau provided the depots with thousands of blocks of ice to keep the beer stocked in the depots refrigerated. The Central Bureau also provided them with an allowance of two and a half pounds for the maintenance of their depots and offered them three days of credit if they wanted it.[78]

In the suburbs of Alexandria, the two agents of Crown, who operated exclusively in the Ramleh suburb, were tasked with both the sale and the delivery of beer to customers. The agents would buy the beer from the Central Bureau at the standard rate and would incur all the costs of transportation to one of their four depots. However, the agreement was definitely in favor of the agents. For every dozen bottles they sold, they would receive a commission of five Egyptian pounds, a huge sum. They also received an eight-millieme commission on every successfully delivered dozen and two thousand blocks of ice from the Central Bureau.[79] Nevertheless, Crown was more successful than Bomonti-Pyramid at exploiting the suburban market.

This success was built on Crown's sales in the villages outside of the city and its suburbs. For example, in 1934 Crown sold more beer in Port Said and Ismailia, 1,477 hectoliters, than Bomonti-Pyramid sold in all Upper Egypt, roughly 1,300 hectoliters. These superior sales probably had to do with the fact that Crown had excellent agents in both cities. These peripheral agents were left a great deal of autonomy, so they were the ultimate determinants of the success or failure of the brewery there. Fortunately, the agent in Port Said, Mr. Garangiotis, was active and intelligent, and he had the support of his son, who was fully committed to selling beer. On top of these personal characteristics, Garangiotis had lived in Port Said for more than forty years and was embedded in the community as a municipal councilor.[80]

In addition to serving villages, Crown also, as part of its agreement with Bomonti-Pyramid, exported to all clients in foreign markets. With Crown running exports, it was easier to ensure that the beer exported was of a good quality. The beer could go straight from the factory onto boats and trucks headed out of Egypt, instead of making the hard journey between Cairo and Alexandria, which added an extra chance of breakage or spoilage. In the 1920s, the three largest export markets were Syria, Palestine, and the Dodecanese, the group of 12 larger and 150 smaller islands in the Aegean. By the 1930s, however, these three markets were in decline; they went from consuming nearly 1,500 hectoliters in 1930 to consuming 856 hectoliters in 1934. This decline was the result of three factors: more organized local competitors offering their beer at lower prices, foreign countries raising tariffs and other barriers to the import of beer, and Egypt's overall decreased trade with these countries.[81]

## The Results

A 1934 study on the beer market in Egypt reasoned that there were more than three hundred thousand Egyptians and "foreigners" who drank beer.[82] These foreigners were composed primarily of *mutamaṣṣirūn* (Egyptianized foreigners).[83] This grouping did not include the seventy-five hundred British soldiers who were stationed throughout Egypt. The analyst separated them from the rest of the foreigners because their consumption was rather prolific. They consumed approximately 17,000 hectoliters per year, which put their per capita consumption at 220 liters per year.[84]

Despite being a minority of the population of roughly fourteen million people living in Egypt, this group of beer drinkers was a profitable market. For example, in 1929, residents of Egypt drank more than 130,000 hectoliters of beer, of which more than 70,000 came from local brewers. These would be high-water marks for nearly a decade, as the Great Depression would hit in that same year. By 1933 total beer consumption had dropped to its lowest level during the decade, at 71,000 hectoliters, with local production making up roughly 42,000 hectoliters.[85] Despite the continuing poor economic conditions, consumption would only rise from 1933 to the end of the decade.

Of the breweries that were selling their beer in Egypt, it was Crown and Bomonti-Pyramid that supplied the majority of the beer consumed. For example, in 1934, these two breweries sold 59 percent of the roughly 85,000 hectoliters that were consumed in the country, of which Bomonti-Pyramid sold 33 percent and Crown sold 26 percent.[86] When we look at consumption of non–British army personnel, the Crown and Bomonti-Pyramid dominance becomes even starker. In 1934 non–British army personnel consumed more than 68,000 hectoliters of beer. Bomonti-Pyramid and Crown of the Egyptian market sold 77 percent of this beer, with Bomonti-Pyramid accounting for 44 percent.[87]

It is hardly surprising, then, that Bomonti-Pyramid did quite well during the Depression. That is not to say that the breweries weathered the Depression unscathed. In order to maintain investment in the company during this time, it had to offer a dividend that paid 6 percent, which impeded its ability to replenish its reserve capital and made the company financially vulnerable. However, outside of the three-year period from 1930 to 1933, the company maintained a relatively stable rate of profit between 4.5 and 6 percent.[88] It is important to remember that while the Bomonti-Pyramid Brewing Company was consistently profitable during this period, it was arguably less profitable than other "core" industries, such as the Egyptian Salt and Soda company, which was capitalized at 485,347 Egyptian pounds in 1937 and saw profits at 11.3 percent, as compared to the 192,875 Egyptian pounds of the Bomonti-Pyramid company and its 6 percent profit margin.[89]

Even still, one cannot look at the years from 1920 to 1940 as anything but a success for Bomonti-Pyramid and Crown. In this twenty-year period, they devised an organizational plan, an effective and efficient sales system, and a brand, Stella, that could beat back competitors, local and foreign. Stella dominated other local brews with its quality, it was on par with the imported brands, and it outmaneuvered the imported brands with its price. It is, then, no surprise that the story from Stella from this point forward is one of success. The next few chapters describe how, with the backing of one of the most important brewers in the world, Heineken, it would come to reach the summit of the Egyptian beer industry and become the beer of Egypt. But it is worthwhile to ruminate over the story in this chapter, as it displays how this success was not accidental. From its inception, Stella was meant to do what no other Egyptian beer had done before it, to find the market sweet spot. It was exclusive, yet attainable. It was of a high quality, yet relatively affordable. It also, as we will see, co-opted and expanded on the marketing strategies foreign beers had first deployed. It would become the fun, refreshing alcoholic beverage of the Egyptian middle stratum that so many other beers tried to be. Nevertheless, because of the work of Islamic modernist thinkers, this fun would always be tinged with a sense of danger.

# Crowning the Pyramid

*The Egyptian Beer Industry's "Mature" Period, 1940–1952*

By the late 1930s, beer had become a significant, though contentious, element of "modern" Egyptian culture. A prominent example of the growing cultural presence of beer in Egypt is the appearance of a beer-centered ritual in Egyptian nightclubs. As Karin van Nieuwkerk describes, inside clubs in the 1920s and 1930s, female entertainers were tasked with the *fatḥ* (Arabic: "opening"), whereby the entertainers would walk from customer to customer and ask if he would like to drink with her. This *fatḥ* would often turn into a competition between men to exhibit their wealth and masculinity, with the beer bottle serving as the ostensible measure of power. A male customer might, for example, order a dozen bottles of beer and have them brought by a train of attendants to show off.[1]

Stella, the upscale joint venture of Egypt's biggest brewers, Crown Brewery and Bomonti-Pyramid Brewery, however, had yet to reach its status as *the* beer of Egypt. It would begin its journey to the top in the 1940s as the companies who sold it entered what I call their "mature period." In the span from 1940 to 1952, these companies would take the form that they would maintain until 1963, that is, a partnership with converging executive structures, shareholders, and business practices. This convergence was spearheaded by the Amsterdam-based multinational corporation Heineken Brewing Company (Heineken Bierbrouwerij-Maatschappij). Heineken had targeted the Crown and Pyramid Breweries for inclusion in their ever-expanding empire after having seen the developments and profits of these two companies up to 1940. A third feature of the companies' mature period, in addition to being characterized by partnership and by Heineken's influence, was their struggle to maintain their hybrid identities as truly transnational ventures. The companies could not be classified either as strictly Dutch or as strictly Egyptian ventures. This hybrid state was crucial to the companies' success prior to

1940, but it became problematic in the 1940s, as the world was far less accepting of ambiguity in nationality and economics.

The transformation of the companies from relative autonomous entities
to Heineken-guided ventures stemmed from a single catastrophic event:
World War II, the largest war that the world had yet seen. Heineken's push
to consolidate the Crown and Pyramid Breweries represented its unwillingness to continue to suffer the inefficiency, of which it had become acutely
aware of during the war, of being a passive shareholder a continent away.
After the war, Heineken sought greater control over its assets to maximize
profits and ease the exploitation of the Egyptian market.[2]

Heineken was not the only party that was inspired by the extraordinary
circumstances of the war to demand greater control of the breweries. The
Egyptian government, too, came to interact and control businesses in a way
that it had never before. Since the 1920s, there had been growing demand
among Egyptian politicians for greater control of their economy, especially
vis-à-vis the "foreign" elements present. These two trends, toward greater
control and targeting the foreign element, converged in 1947 in the Company
Law, which granted unprecedented powers to the Egyptian government to
deal with joint-stock companies that it classified as "foreign." Whereas in
the 1920s and 1930s these companies and their actions had been relatively
unsupervised, starting in 1947 they had to reckon with a more invasive and
self-assured government that had a very narrow idea of what an Egyptian
company was.

As both forces, Heineken and the Egyptian government, exerted greater
control over Pyramid and Crown Breweries, they did not sit by passively.
Rather, they fought both actively and surreptitiously against outside control.
In both companies' interactions with Heineken, they used the geographic
distance between them and the Amsterdam headquarters to reject or slow
down actions that they found distasteful; thus, they could negotiate from a
position of weakness. In the breweries' interactions with the Egyptian government, despite the rising political tide of economic nationalism, they were
able, with the aid of their Dutch backers, to maintain their hybridity.

## Celluloid Consumption

In tracing the place of beer in Egyptian culture, film is an excellent place to
look, as its development in Egypt tracked a parallel path to the development
of the nation's beer industry. Film entered Egypt before the beer industry, in

1896.[3] Both Egypt's beer industry and its film industry adopted technological advances from Europe. The first films, recorded on a cinematograph by the Lumière brothers, Auguste and Louis, had been played for Paris audiences in 1895.[4] Less than thirty years later, the first full-length film produced in Egypt, *Fi bilad Tut'Ankh Amun* (In the land of Tutankhamen), premiered in 1923.[5] This section traces how cinematic portrayals of beer signaled a new cultural acceptance of the beverage in Egypt.

By the 1930s, the film industry, like the beer industry, had become a modern industry; by the 1940s, it had become a powerful force in Egyptian culture. Between 1945 and 1952, the film industry produced more than four hundred films.[6] It was in this same period that film became an art form that was crafting a new "middle-class bourgeois nationalist identity."[7] It stands to reason that beer would appear in films, as it too was becoming a cultural force in this period. Indeed, from 1940 to 1952, the beer industry experienced sustained success. In 1946, for example, Crown Brewery's net profits totaled the significant sum of LE 106,000.[8]

The films discussed in this section tend to show that beer drinkers were coming from the old groupings of the *effendiyya* and the urban underclass. However, as Lucie Ryzova notes, the boundaries of these groupings had shifted by the 1940s. The *effendiyya*, the urban office class, in the period following Egypt's semi-independence in 1922 came to represent, at least for the liberal nationalists, the perceived middle of Egyptian society. The *effendiyya* were the bearers of the national mission, and they were distinct from the *awlād al-balad* (native sons, "the good guys"), the fellahin, and the *awlād al-dhawāt* (Arabic: "sons of distinction," the "elite"). In practice, to be an effendi was to inhabit a liminal place between the lower and upper classes, to be a secular, modern, and liberally educated person who strove for the modern, secular, elite lifestyle, but whose background and financial status kept one separate from that elite.[9]

With this shift from broad to specific characterizations, the *effendiyya* became distinct from the classes above and below, at least in the minds of intellectuals. Whereas previously the *effendiyya* included both the elite and the Western educated nonelite, the term came more and more to refer to those urban subalterns who had undertaken "effendification," while the Westernized elite took the name of *awlād al-dhawāt*. Likewise, with most of the new effendi transitioning from the urban subaltern, what it meant to be a noneffendi resident of a town or a city came to be encapsulated in the concepts of the *awlād al-balad* and *al-futūwwāt* (Arabic: "youths"). As Wilson Chacko Jacob has shown, despite the term *futūwwa*'s multivalent and complicated

history, by the 1930s the term was divested of much of its positive characteristics and came to resemble the concept of *al-balṭagī* (thug, tough, etc.).[10]

Like the depiction of cigarettes in films, it was these imagined groups
(*awlād al-dhawāt, awlād al-balad, futūwwāt*, and the *effendiyya*) that shaped
depictions of beer consumption in Egypt in the postindependence period.[11]
For the elite, their consumption of alcohol was assumed and unquestioned.
Many movies from the period 1930 to 1950 show upper-crust men and
women dressed in fine Western clothing, listening to music and dancing
while enjoying alcoholic beverages. While generally the type of alcohol remains obscure, in a few notable exceptions, beer takes center stage. For example, in *Al-ʿAzima* (Determination [1939]), as ʿAdli Bey (Anwar Wagdi) talks
to Muhammad Hanafi (Husayn Sidqi) about their joint business venture,
using a phone located in a bar, a Stella advertisement sits prominently in the
background. The advertisement is so legible and prominent that it can only
have been intentionally placed in the frame.

In an even more prominent example, from the movie *ʿUsta Hasan* (Boss
Hasan [1952]), the rich Svengali, Kawsar (Zuzu Madi), has a refrigerator
stocked with beer bottles bearing the unmistakable star logo of Stella beer.
The bottle is fetishized, with the camera making it one of the most prominent images on the screen. In addition, the bottle is used as a metonymy for
beer and alcohol more generally. This ability to have the branded bottle serve
as a signifier of alcohol in general is evidence of the effectiveness of the beer
advertisements of the 1930s. By the 1940s, these advertisers had achieved
what they desired: the bottle, a symbol of what I call total-control brewing,
had entered Egyptian culture as *the* symbol of beer. Total-control brewing
was the idea that a company could produce a standardized, sturdy, and sanitary product by assiduously applying the latest in brewing technologies. The
scene in *ʿUsta Hasan* is important in showing the cultural footprint of the
beer bottle and of beer in general. The film again links the consumption of
beer to the elite, although it adds a layer of complexity by portraying upper-
class women's consumption of it as normative. This portrayal was atypical
for the time, as alcohol was still generally reserved for men.

Egyptian films also portrayed urban subalterns as drinkers of beer. The
two most prominent examples of such characters are Hamida (Shukri Sarhan) in *Ibn al-Nil* (Nile boy [1951]) and Hasan (Farid Shawqi) in *ʿUsta Hasan*.
In *Ibn al-Nil*, whose very title evokes the idea of the *awlād al-balad*, a *fellah*
named Hamida travels to Cairo to escape his life in the village. Fresh off the
train, Hamida searches for a place to spend the night and ends up in a dance
club. Unsurprisingly, he is enticed by the vices of the club, and in an act that

sets off a terrible chain of events, he succumbs to a dancer and to beer and eventually loses all his money. In the scene, beer, depicted in an overflowing stein, is closely associated with the dancer (Samiha Tawfiq) through interspersing of images of the frothy mug with her gyrating. In the case of Hasan, Kawsar entices him to abandon his humble lifestyle and become her paramour with gifts and plentiful food and drink. In one of the film's pivotal scenes, in which the protagonist begins to realize the pleasures possible in this new life, Hasan gorges himself on a whole turkey and drinks three bottles of beer. This plenty appears in stark contrast to the penurious lifestyle he lived in his humble home.

The blatant consumption of beer in the film is not without consequences for the two main characters. A common refrain in these and other pre-1960s Egyptian films is that the *ibn al-balad* who drinks ultimately suffers for doing so. In the case of Hamida, his first night of drinking transforms him from the naive yet authentic *ibn al-balad* into a cynical and violent *futūwwa*. Eventually, his new lifestyle leads him to jail, although he is later freed and returns home. As for Hasan, beer marks an even more tragic transformation. He leaves his life as a hardworking mechanic to become a morally corrupt bon vivant. There he has two unhappy relationships (with his wife and Kawsar) and sees his son come to physical harm and Kawsar murdered. Hasan is freed, only to learn from his mistakes and resume his original life because of the surprise confession of Kawsar's invalid husband to the woman's murder. These films emphasize the dangers of modernity to the uneducated but authentic *awlād al-balad*, with the transformative power of beer emerging as a key theme. In each case, beer has caused the protagonist to make the incorrect transition. Neither character has moved from authentic native son to hardworking and respectable member of the middle class. Instead, they both transition to more profitable but morally bankrupt phases.

This narrative of the drinking-led downfall for the *ibn al-balad* is echoed in other media as well. For example, we see this narrative in Bayram al-Tunsi's *zajal* poems, "rhymed strophic poems composed in non-classical Arabic based rhythmically on metrical patterns adapted from the classical tradition." In his massive 1924 *zajal* poem *Il Baladi*, "'Abd al-Salam, the writer, is brought down by his ever-increasing consumption of beer and whiskey."[12]

The idea that the consumption of beer and alcohol is dangerous is supported by the depiction of the *effendiyya* in movies, who generally remain teetotalers. For example, the main protagonist (and arch-hero) of *Al-ʿAzima*, Muhammad Hanafi, avoids drinking even when he visits his good friend the elite playboy ʿAdli in a bar. This abstemiousness is seen in other effendi protagonists like Hamid ('Imad Hamdi) in *Al-Suq al-Sawda'* (Black market

[1945]) and Taha Effendi (Yusuf Wahbi) in *Ibn al-Haddad* (Son of the black-smith [1944]). The middle-class protagonist is not always strictly abstemious; for example, Munir (Farid al-ʿAtrash) in *Uhibbuka Anta* (I love you only [1949]) is a telegraph operator and part-time singer, who in the course of his work consumes alcohol. In this role and many others, Farid al-ʿAtrash's characters are notable for their entirely normative relationships with alcohol. The different depictions of alcohol consumption vis-à-vis the imagined middle class or *effendiyya* reflected Egyptian intellectuals' uncertainty over what the ideal mix of modern and traditional should be, particularly for the group whom they envisioned to be the true bearers of Egypt's future.[13] They likewise represent the multifaceted cultural image of beer in Egypt, equal parts refreshing and corrupting.

## In the Hands of a Dutch Giant

While the depiction of beer and alcohol in film was somewhat ambiguous, there was no ambiguity about who controlled the beer industry in Egypt in this period: it was Heineken. As discussed in chapter 2, Crown and Bomonti-Pyramid embarked on a new unified plan of selling beer, Stella specifically, to Egyptians in the 1920s and 1930s, under the leadership of French entrepreneur René Gaston-Dreyfus. As an entrepreneur is wont to do, Gaston-Dreyfus continued to look to grow his beer empire and his profits.

His main project after Crown and Bomonti-Pyramid was increasing his presence in Indonesia by establishing a brewery in Java. Since it was a Dutch colony at the time, Gaston-Dreyfus aimed to partner with a Dutch brewery in the venture. He found a willing partner in Heineken Brewing Company, one of the largest brewers in the world, and its representative in the area, Jonkheer Pieter R. Feith. When Gaston-Dreyfus's Sofibra and Heineken went to Java, they agreed that the only place suitable for a new brewery was the city of Surabaya. Unfortunately, another company, Coloniale Brasserie (Cobra), had purchased land there in hopes of building their own. Although they were initially discouraged, Sofibra and Heineken came upon a solution when, in the 1930s, they encountered another multinational brewing interest looking to expand its brand, Société Anonyme Internationale de Brasserie (Interbra). This Belgian company had interests in Belgium, France, Belgian Congo, and Angola and, incidentally, owned Cobra.[14]

In line with Heineken's aggressive international expansion plan of the 1930s, the brewing giant purchased all three of the companies (Sofibra, Interbra, and Cobra). With regard to Egypt, the investment in Gaston-Dreyfus's

Sofibra provided an entrance into a market that it coveted; the chairman of Heineken had visited Egypt after World War I and was impressed by the rapid development that the beer companies had made during that time.[15] Heineken's entrance into the Egyptian beer industry thus began in 1937 and was spearheaded by the investment company Cobra, renamed N. V. Koloniale Brouwerijen and relocated to Amsterdam.[16] Cobra had become, after the purchase of and incorporation of Sofibra and Interbra, the main vector for Heineken's international expansion. It had investments not only in Egypt but also in Indonesia (Heineken Netherlands-Indonesian Brewing Company in Surabaya), Singapore (Malayan Breweries), and Brussels (Société Internationale de Brasserie). This last brewery even had its own international holdings in France (Metz and Tours) and in Belgian Congo (Leopoldville).[17]

Instead of purchasing the breweries outright, Cobra bought shares in Bomonti-Pyramid (which dropped Bomonti after the purchase) and Crown Brewery. Although this might sound like a rather straightforward process, the acquisition of the shares was a multistep venture. Heineken, acting through Cobra, as a Dutch company, bought shares in companies whose main bases of operation were in Egypt but were registered as Belgian companies in Brussels. The multinational nature of the new enterprise meant that the movement of information was not a frictionless process and was often held up by language barriers. For example, if Heineken wanted to implement a new policy on the ground in Cairo, it had to go through a multistep and multilingual process. Heineken, located in Rotterdam, would send a directive to Cobra, located in Amsterdam, via a letter written in Dutch. Cobra would then relay this information to the managing directors of the Crown and Pyramid Breweries, who were in Alexandria and Cairo, respectively; this communication would again go by letter, but this time in French. The managing directors would then relay the message to their respective boards in Brussels, through letters or telegrams in French. Finally, after approval by the boards in Brussels, the policy would be implemented through the aid of workers who had been informed of the plan either orally or through written Arabic.

Despite the added layer of administrative inefficiency, the involvement of one of the largest brewers in the world was a positive development for the companies and their beer, Stella. This relationship provided Pyramid and Crown access to the expertise of Heineken, which was on the cutting edge of brewing. In addition, Heineken was a multinational company with worldwide business interests and thus was well acquainted with the particularities of brewing in all manner of climates and regions. In fact, the procedures that it enforced were like those it implemented everywhere else in its beer empire.[18]

Heineken's main base of operations within Egypt was Pyramid Brewery. It would then use Pyramid to advise Crown. Its services to Pyramid came in five forms: advising, control, staff, yeast, and supplies. Heineken advised on all technical matters ranging from the first step of brewing (raw materials used) to the last (refrigeration). Through this advisory role, Heineken pushed Pyramid and Crown Breweries to implement the latest innovations in brewing in the name of maintaining a healthy bottom line and a product, Stella, befitting the Heineken label. For example, it not only advised Pyramid on what products (the type of malt) and production methods (new malting systems) they should use, but also directed them on how to conduct their own lab-based analysis of the raw materials and the beer produced. This advice was generally rendered in monthly technical reports exchanged between Pyramid and Heineken. For more complex matters, however, Heineken either sent a representative to Pyramid or requested that Pyramid send one to Holland.[19]

This system of monthly technical reports and visits was at once how Heineken advised Pyramid and controlled them. While the technical reports were an important way for Heineken and Pyramid to discuss best practices, they were also a way to keep constant tabs. These reports were usually written by one of the men whom Heineken had placed on the board. These reports were supplemented by the visits of Heineken employees who would not only advise on technical matters but also monitor and report on the operations and workers of the company. Heineken also had Pyramid send a monthly sample of beer to be analyzed in one of Heineken's laboratories.[20] This service was meant to ensure that the beer produced in Egypt matched Heineken's exacting standards.

Heineken not only relied on reports, visits, samples, and members of the executive board to ensure that Pyramid put out a product worthy of the Heineken name, but also placed a man highly trained in Heineken's methods of making beer as the brewmaster. While the industrialization of beer making allowed companies to produce beer with fewer well-trained workers, it did not eliminate the craft in making beer entirely. A person with a large knowledge base, the brewmaster, was still needed to ensure that the product tasted the way the company wanted. The brewmaster was massively important to the direction of the company, and it is for this reason that, as I discuss below, one of the major issues in the nationalization of the beer industry was the expulsion of the foreign-trained brewmasters.

The placement of a Heineken-trained brewmaster at Pyramid was especially important because of another service Heineken rendered, sending their strain of yeast to Pyramid. As discussed above, the greater understanding and subsequent control of the life cycle of yeast inaugurated the scientification and mechanization of brewing. With this new understanding, breweries could optimize the brewing process and even begin to breed proprietary strains of yeast. Thus, the yeast Heineken used to make its beer was unique to the company, a closely guarded secret that differentiated it from other brands. The brewmaster had to be Heineken trained so that, having learned to brew using Heineken's strain, he could maximize its output in a different setting. Beyond the brewmaster, Heineken also aimed, when it could, to place people whom it had trained within Pyramid.

In addition to sending part of the workforce, Heineken also served as the broker for Pyramid's acquisition of new materials. Heineken sent pro forma invoices to Pyramid for any raw or auxiliary materials and machines and installations that were not present in the local market. When possible, Heineken's engineers inspected anything before it was sent to Pyramid. For those materials available in the local market, like crown corks (bottle corks), Heineken insisted that Pyramid send them to Holland for inspection.[21]

As noted above, Heineken very often matched these services to Pyramid with a strong amount of surveillance. Even greater surveillance was demanded by the financial and administrative happenings of the company. Pyramid was responsible for sending Heineken monthly reports on the price of beer, Pyramid and Crown sales, share prices, their cash situation, and meetings of the administrative board. Beyond these monthly check-ins, Pyramid also had to send a quarterly budget and feasibility study of that budget, a yearly inventory, the position and cost of any imports, any lawsuits raised against the company, any regulations passed by the government that would affect the company, and, finally, the status of Pyramid's relationship with Crown.[22]

Heineken tried, when possible, to use its power in Pyramid to influence the direction of Crown, which was also selling Stella. These efforts came into focus when, for example, Crown Brewery invested in kegs in 1938. Given the importance of kegs to the overall brewing process, when Crown wanted to purchase kegs in 1938, they turned to their new multinational partner for their expertise. Heineken, speaking through Cobra, offered two recommendations for companies from whom Crown Brewery could purchase their kegs: a Dutch firm, T. Knape, located in Wassenaar, Netherlands, and a German firm, Rosista, located in Dortmund.[23]

Beyond merely suggesting the two firms from which the brewery could buy its kegs, Heineken also advised Crown to go with the much more expensive kegs from Rosista in Dortmund. Despite the more significant financial outlay, Rosista's kegs were made from stainless steel, meaning that they did not require any pretreatment before they could be used. Another benefit of the Rosista model was that it came with its own specially designed method of closing the keg.[24] This meant there was no fear of mismatched caps and kegs. Although the suggestion came with the implication that Crown was not up to the task of meeting the demanding conditions required for the T. Knape kegs, Crown Brewery proved very receptive to the advice of Heineken.[25]

This interaction between Heineken and Crown illustrates how Heineken's investment in the Crown and Pyramid Breweries paid significant dividends for the Egyptian companies. Being a part of a multinational corporation gave the breweries access to the latest in brewing technology and techniques and thus allowed for the smarter importation of technologies. The breweries could tailor their imports to the particularities of the country before spending any money, in contrast to previous attempts by entrepreneurs to bring technology into Egypt. Such entrepreneurs often assumed that the import process would be frictionless, only to find difficulties in applying technology. So Crown, on the advice of Heineken, instead of going for the "cheaper" keg option and suffering from their false economy, chose the "more expensive" option that was better suited to their needs.

## World War II and the Desire for More Control

Heineken's advice to Crown did not arise solely from a desire to build up the Egyptian beer industry; it also came from its desire to preserve the bottom line for an investment that was almost immediately profitable. In 1939 Heineken received a total dividend payment of more than 23,000 pounds sterling from the 8,968 shares it owned in Crown Brewery.[26] This profitability was immediately threatened by a global conflict that was slowly starting to engulf the world, what would eventually be called World War II. This war caused numerous difficulties for Heineken. Because of British regulations on money leaving Egypt, they were unable to transfer dividends from Crown Brewery to Heineken. Another difficulty was the loss of German employees. After the war began, Crown very quickly lost its German brewmaster and its cooper (the man in charge of making wooden barrels or casks for aging the beer), as both abandoned their jobs to return to their homeland.[27] An even greater difficulty that Crown faced after the outbreak of the war was that all of its activities involving the governments or citizens of any occupied countries (e.g., Belgium, the Netherlands, and France) came under the purview of an Egyptian governmental body created during the war, the Office des Territoires Occupés et Contrôles (Maktab al-Bilad al-Muhtala wa al-Khadiʿ li-l-Riqaba; Office of Occupied and Controlled Territories).[28] The OTOC served as a watchdog of any action the breweries took with regard to Belgium or the Netherlands and also had full control of Crown and Pyramid's transactions with these countries. For example, during the war, the OTOC not only blocked any Crown funds going from Egypt to Holland but also kept them in their own coffers.[29] Thus, in 1945, when the OTOC informed Crown that it could start paying out to its stockholders, the money came from the OTOC.[30] When, in 1948, the OTOC did unblock funds flowing to Holland, an agreement between the Egyptian and Dutch governments enabled the Egyptian government to control the bases through which companies could transfer the money from one country to the other. In total, the OTOC held nearly 48,000 pounds sterling during the war that was meant to be transferred from Crown to Cobra.[31]

The OTOC's involvement with Crown was emblematic of how World War II allowed governmental bodies in Egypt to become more involved in private businesses in the name of national interest. Despite the disruption of the war, the breweries were still able to maintain their financial viability. In an internal memo, one of its administrators noted that during the war, Crown used its brewery machinery nonstop.[32]

The wartime loss of control spurred Heineken to take greater control of their profitable property. The main avenue for this push was the placement of Cobra and Heineken employees on the Crown board. As is clear from the above discussion, the communication chain between Heineken and Crown and Pyramid was highly inefficient. For example, if Cobra wanted to be represented at shareholders' meetings, it had to go through significant hurdles, giving power of attorney to an employee of Pyramid Brewery to represent Cobra at Crown's shareholder meetings. In addition, according to the regulations of Crown, this employee had to be a shareholder in Crown and thus had to buy shares in Crown before attending a meeting.[33]

After 1947 Cobra aimed to eliminate this inefficiency and worked to have a Cobra employee on the board of Crown.[34] As discussed in chapter 2, Mouratiadis and Crown had fought for and secured a large degree of autonomy in their battle with René Gaston-Dreyfus. They were not keen on any encroachment from Cobra, especially Cobra's request for representation on their board. The only way Crown would even consider the concession was if they could have a representative on the Pyramid board.[35] This request illustrates that, despite the external appearance of unanimity between Crown and Pyramid, people within both companies viewed them as autonomous bodies.[36]

So how did Cobra attempt to circumvent Crown's protestations about Cobra's representation on their board? It appears that Cobra used the other brewery, Pyramid, against Crown. Their basic strategy was to give 4,860 shares of Crown Brewery, from among the 8,978 it owned, to the Pyramid Brewery in exchange for 50,000 shares of Nigerian Brewery Limited in Lagos that Pyramid owned.[37] With control of these shares, Pyramid would become the largest shareholder in Crown Brewery. This was a backdoor for Cobra to acquire local representation in Crown without forcing their hand and souring the relationship. Cobra was the largest stockholder in Pyramid, and because Pyramid had not been as recalcitrant to members of Cobra sitting on their board, it had handpicked representatives on the board, who were consulted on all major decisions.[38] In particular, an executive named Oscar Adrian Eduard Egbert Lewe Wittert van Hoogland had taken a large leadership role in Pyramid after his appointment, assuming the title of managing director. With these Cobra employees embedded in the upper executive realm of Pyramid, Pyramid's new stake in Crown meant that Cobra could have an indirect way of influencing Crown.

Pyramid looked askance at the dealings of Cobra, and this influenced the negotiations between the five main parties involved: Ahmad Farghali Pasha, Yusuf Dhu-l-Fiqar Pasha, and René Ismalun, all of whom were of Egyptian nationality and sat on the board of Pyramid; Wittert van Hoogland, who also sat on the Pyramid board; and G. A. Martin, a British shareholder. The three Egyptians represented the interests of Pyramid, while Wittert van Hoogland and Martin spoke for Cobra. When Wittert van Hoogland was able to gather all the Egyptians together in April at a board meeting, it was Farghali Pasha who held up the deal, doing so by raising questions about the deal's fairness.

Cobra would exchange the Crown shares for the Nigerian shares at a price of 120 piasters per share, a sum that covered both Pyramid's original investment in the shares and a 3 percent yearly interest on them. Although there would be a loss of about 863 Egyptian pounds, this was covered by Cobra's 1-sterling discount on the Crown shares that Pyramid was receiving. Farghali Pasha was unconvinced, however, and believed that because Pyramid was giving Cobra such a below-market price on the Nigerian stock, the least Cobra could do was pay 4 percent yearly interest instead of 3 percent. After months of stalemate, Wittert van Hoogland eventually conceded to 4 percent, and this concession, plus the direct contact that Cobra made with the

Egyptians at Wittert van Hoogland's request, was instrumental in getting the deal pushed through.[39] With the deal completed, some questions remained about who would represent Pyramid Brewery at the shareholders' meeting for Crown Brewery.[40] Unsurprisingly, Cobra chose the man who had done so much work for them in this matter, Wittert van Hoogland.[41] He would have a powerful role to play in both of the companies from 1953 to 1957, serving as Cobra's main man on the ground.[42]

The great difficulty in finishing this deal, which ultimately benefited both parties, evinces a deeper rift between the Egypt-based entrepreneurs and their European counterparts. Wittert van Hoogland remarked on this rift in discussing the particularities of the deal. He stated, "When one proposes something to an Egyptian he generally thinks there is something that he does not see behind the proposal and therefore that he is being had."[43] From the European side, this statement speaks to the essentialized view that Europeans had of Egyptians. Nevertheless, the statement and the actions of Farghali Pasha also hint at a sense of distrust among Egyptian business elites vis-à-vis Europeans.[44] Of course, Farghali Pasha's intuition may have been correct, as Cobra was using this deal to manipulate Egyptians, just not him.

These hard dealings also tell us something more personal about Farghali Pasha. As he was arguing with Wittert van Hoogland over the percentage interest on the Nigerian shares, he made a statement to René Ismalun, his fellow Egyptian on the board and a member of the Egyptian Jewish community: "I think we should be like the jew [sic] and ask Cobra to compensate us on the basis of 4 percent interest." This bit of off-the-cuff anti-Semitism was meant as a way to justify Farghali Pasha's hard line, but to the modern reader it is jarring. The breeziness with which Farghali Pasha mentions "jew" as a joke signals his, and perhaps his cohorts', use of casual anti-Semitism as a source of humor. Ismalun's response to Farghali Pasha only affirms the point, as he notes in a quick rejoinder, "That would not be like the jew [sic] but like Farghaly [sic]."[45] This response confirms not only that the anti-Semitism was expressed in jest, but that this was probably not the first instance in which Ismalun had heard such a statement.

## (Partial) Egyptianization

Despite the push for greater control, as we saw with the negotiations with Farghali Pasha, the people on the ground still had a massive influence on the direction of the companies. Heineken and its representatives in the companies could map out whatever best practices they wanted, but, ultimately, the decision on whether policies were implemented relied on the local leadership. As I discuss later, despite all of Heineken's advantages, it was never able to control Crown like it did Pyramid.

Heineken's lack of complete control over Crown and Pyramid was exactly what the Egyptian government of the time wanted. As Heineken was trying to gain great control over Crown and Pyramid Breweries, the Egyptian government was instituting policies that were pushing private industries toward a singular goal, Egyptianization. This push grew out of a series of concurrent trends. The first trend was the slow erosion of the Capitulations and their main manifestation, the Mixed Courts. The Capitulations were "a set of privileges granted to nationals of certain countries that effectively exempted them from Egyptian law and judicial institutions." The Mixed Courts was the body that attempted to manage the judicial needs of two antagonistic forces in Egypt, the Egyptian government and the capitulatory powers. What the courts became in practice was a dual legal system, in which Egyptian and foreign companies were tried separately. Regarding private European companies like Crown and Pyramid, this dual system made them practically inviolate. However, the Mixed Courts had, from their founding, been continually under attack by both the Egyptians and the British.[46] Opposition reached a critical mass in 1937, when the Montreux Conference established a phasing out of the Capitulations, which was then followed by the abolition of the Mixed Courts in 1949. Without this impediment, the Egyptian government could now deal with foreign businesses that for so long had resided in Egypt as judicial blind spots that were exempt from tariffs and taxes.[47]

At the same time, World War II emboldened the Egyptian government to deal with foreign companies in a new, more invasive way. As with the actions of the OTOC, the Egyptian government, acting under the auspices of martial law, honed its new methods in regulating businesses and their profits. The tactics that the government used to ensure that no money flowed to British enemies, i.e., requesting lists of shareholders, bank statements, and letters and statements from executives, were some of the same tactics they utilized to encourage the Egyptianization of the economy.

The desire to Egyptianize the economy grew out of a sense of economic nationalism, the belief that Egyptians should run the Egyptian economy. This idea originated in the 1920s with the Sidqi Commission on Commerce and Industry, Bank Misr, and the Egyptian Federation of Industries, all of which formed during the period from 1916 to 1922. Bank Misr ("Bank of Egypt" in Arabic), which was founded and headed by Egyptians, seemed to be the example par excellence of Egypt's new economic nationalism. However, these institutions were gradualist and were still intimately tied to non-

Egyptian capital. In the 1920s, business nationalism was merely a convenient way to support new ventures and garner public support for the multinational business groups that were forming around certain enterprising Egyptian individuals.[48]

However, beginning in the 1930s and culminating with the Joint-Stock Company Law of 1947, the ideals of 1920s Egyptian economic nationalism became more of a reality. In fact, the removal of the Capitulations and the eventual abolishment of the Mixed Courts were framed, on the Egyptian side, by the rhetoric of economic nationalism.[49] The Company Law of 1947, however, represented the first powerful push by the Egyptian government for Egyptianization. It required Egyptian companies (those with major bases in Egypt) "to offer 51 percent of their stock to Egyptians and to place Egyptian nationals on 40 percent of the board seats."[50] These moves pushed many multinational companies, including the beer companies, to employ more Egyptian citizens. With regard to the beer industry, it is indisputable that the main leadership became more Egyptian. The presidents of each of the breweries after 1950 were native-born Egyptian citizens: Farghali Pasha for Pyramid Brewery and Muhammad 'Aziz Abaza for Crown Brewery. Both men were exemplary business oligarchs who came to dominate the private sector in the 1940s and the 1950s.[51]

Farghali Pasha's father was a successful Alexandrian cotton merchant who, with the help of foreign investors, established Farghali Cotton and Investment Company. Using the connections afforded by his father's business, as well as his own business acumen and a familiarity with European business practices gleaned from his education in England, Farghali Pasha could sit on many different executive boards. In 1946 he sat on the boards of twenty-nine companies.[52] 'Aziz Abaza, a member of one of Egypt's largest landholding families and the head of Crown Brewery, also sat on numerous boards, including the Land Bank of Egypt, the Société Anonyme de Misr pour le théâtre et cinéma (Corporation for Egyptian theater and cinema), and SEP (a petrol company).[53]

Several other Egyptian citizens joined Farghali Pasha and 'Aziz Abaza on these boards. Of the six other members on the Pyramid Brewery board, three were Egyptian citizens.[54] Meanwhile, Crown Brewery had a similar percentage of Egyptian citizens on its board.[55] Some of the board members shared a similar involvement in business groups; the Jewish-Egyptian René Ismalun of the Pyramid Brewery sat on the boards of seven other companies.[56] Moreover, the "foreign" elements were not as foreign as the government led observers to believe. For example, in the cases of Zenon and Katerina Pilavachi and Spiro Spiridis on the Crown Brewery board, these board members not only lived in Egypt but also spoke Arabic and were integral to the large Greek Egyptian community, which had ancient roots and had grown steadily since the 1860s.[57] Thus, the "foreigners" were as invested in a successful and prosperous Egypt as was a man like Farghali Pasha; they also had a distinctly different relationship with the country than, for example, the Cobra representatives who sat on the Pyramid board. A useful term for them is the *mutamaṣṣirūn*, those "people of foreign origin who had become permanent residents" and in their language and habits had become "Egyptianized."[58] Nevertheless, the *mutamaṣṣirūn* did not have Egyptian citizenship, and thus the government grouped them with men like Wittert van Hoogland and Feith.

The Egyptian government's grouping of the *mutamaṣṣirūn* with foreign-born industrialists was based on two factors: the transnational character of the *mutamaṣṣirūn* and the citizenship process as it existed from the 1930s to the 1950s. Until the late 1930s, the prospects of legal and fiscal exemption through the Capitulations and the Mixed Courts made it much more attractive for local minorities to apply for foreign rather than Egyptian nationality. As a result, there was a mass of residents in Egypt who had spent their entire lives in the country but were not citizens. This trend was particularly pronounced among the religious minority communities; as Gudrun Krämer notes, "The majority of Jews living in Egypt in the twentieth century did not have Egyptian citizenship."[59] An excellent example of such residents is the Suareses, a prominent Jewish family who were also Italian citizens.[60] The linguistic, cultural, and economic heterogeneity of this mass of residents makes any attempts to place them into the "foreign" or "Egyptian" dichotomy reductive. However, that is exactly what the Egyptian state, with legislation like the Company Law of 1947, attempted to do.

As a result of this legislation, these *mutamaṣṣirūn* and the companies that employed them were faced with the dilemma that one of their greatest strengths—their cultural dynamism and multicultural familiarity—had become a major threat to their employment.[61] For the individual citizen, in order to save his job he often had to seek Egyptian citizenship. The path to Egyptian citizenship for these local minorities before 1947 was very difficult. In particular, despite the 1929 Nationality Law's Western liberal basis, the burden of proof needed to become a citizen and the institutional bias against *mutamaṣṣirūn* prevented many minorities from gaining Egyptian citizenship even if they wanted it.[62] Despite pressure from the government, the breweries were able to avoid any traumatic losses of executives or employees. In fact, prior to 1952, the companies had some success with their employees gaining, or rather confirming, their Egyptian citizenship. For example,

Crown Brewery's auditor, Hanna Yusuf Hanna, a Coptic Christian, whose declaration of state-recognized Egyptianness is contained in the Pyramid Brewery records, did succeed in gaining citizenship.[63] However, citizenship would become less attainable after the ascension of the Free Officers, the cabal of disaffected army officers who would overthrow King Farouk in 1952, as they would take what had been laid down in 1947 and build upon it until they had removed all the "foreign" elements.

This chapter has tracked the maturation of the Pyramid and Crown Breweries before, during, and after World War II. This phase was marked by two new sources of power and intrusion, Heineken Brewing Company and the Egyptian government. Heineken's involvement went from investment in an attractive asset to active participation in the beer companies' daily operations. Although Heineken ultimately acted like any business enterprise works, prioritizing their interests above all, its dealings with Pyramid and Crown Breweries were generally conducted diplomatically and with an eye toward consensus. Heineken was more than willing to volunteer, rather than force, its expertise upon Crown and Pyramid, and these two breweries benefited from the technical expertise of the multinational. The balanced dynamic is noteworthy considering the significant power differential between the multinational and the Egyptian beer companies. The relative balance of power can be attributed to the Egyptian breweries' control of the situation on the ground and to the fact that the parties ultimately shared the same goal of profiting from the sale of beer in Egypt.

As for these companies' relationships with the Egyptian government, they were not based on mutual interest; rather, they were characterized by tension that arose from opposing desires. As the government pushed for a more Egyptian economy, the beer companies had a vested interest in maintaining a hybrid and ambiguous national identity. In this case, it was the beer companies that had the advantage: they had a decades-long history of government noninterference as well as multinational connections to deal with the demands of the newly empowered government. Meanwhile, the government was only just starting to escape its colonial/semicolonial past and was only beginning to map out what it could demand from these "foreign" businesses that for so long had remained inviolate.

# Stella Is Always Delicious

## *Selling Beer in the Time of Nasser, 1952–1958*

You write me furthermore about the shortcomings of Hafiz and his
intrigues as well as those of your other employees. While this is of course
most unpleasant, I believe that in Egypt this is actually more or less normal
as the Egyptian Mohammedan urbanite, the so-called effendi, is simply a
highly unreliable and incompetent person. While the Copt, as an always-
cornered minority, is so accustomed to the intrigue that he cannot but
be branded guilty.
—Wittert van Hoogland to Erick Carl Kettner, July 17, 1957

The period from 1952 to 1958 in Egypt was one of massive change. During
this time, the newly installed government of Gamal Abdel Nasser worked
to punish the "foreign" capitalists and their Egyptian conspirators, who, in
Nasser's eyes, had stifled the progress of the country. The government also
worked to assert Egypt's place in the world, a pursuit that involved political posturing (the Suez Crisis), economic restructuring (land reform and
nationalization), and grand architectural ventures (the Aswan High Dam).
For the two major Egyptian beer companies, the Crown and Pyramid Breweries, this was one of their most successful periods, as they witnessed banner profits and brand consolidation behind the breweries' flagship product,
Stella beer. Behind the success, though, the company was troubled by internal conflicts among its Dutch technocrats, who had been sent by Heineken to make sure the company ran "properly," and the Egyptian executives,
managers, and workers. These conflicts grew out of the policies of an activist
Egyptian government that was overt in its favoritism for Muslim Egyptians
and that framed all business interactions as struggles between the "foreign"
and the "Egyptian." It is within this atmosphere that Wittert van Hoogland,
the managing director of Pyramid Brewery, produced the epigraph for this
chapter, which painted all his employees as incompetent urbanites or du-
plicitous Christians. As we shall see, despite Nasser's turbulent early years
of rule, the beer companies' external success managed to coexist with internal strife.

## Crafting a Brand

The year 1952 was a traumatic one for Egypt. On January 26, 1952, antiregime protesters rioted and set fires throughout the city of Cairo, the beating heart of the country. In total, twenty-six were killed, five hundred were wounded, and the cost of the damage was 15 million Egyptian pounds.[1] These fires meant not just protest but violent reaction against the perceived pernicious influence of "foreign" elements in Egypt.[2] Many of these protesters were members of the Muslim Brotherhood and Young Egypt, or at least sympathized with the groups' core belief that the foreign presence in Egypt needed to be excised in order for the country to return to greatness. Many protesters directed their attacks at establishments that were symbols of the foreign presence in Egypt, especially British. Not coincidentally, many of these foreign places under attack, such as sports clubs, bars, hotels, and dance halls, also sold alcohol. These fires represented the literal and figurative explosion of the jingoistic, nationalistic, Islamic modernist feelings that had been bubbling in Egypt since the 1920s, and they also signified the demise of the monarchal Mehmet Ali regime in Egypt. Later that same year, in July, a small group of young, midlevel military officers seized power. In what would come to be called the Free Officers Movement, this group of ninety to one hundred officers seized control of the country from King Farouk and set out to dismantle the regime and its elite support, which they deemed to have been exploiting the country for too long.[3]

Immediately after the Free Officers Movement, the breweries managed to continue business as usual and even to remain profitable. Crown made a profit of 23,000 Egyptian pounds in 1953. Most of this profit, 22,000 pounds, came from the sale of beer, which at the time was going at 34 Egyptian pounds per hectoliter. From this sum, the company was profitable enough to distribute a dividend of 203 piasters, making Cobra's income from Crown in 1953 around 30,000 Egyptian pounds.[4] Still, this profit was less than the company was expecting, a fact that is surely attributable to the country's volatility at the time.

The success of the two companies despite the volatility of this period can be attributed to the fact that Stella had become the beer of Egypt. One of the most significant spurs for the realization of this market control came in 1952 with an important technical innovation, a strain of barley specifically designed to grow in Egypt. Malted barley, which was soaked in water to begin germination and then roasted to arrest this germination, was one of the essential ingredients of modern beer, along with hops and water. Before the innovation of "Egyptian" barley, the Egyptian breweries had to import the malted barley from the Netherlands, where Heineken carefully chose and roasted it. The import of malt from the Netherlands was problematic, as it was inefficient and costly and exposed the malt to the possibility of spoilage or contamination.

These problems with barley supply were resolved when a Dutch brewmaster who had trained at the Heineken Brewing Company, Gerardus Hubertus Ulenberg, became the chief of beer making at the Pyramid Brewery and created a strain of barley in 1952.[5] This new strain of barley was two rowed; barley generally comes in two forms, two and six rowed, depending on how many rows of seeds it has along its flowering head.[6] Although more expensive than six-rowed barley, this two-rowed barley was better suited to growing conditions in Egypt. Ultimately, the breweries came to maximize both quality and price by using a two-rowed/six-rowed mix for making their malt.[7] With this new strain, Pyramid could produce malt that was up to Heineken's standards and differentiated their beer from foreign competitors in Egypt. This innovation not only freed Pyramid from the major manufacturing bottleneck of importing large amounts of barley, but also meant that Pyramid could become a hub of malt production in Egypt and the Middle East.

One of the first results of this innovation was that Pyramid could now send malt to Crown Brewery to produce a similar product. These malt deliveries even went beyond the borders of Egypt. One of the main recipients of this new Egyptian malt was a brewery in the Sudan that had also come under the control of Cobra in the 1950s, Blue Nile Brewery. For example, in 1958, Pyramid sent around 570 metric tons of malted barley to this brewery.[8] The creation of this Egyptian variety of barley was another example of the benefits of Heineken's ownership of Crown and Pyramid. Counter to Nasser's narrative of foreign influences suffocating local industry, the inventiveness of a Dutch brewmaster had created a beer, and thus a beer industry, that was more Egyptian than not.

Even as the barley was being standardized, so too was the bottle that contained the beer. The breweries started using standard-size bottles in 1952. These bottles were imported in two standard sizes, small (330 ml) and large (660 ml). The companies had imported bottles since their founding because it was cheaper to import repurposed bottles from Europe than to purchase new bottles in Egypt. However, the breweries started using standardized bottles only in the 1950s, when it became cheaper than using nonstandard bottles. The government-levied duty on the bottles was based on the metric of "bottles per hectoliter." Thus, for a certain duty paid, a company was able to bring in a certain number of bottles. In 1952 the government made the number of bottles per hectoliter greater for standard bottles than nonstandard. The shift was not without difficulty, as the breweries had built up a tertiary market of selling the bottles. They thus had to either exchange the nonstandard bottles at cost to the breweries (the standard bottles cost 5 milliemes more [20 milliemes] than the nonstandard bottles [15 milliemes]), which they did in Cairo and Suez, or they had to deliver the bottles on consignment, which they did in Cairo and Assiout.[9]

In a trend that occurred in food industries around the world, as both the product within the packages as well as the packages themselves became more standardized and homogenous, companies like Pyramid and Crown had to find ways to differentiate themselves from competitors.[10] In the Egyptian case, there were three distinct reasons that after 1952 the breweries were looking for ways to stand out. Prior to 1952, the beers that the Crown and Pyramid Breweries sold, including Stella, were marked with a label that merely stated the brewery's name. This was not an unusual branding practice for beer companies; Heineken still uses it to this day. Nevertheless, this reliance on the name of the breweries was not the most effective way to sell beers in the dual-brewery model. Selling similar beers under different names in Egypt's two biggest markets created the very real possibility that Heineken would be cannibalizing its market share in both cities. Another motive for creating a brand was that after changing their name from Pyramid to al-Ahram Brewing as part of the Egyptianization process, Pyramid had made their own name less distinctive. One of Egypt's main daily newspapers even shared the name of al-Ahram. The third reason for creating a recognizable brand is that in the 1950s Crown and Pyramid's first real challenger, Nile Brewery, appeared on the market selling similar beers.

For these breweries to differentiate themselves, they turned to a nascent field in the business world, marketing. The breweries contracted an advertising agency, al-Shark, to produce their advertising materials. The owner, a Mr. Maggyar, was excellent, as he had trained at J. Walter Thompson, one of the world's leading advertisers. Al-Shark handled the advertising for almost all major international groups in Egypt, and it even had a department for market research.[11] However, this marketing firm could only do so much without a clear brand message from the company.

Therefore, in the 1950s, these two beer companies, with the help of Heineken, developed the Stella brand. They took the industrially produced lager beer they had been selling under the name Stella since the 1920s and built a brand around a beer that was golden in color and had a light, crisp taste; that had an alcohol by volume between 4 and 5 percent; and that was brewed from Egyptian-made malt (a proprietary mix of two-rowed barley, six-rowed barley, and rice), imported hops, and Egyptian water.[12]

The brand that was featured on bottles and company letterhead was truly a marketing masterpiece. It was simple—a black and white star with the name "Stella beer" circling around it in both Arabic and French—but packed with numerous layers of meaning that resonated with the Egyptian market. The bilingual nature of the brand clearly evoked the imagined consumer of the beer as the middle- to upper-class Egyptian, but the power of this brand went beyond the use of French and Arabic, which was a very common advertising ploy at the time. As I discussed in chapter 2, using the Italian word for "star," *stella*, was a masterful way to craft the product for the Egyptian market. The Italian language, like the culture itself, was perceived as exclusive, as only the truly "educated" Egyptians would know Italian, yet familiar.

Al-Shark publicized this brand through two avenues: large public signs and newspaper advertisements. One particularly prominent electrical sign for Stella sat atop a building owned by a shareholder of the National Bottling Company, the company in charge of selling carbonated soda, Pepsi, in Egypt.[13] While the signage was a public testament to the Stella brand, it was the newspaper advertisements that provided a clear articulation of what the Stella brand was intended to represent.

All the attributes that advertisements ascribed to Stella were properties commonly associated with beer in the earliest Egyptian beer advertisements. Advertisements by beer importers like Dressler, Amstel, and Guinness in the 1930s focused on the beverage's refreshing nature, its healthfulness, and its curative properties.[14] These advertising directives grew out of advances in both the beer industry and the advertising business. Regarding beer, due to advances in refrigeration technology, yeast biology, and bottling, advertisers could put forth a beer that was limpid, temperature controlled, and free from "impurities." Likewise, as advertisers sought to distance their products from the quackery of patent medicines, they aimed to imbue industrial-produced products like beer with medicinal properties.[15] All of this messaging was targeted at the "modern" consumer, who now invested consumer goods with the ability to signal their lifestyle and aid them in their quest for self-improvement.

The Stella advertisements were noticeably more targeted than those that had preceded them. Instead of merely showing "modern" Egyptians in their advertisements, these advertisements illustrated how beer could fit into the everyday lives of the Egyptians. For example, a set of advertisements that featured "the Stella Fairy" argued that Stella could be a normative part of

Egyptian life and even improve upon it. This campaign opened with an advertisement (fig. 04.01) depicting a buxom fairy floating in front of the Stella star and declaring:

> I am a healthful fairy, full of magic and happy things
> I am Stella, I am Stella, and everyone knows who I am.
> My wand refreshes and revives anyone it touches
> It fills one's heart with joy, gives one succor, and quenches one's thirst.[16]

In this advertisement, the healthful properties of beer are equated with magic and wonder. The other advertisements in this series built upon the magical premise established in this advertisement. One advertisement (fig. 04.02) depicted four people on a date, two women sitting on a couch and two men in chairs on either side. Rather than enjoying themselves, they are sitting in bored silence. In the text above and below the image, the men call for the help of the fairy, "They [the women] are racked with boredom and lack of interest and there is no hope in sight. We call for the enchanting fairy. Stella, the shining star." Below this line is another image, in which, with the help of the fairy sitting atop the panel and touching the scene with her wand, and Stella, which sits in the foreground, one couple is dancing and the other is engaged in enjoyable conversation about the music. The men in the advertisement exclaim, "Stella. Thank You! Thank You! Now we know the secret. They have come alive."[17] At the bottom of the advertisements is a picture of the beer bottle standing next to a foaming glass of beer, with the slogan "Stella Is Always Delicious" (Bīrat Stella, al-Bīra al-Ladhīdha).

Above that image is a declaration of why Stella beer is the best:

> Stella beer is made from nutritious (mughadhdhī) Egyptian barley
> And other choice ingredients. Stella beer is the freshest.
> It's a cool, refreshing, and healthful drink.

This was not the only advertisement that focused on Stella's role as a sort of social lubricant. In another advertisement with a similar setup, two young couples sit on the beach in their modern swimsuits, the men in swim trunks and the women in bikinis, all of them looking dreadfully bored. One woman is even reading a book underneath a beach umbrella. This boredom is a shame because the "weather is beautiful as the waves are rolling in and a gentle breeze is blowing." However, when they say the magic words: "We call for the enchanting fairy. Stella, the shining star," the dour scene is transformed, with one couple playing with a ball in the sand and the other snuggled up underneath the beach umbrella.[18] Another advertisement uses

أنا الجنية المذهبية ، ذات الشعر والحسن
أنا ستلا ، أنا ستلا ، وكل البناس تعرفني
وتلك عصاي من لمستَهُ تنعشه وتخفيه
وتملأ قلبَهُ بشرا وتسعدُهُ وتروبه

Figure 04.01. The Stella fairy (*Akhir Saʿa*, May 8, 1957, 5)

Figure 04.02. The Stella fairy (*Akhir Sa‘a*, May 15, 1957, 11)

a similar format (problem, request for the fairy, solution) to show how Stella could even aid adults at work. In this third advertisement, the fairy, after hearing the magic words, blesses two men arguing over a difference of opinion about a contract, bestowing upon them bottles of Stella that immediately resolve the conflict and allow the two to sign the contract.[19] Thus, Stella can even "clear the air and resolve arguments" between feuding businessmen.

Another advertisement in the fairy series takes aim again at the youth, showing Stella as a beverage for the tired athlete. The advertisement begins with a picture of men walking off a soccer pitch exhausted by their exertion in the gleaming sun and saying, "Playing has tired us out. We want something refreshing and revitalizing." When they say the magic words, the fairy blesses them with Stella, and then we see them in the clubhouse celebrating and raising their glasses of cool Stella beer. The players explain their new feeling by saying to the fairy, "A gulp from your health-giving cup is magical and intoxicating. It reactivates the body and fills it with power and health." This advertisement is particularly interesting for two reasons. First, it portrays beer as the ideal after-sports drink. Although this advertisement predates sports drinks by decades, it trades on the same promises of revitalization after sweaty exertion that advertisements for sports drinks use today. While it may seem odd to the modern viewer to imagine beer as a sports drink, this is really no different from parading flavored, artificially colored water that is high in both salt and sugar as a "sports drink." Most interestingly, this advertisement also mentions the intoxicating (*nashwa*) power of beer. Although it is meant in the figurative sense, this is one of few advertisements that even hinted at the reason many consumers bought and drank beer.[20]

In two especially striking advertisements from the series, the fairy is not transformative but merely an observer placed in the corner of a vignette. One depicts a well-dressed couple (the man wearing a tuxedo, the woman a ball gown) dancing at a club as a band plays in the background. The other depicts a man exhausted from the day at work, lying in his reclining chair with the newspaper on his lap and a Stella in his hand. In addition to the lack of the mininarrative of transformation, these advertisements are also distinct because the main text is a colloquial poem perfectly suited to the advertisements' subject matter. Accompanying the couple dancing is a poem with an *aabb* rhyme scheme:

> Dance and enjoy this happy day
> For the day will pass and go away
> Stella opens the way for your day of celebration

As the delicious beer that gives you what you want
Oh, how Stella pairs with songs
And sets the mood for a beautiful evening
For nothing can compare to it
In its quality.[21]

The vignette of the man relaxing is accompanied by a poem with an end-line rhyme of -*ak*.

After the strain and toil of the day
Drink Stella to ease your mind
You will forget all your cares and worries
And the world will always look better
Your normal energy level will return
And it will immediately soothe your nerves
Drink Stella whenever
For it's just what your health needs.[22]

These themes ran through many of Stella's advertisements, as can be seen in another campaign from the 1950s. As figures 04.03, 04.04, and 04.05 show, Stella was often depicted as the perfect accompaniment for a party or a provider of stress relief and relaxation.

The fairy series thus shows that Stella beer could be an important aspect of the modern Egyptian's lifestyle and even add an element of magic. This turn to the magical represents a return to the origins of advertising, in which huge claims were made for patent medicines that were generally of dubious quality and effectiveness. The magic in these beer advertisements is more maturely rendered, however. An Egyptian reading these advertisements would not have imagined that Stella beer had magical powers, but the advertisers do show potential consumers that beer did have the ability to revive, refresh, and, most important, bring people together. This last point was particularly of concern to the newly imagined consumer, the middle- and upper-class youth.

Four out of the six advertisements (the party, the beach party, the sports field, and the dance club) were targeted at youthful audiences. The people depicted in these advertisements appear younger and are rendered in more cartoonish forms. The magic that the "fairy" brought was generally relevant to the lives of younger people; in two of the advertisements, Stella appears as the ultimate icebreaker between men and women. This line of advertisement also does much to focus on another aspect of beer, its cool refreshment. As discussed above, this was a characteristic of beer that was emphasized even

Figure 04.03. Stella advertisement, ca. 1950 (Omar Foda)

Figure 04.04. Stella advertisement, ca. 1950 (Omar Foda)

Figure 04.05. Stella advertisement, ca. 1950 (Omar Foda)

in the first beer advertisements in Egypt. Yet these advertisements transformed beer into a sports drink, the quintessential refreshing beverage. It is these three aspects—that beer is young and fun and refreshing—that would become the essential characteristics of beer in Egyptian advertisements, movies, and literature in the 1960s and 1970s.

## Egyptianization

The ease with which the Stella brand was Egyptianized was not mirrored in the Egyptianization of the companies that sold it. In fact, the government push for Egyptianization inflamed internal divisions, framing interactions between the Dutch, Egyptian Muslims, Christians, and Jews with an "us-versus-them" mind-set.

Prior to the Free Officers Movement, the breweries had taken the first step toward Egyptianization by keeping their headquarters in Egypt, where they had relocated during World War II. This decision was not out of any sense of nationalism but from Heineken's worry that they would have to pay the 150,000 Egyptian pounds they owed to the Belgian fiscal authorities in back taxes if they remained there.[23] However, the decision was not accompanied by any other changes that resembled "Egyptianization." Heineken started to formulate a policy for Egyptianizing both companies in earnest, such as changing their name to al-Ahram, only after 1953, with the rise of the leader who cast a shadow over Egypt and Crown and Pyramid for the rest of his life, the new president of the republic, Gamal Abdel Nasser (1918–1970).[24]

The most telling sign of the activist bent of the Nasser regime vis-à-vis the private sector was his nationalization of the Suez Canal Company in 1956. Since the handover of control to the British in 1875, the canal had served as a constant reminder to Egyptian nationalists of the economic control that foreign interests maintained in Egypt. There was thus broad consensus in Egyptian society at the time of the Free Officers Movement that the Suez Canal Company's control of the canal must eventually come to an end.[25] While the issue of the canal's nationalization was openly discussed, Nasser's desire to use revenues from the canal to fund the Aswan High Dam project accelerated the time line of that nationalization. The British, American, and World Bank's initial overtures to help fund the project and then quick turnaround may have spurred Gamal Abdel Nasser, who by that time had seized power from the Revolutionary Command Council (RCC), the body formed by the Free Officers to rule Egypt, to nationalize the Suez Canal.

Of course, the British and French did not accept laying down the nationalization of one of their most profitable assets, and the policy response they pursued was one of economic deterrence, employing banking and currency restrictions. Their most audacious countermeasure was a failed tripartite (British, French, and Israeli) military excursion that involved the bombing of Port Said and the advancement of troops into the Canal Zone. The invasion only emboldened the Nasser government to expand its nationalization plans. After the failed invasion, the Egyptian government sequestered and then nationalized the companies that had significant British or French capital. This move was accompanied by actions aimed at expelling all British, French, and Jewish residents from Egypt. What really marks 1956 as the start of the new era, though, was what Robert L. Tignor calls a "rupture," as the Nasser government extended these policies to the rest of the Egyptian private sector. The government, backed by "socialist" laws that gave them unchallenged power in the corporate sector and headed by the Egyptian Economic Organization (al-Mu'assa al-Iqtisadiyya), sequestered and nationalized more than 250 million pounds' worth of assets from the private sector.[26]

From that point onward, Cobra, Crown, and Pyramid tried not to go, as one Dutch board member of the Pyramid brewery phrased it, the way of the Suez Canal by adhering to all regulations put forth by the Egyptian government.[27] It was Wittert van Hoogland—Cobra and Heineken's representative on both the Crown and the Pyramid Breweries' boards—who was tasked with this goal. The most pertinent example of the companies' commitment to avoiding the watchful eye of the government was their willingness to comply with the multiple updates and amendments that the Nasser government made to the Company Law of 1947, which required Egyptian companies (those with major bases in Egypt) "to offer 51 percent of their stock to Egyptians and to place Egyptian nationals on 40 percent of the board seats."[28] In 1955 the government modified the Company Law by requiring anyone who sat on the board of companies (*administrateur*) to retire at the age of sixty, unless otherwise approved by the government. This law was intended to free the economy from the domination of "predatory" capitalists.[29]

To comply, Crown had to appoint a new Egyptian member of the board. The person chosen was Samih Muhammad Musa, a lawyer who served as a member of the boards of several other limited liability companies. Importantly, he was a friend of Farghali Pasha.[30] While Cobra and Wittert van Hoogland did not realize it at the time, the placement of a good friend of Farghali Pasha on the Crown board was a signal of the new hiring practices that the breweries would come to adopt under the Nasser-led government.

Although the law had a significant effect on the executive level, it was a blunt-force object when it came to those below the executive. Both the *muta-*

*maṣṣirūn* (Egyptianized foreigners, as Joel Beinin refers to those Arabic-speaking Greeks, Italians, and Jews) and the companies that employed them were faced with the dilemma that one of their greatest strengths—their cultural dynamism and multicultural familiarity—had become a major threat to their employment.[31] As discussed above, some workers applied for citizenship and were able to get it, but many were not. The large companies had two options in dealing with the cases of those who did not get citizenship: either replace them (i.e., fire them) or "move" them through a manipulation of the records produced for the Department of Companies.

In the case of the Egyptian beer industry, we are privileged with a view into the companies' "creative" accounting practices because they were caught in flagrante delicto. As a 1962 report shows, the two beer companies attempted to circumvent the watchful eye of the Ministry of Trade (Wizarat al-Tijara), which housed the Department of Companies, by setting up a distribution office that was shared by both companies but not formally part of either. Through this distribution office, the companies paid employees like Michel Elias, who would otherwise have raised the percentage of foreigners' pay to an unacceptable level. Dealings such as this led the Ministry of Trade to look further into the companies' books, where numerous inconsistencies were discovered, including the gifting of villas and unreported bonuses to foreign employees. All this malfeasance was evidence of the beer companies' flaunting of the Company Law of 1947. As punishment, the companies were forced to let go of some of their "foreign" workers.[32]

The bolstering of the Company Law, which reified the differences between "foreign" and "Egyptian," placed the foreigner in a disadvantaged position. While this turn against foreign elements could not compare to the long history of favor that these elements had received in Egypt, the turn certainly engendered a sense of beleaguerment in men like Wittert van Hoogland. This sense was compounded by the stark reality that the imagined citizen of Nasser's Egypt and the one most likely to maintain his status and advance was the Muslim Egyptian.

This reality was due to the complicated secularism of Nasser's regime. On the social and cultural level, Nasser's push for secularism was apparent. The reform programs he endorsed and championed, like increasing women's political rights and expanding education, were framed as socialist maneuvers. They fitted in line with the overall turn to the left that the government experienced after 1961.[33] Likewise, the cultural productions that the government supported, through newly created organs such as the Ministry of Culture, were nonreligious. The songs of Umm Kalthum and ʿAbd al-Halim Hafiz, the writings of Naguib Mahfouz, and the movies of Ihsan ʿAbd al-Qaddus were all, to varying degrees, constructed in a world where religion was background scenery.[34]

Nasser's social secularism belied his political actions as the leader of Egypt. Despite its claims to be secular, Nasser's government still followed policies that marginalized Coptic Christians and Jewish Egyptians. When he struck at al-Azhār, it was not to lessen the role of Islam in society but to co-opt the preeminent Islamic institution in Egypt. Nasser recognized the importance of Islam to Egyptian society and did not "hesitate to utilize Islamic institutions to legitimize" his policies. He commissioned government propagandists to laud the government's goals and their compatibility with Islam in the *khutba* (sermons) in Friday mosques, and he encouraged members of the government-appointed ulema to write tracts on the harmony of Islam and Arab socialism. With regard to social issues, although he passed laws that equalized gender relations somewhat, he was "extremely cautious" in his attitude toward family law and made no attempts to reform the Islamic institutions of polygamy or divorce.[35] Nasser's policies were also unfavorable to the minority religious communities. As compared to the constitutional period, far fewer non-Muslims could achieve high levels of power under Nasser. As Heineken noted, in the elections of 1957, "about half of the candidates were not approved by the government until the election (the bulk being Copts)." In many districts, the government candidates were victorious in unopposed races.[36] The contrast in the treatment of religious minorities was so stark that many non-Muslims came to regard pre-Nasser Egypt as a golden age for religious tolerance.[37]

Internal realities of the Crown and Pyramid Breweries only widened the rifts caused by these external policies. One of the biggest factors in the hardening of an "us-versus-them" mentality was the appointment of a new managing director in 1957. From Heineken's first involvement in Pyramid in the late 1930s, Wittert van Hoogland served in this position. However, in 1957, due to his excellent work with the company in Egypt, he was appointed to a better position as head of Cobra.[38] Although Wittert van Hoogland remained on the executive board of Pyramid, he would return to Amsterdam to serve as an adviser for breweries worldwide. He would cede his role as managing director and representative of Cobra in Egypt to Erick Carl Kettner, another Dutch national who had trained at Heineken in the beer business. He was a true technocrat and was fully committed to what I call total-control brewing, that is, the application of the most cutting-edge techniques and technology to create a standardized and durable product that could be delivered uniformly to all its consumers.

Emblematic of Kettner's commitment to the product's quality was his response when he once spotted imported Heineken beers in an Egyptian market. He bought four and put them through a blind testing to see if they lived up to the standards of Heineken beer. During the test, he discovered that the bottles of Heineken, when turned, would produce a cloud of particulate that whirled around inside the bottle. This occurrence was deeply troubling to Kettner because it violated a major selling point of beer in the Egyptian market, that it be clear, clean, and free of particulates. Although the cloud was benign from a health perspective, modern Egyptian advertisements' focus on the "purity" of industrially produced beer meant that this cloud was a symbol of "impurity" and a deterrent to purchase. In response to this violation of the total-brewing ethos, Kettner asked the Heineken representative, who happened to be Wittert van Hoogland, if he should buy back all the Heineken that was on the market.[39]

His officiousness extended to interpersonal relations, as seen in the case of another victim of the stricter enforcement of the Company Law, Victor Moreno. Not only was Moreno, a Coptic Christian, unable to secure citizenship, but the company also made no effort to "move" him. Instead, Pyramid removed him from his post, and the government forced him to leave the country. Moreno's case was a very sad and tricky one because he had worked for Pyramid for more than twenty-five years, and his dismissal left him penniless. Heineken offered employment with their brewery in the Belgian Congo, but Moreno refused, not willing to move to such a distant and unfamiliar location. Despite Moreno's long tenure with Pyramid, the company, and its mother company, Heineken, showed very little compassion when discussing his exit. Upon Moreno's termination, the Pyramid board agreed to pay 2,000 Egyptian pounds in indemnity to Moreno, while Heineken agreed to pay 9,000 francs.[40] Moreno found this sum far too low, and he requested, in several seven-page letters, that Heineken pay him approximately 25,000 francs. This request not only was rejected by Kettner, who sent a letter to Moreno expressing that the calculations behind this claim were simply incorrect, but also led Wittert van Hoogland to assert that Moreno's claims were no longer of any importance to Kettner and that he must cut off the correspondence with him, which Kettner did.[41]

If Kettner was ruthlessly business minded in his dealings with Moreno, his search for Moreno's replacement was no less informed by shrewd management tactics. Kettner was willing to use any means necessary to find the right fit for the position. Beyond talking to candidates and their references, Kettner also subjected them to handwriting tests. Implementing a theory that was used by the Egyptian army, Kettner had a handwriting specialist named Deen analyze potential employees' handwriting to determine their employability.[42] Kettner also consulted with Egyptians who could suggest other Egyptians as potential employees, as at this point Pyramid could hire only Egyptians.

## Us versus Them

Kettner's personality proved toxic when coupled with Pyramid's organizational structure. From the outside, it appeared relatively clear. Kettner, as a managing director, served as the direct link between the executive, headed by Farghali Pasha, and the management of the company. Three directors sat below Kettner: Alber Farag, Emil Natti, and Gerardus Hubertus Ulenberg. Farag, a Coptic Christian, oversaw the communication department, which contained the secretariat and the accounting section. Natti was at the head of the engineering division of the company, which included the workshop where all the brewery's machinery was repaired, the garage housing the cars and trucks that transported the beer, the department where labels were made and affixed to the bottles, and the electrical department. A Dutch national trained at Heineken, Ulenberg was the head brewmaster and head of the brewing department, which covered malting, fermenting, brewing, refrigeration, storage, and bottling.[43]

Originally, Ulenberg and the rest of the brewing department were under the watch of Natti, but Ulenberg proved so vital to the company that Kettner elevated him to the level of director.[44] Below the three directors were the heads of each of the separate subdepartments, most of whom had Egyptian citizenship. For example, underneath Ulenberg were Fathi al-Malt, the assistant brewmaster; Ahmad Hamdi Abu Khatwa, head of malting; Muhammad Ihab al-Shammaʿ, head of fermenting; Muhammad Ramses ʿAwad, head of the cellars; and Hafiz Zaklama, head of bottling.[45] Below these subdepartment heads were two sets of company employees: salaried employees and workers. The salaried employees, who were paid monthly, were classified by the Department of Companies as *muwaẓẓafin* (employees). The rest of the people working for the company were paid a daily wage and were classified as workers (*ʿummāl*). These groups were differentiated both by their salary structure and by the type of jobs they filled. The *muwaẓẓafin*, who included the chiefs of the subdepartments, were generally white-collar workers (supervisors, company doctors, lawyers, secretarial staff, translators, brewers, accountants, and so on), while the *ʿummāl* were the blue-collar types (bottle fillers, bottle cleaners, label attachers, drivers, and assistant drivers). Many daily wageworkers did have long-standing relationships with the company, but their turnover rates were higher than those of the *muwaẓẓafīn*.

One notable omission from the above description of the organizational structure of Pyramid is the Egyptian Ismaʿil Hafiz. From the very first moment that Kettner arrived in Egypt and assumed his position in 1957, Hafiz was an issue for him. One of the first instances of discord between the two occurred when Hafiz, with the supposed aim of making Pyramid appear more vital to the Egyptian economy, suggested that the beer company branch out into partnerships with other industries, including making feed for cattle from their spent grain. Kettner rejected his suggestion, citing the proverb "Schoenmaker houd je bij je leest" (Cobbler, stick to thy last). Nevertheless, Kettner conceded, in a letter to Wittert van Hoogland, that the company would probably have to do its "patriotic duty" and contribute in some way to the promotion of the "national economy."[46]

If Kettner and Hafiz had disagreed only over the investments the brewery should make, then the friction would have been resolved quickly. However, Kettner's issues with Hafiz stemmed more deeply from Kettner's belief that Hafiz was actively sabotaging the company. For Kettner, one notable incident was the feud between Hafiz and the head of the garages, Hasan Tawfiq. As Kettner described it, the dispute began when Tawfiq had the temerity to deny Hafiz the use of a company car, an act that won Tawfiq the "eternal hatred" of Hafiz. According to Kettner, this act, in addition to the simmering envy that Hafiz felt toward Hasan Tawfiq for having been elected vice president of the workers' syndicate instead of Hafiz, led Hafiz to ignore the reasonable requests of Tawfiq and actively sow discord among those who worked below Tawfiq at the garage. The situation reached such a level of discord that Kettner had to step in and arbitrate among Hafiz, Tawfiq, the workers' syndicate, and the other heads of departments. Although a great number of accusations were made, the squabble was settled when Kettner threatened to not pay out any Ramadan bonuses.[47]

Kettner believed that, while Hafiz "on the surface was an extremely dedicated and jovial friend," he was, in reality, very dangerous. This danger stemmed from Hafiz's status as an "untrustworthy, vain, ambitious, and overall a substandard individual." These characteristics were only to be expected from Hafiz because, as Kettner stated bluntly, he was an Egyptian. Kettner was particularly worried that if ever the day came that Hafiz did acquire a leadership position in the company (which as we know he did) and had full say in personnel policies, the Coptic Christians would suffer.[48] In

Kettner's eyes, how could the Coptic Christian not suffer when a Muslim like Hafiz controlled all personnel decisions?

Pyramid's policy regarding Hafiz did very little to assuage Kettner's worries about this Egyptian, which was apparent from another Heineken employee's 1959 report on the company. As the report noted, during his time at the company, Hafiz served both as a managing director, a position that was equal to Kettner's, and as a head of two departments, the personnel and public relations departments. Where exactly he sat within the company hierarchy was not particularly clear. In his dual position, he was both underneath and the equal of Kettner. The lack of definition was particularly troubling to the heads of the other departments—Natti, Ulenberg, and Farag—who were unsure whether Hafiz was their superior or equal. Hafiz used this ambiguity to continually assert his authority. In particular, he was focused more on being a managing director, like Kettner, and delegated the personnel and public relations work to his subordinates. All of these statements seem to at least signal that Kettner was not being paranoid about Hafiz's plans for him.[49]

While Kettner may have had an enemy in Hafiz, the enmity that he expressed toward Egyptians was not limited to Hafiz. Kettner also noted that he did not trust Tawfiq any more than he did Hafiz. In Kettner's opinion, Hafiz was a dangerous person, who could only be trusted up until the point that he showed himself as an enemy. Kettner believed that Tawfiq was even more dangerous than Hafiz "because he [was] more intelligent."[50] This general distrust of Egyptians was a reflection of the "us-versus-them" mentality that Kettner harbored. He believed that men like Hafiz and Tawfiq would always be on the ready to use the anti-Western sentiment that permeated Egypt at the time to get ahead. In fact, Kettner referred to this type of ladder climbing using nationalist sympathies as "Farghalism," using the name of the man who, in his mind, was the progenitor of this maneuver in the company.[51]

In fact, Kettner's negative opinion of Egyptians may have reflected a general distrust of Egyptians among European Heineken workers in Egypt. We see this feeling in a letter, quoted in the epigraph of this chapter, that Wittert van Hoogland wrote to Kettner responding to the latter's complaints about Hafiz. Wittert van Hoogland stated that Hafiz's shortcomings and intrigues were more or less normal in Egypt because the country was filled with two untrustworthy groups, the effendis and the Copts. For Wittert van Hoogland, the effendis were Mohammaden urbanites who were simply untrustworthy and incompetent. The Copts were equally untrustworthy, but because, as a minority constantly under threat in Egypt, they were so accustomed to intrigue and deceit, such was their default state. This alleged deceitfulness of the Copts was why Kettner, in the eyes of Wittert van Hoogland, should be glad to be rid of Victor Moreno.[52] This prejudice was not mere idle expression; it actively affected the Dutch management of the company. For example, when Kettner was assessing the causes of a dispute between Abu al-ʿAynayn Salim, a Muslim, and Alber Farag, a Copt, Wittert van Hoogland reminded him not to forget that, as a Copt, Farag was inclined toward intrigue.[53] Wittert van Hoogland's inherent distrust of Egyptians was also why, he told Kettner in the same letter, he distanced himself from the Egyptian staff in Cairo when he worked there. He advised the same thing for Kettner, so that Kettner would be able to see "the forest from the trees."[54]

Wittert van Hoogland's comments are shocking to the modern reader for their frank condemnation of Egyptians, but they should not be surprising considering the power dynamics that underpinned them. Wittert van Hoogland and Kettner came to work for the Egyptian breweries with an inherent sense of superiority. Not only were they acting on behalf of the company that ultimately owned the breweries, Heineken, but they were also implementing the policies of one of the preeminent and most powerful brewers in the world. It must, then, have been a massive shock when these Egyptians did not listen to them and even, in the Dutch brewers' eyes, actively worked against them.

On the Egyptian side, Muslim Egyptians realized the advantageous position in which the Company Law and Nasser's policies put them. Kettner noted that Abu al-ʿAynayn Salim had a sense that any legal decision could be ultimately reversed if he found the right lawyer.[55] Likewise, the Egyptians were encouraged by the Dutch to organize along these lines. For example, Kettner freely admitted that one of the roles of Farghali Pasha was to control the other Egyptians on the board.[56] That the Dutch did not know the Arabic language enabled the Egyptians, especially Farghali Pasha and Hafiz, to control all interactions with the government. While this was no doubt easier for Kettner than having to learn Arabic, it also meant that Kettner really could gather only secondhand information on Farghali Pasha's and Hafiz's actions.

The solidarity among Egyptians was not just an outside imposition. Solidarity certainly defined the Egyptian Muslims at Pyramid as well. Nepotism appeared to be a primary way for new executives and directors to be selected; for example, when Samih Muhammad Musa was added to the Crown board, one of his qualifications was that he knew Farghali Pasha. Likewise, Ismaʿil Hafiz's brother was a board member of Farghali Pasha's Cotton Company, and thus he had deeper ties to Farghali Pasha than Kettner would ever have.[57] The numerous times Egyptians, especially Farghali Pasha and Hafiz, refused to accept the commands of "experts" like Kettner may have been the manifestation of their own sense of "us versus them."[58] For Hafiz especially, his refusal to fall in line with Kettner, or with Wittert van Hoogland before him, was partly driven by his sense that management relations were a zero-sum game.

The conflicts between the two groups also arose from causes beyond either of them. People like Kettner and Hafiz were coming from very different worlds, and the mandate to work closely together must inevitably have led to instances of culture shock. An example of culture shock comes from another employee, Alber Farag, who was quite convinced that Heineken did not value him because they did not wish him Happy New Year's or congratulate him when he first signed on to the company.[59] This perceived slight obviously arose from a misalignment of ideas on what a large multinational corporation owes its employees.

## Turning the Workforce

The contentious relationship between the "foreign" and Egyptian extended beyond the management into the workforce, especially between the Dutch management and the workers' union. The Pyramid workers had been unionized since at least the 1940s and now, in the 1950s, had the inspiration of Nasser's legislation on their side. The workers' organization into the workers' syndicate (the Union of Employees and Workers for the Beer Company) included both employees and workers. In a 1949 report by Pieter R. Feith, a Heineken representative sent to report on the beer industry in Egypt, noted that the workers at what he still called Bomonti were better paid than workers in similar positions at other companies and that their union was well organized and accustomed to striking for better treatment. In one strike, Mr. Martin, the man who preceded Wittert van Hoogland as managing director of the brewery, had no choice but to give in to the union's demands for pay increases and bonuses. As a holder of British citizenship, Martin had feared that the union would be able to use the anti-British sentiment that was pervasive in the country during the 1940s to inspire a publicly supported strike. The union was able to achieve tangible goals before the RCC coup because it was well organized and because the company was doing so well. The management of the company considered the seven years between 1942 and 1949 to be fat years and was unable to limit workers' bonuses because the workers, too, were aware of the company's profitability.[60]

The union would be further emboldened by the legislation of the RCC and later the Nasser-led government. As part of Nasser's populist program, he aimed to motivate the working class by greatly increasing their standard of living.[61] In December 1952, the government enacted new labor legislation, which it strengthened in April 1953. In sum, this legislation granted workers "significantly improved material benefits—increased severance compensation, longer annual vacations, free transportation to factories in remote areas, and free medical care." It also gave the workers unprecedented job security by making the dismissal of a worker without cause a "very expensive and bureaucratically cumbersome undertaking."[62]

This new legislation won Nasser and the RCC the immediate support of many workers, although the regime's measures effectively served to thwart the development of a free and powerful labor movement. One reason was that this new legislation was coupled with a ban on labor strikes; in addition, the government passed laws that stifled the activities of trade unions. For example, the government allowed white-collar and blue-collar workers to form separate unions within a single venture and confirmed the practice of having unions form within each company rather than across the industry.[63] Both maneuvers did much to limit the formation of broad-based labor movements. Yet Nasser positioned himself as a populist who sought to mobilize the working class through legislation and through a charged rhetoric attacking "foreign economic imperialists." Nasser and his government portrayed the foreign capitalists as being among the main perpetrators of the exploitation (istighlāl) of the Egyptian people and their economy.[64] He argued that their elimination, coupled with the elevation of the beleaguered Egyptian working class, would set Egypt on a new and prosperous path. Nasser's turn to conspiratorial rhetoric that vilified a single group as the agents of subjugation was yet another example of his combative populism.[65]

These actions on the part of Nasser mobilized and empowered the workers at Pyramid and Crown. The clearest indication of this empowerment was the removal of a Swiss employee and the chief of the engineers, Mr. Eigenheer, in 1957. This event arose out of a disagreement between Eigenheer and his subordinate Antoine ʿAwad, which, in ʿAwad's eyes, was due to Eigenheer's lack of respect for him. The perceived lack of respect boiled over one day when Eigenheer sat in ʿAwad's chair and refused to vacate it when ʿAwad asked him to do so. For ʿAwad, this behavior was all the more galling because Eigenheer did so in front of all of the workers. As a result of this incident, ʿAwad filed a complaint to the board through the union, stating that he could not "stomach" Eigenheer's behavior, which was a clear example of his lack of "class."[66] The union pushed for Eigenheer's removal from his position. Although the union's response may seem extreme, it reflects the cultural differences between those who had been raised in Egypt and new arrivals like Eigenheer.

While sitting in 'Awad's chair may have seemed to be only a minor transgression, 'Awad understood Eigenheer's refusal to move in plain sight of the workers as a violation of the social hierarchy within the workplace and therefore as a significant affront.

Eigenheer's disrespect toward 'Awad was even more embarrassing because Eigenheer was a foreign worker. The Nasser-led government's policies fostered an atmosphere of distrust between Egyptians and the "foreign" elements in the country, portraying the latter as exploitative parasites preventing the advancement of the Egyptian economy. Thus, every interaction between "foreign" and "native" workers was framed with the idea that the two sides were taking part in a zero-sum game. 'Awad interpreted Eigenheer's refusal to move as proof of Nasser's depiction of foreigners. Kettner, for his part, was increasingly aware of the precarious position of foreigners in Egypt. He attributed the union's push for the removal of Eigenheer to the rising tide of "Arab nationalism" in Egypt.[67] The idea of Arab nationalism was at a high point at the time, 1957, in Egypt. Only a year earlier, Nasser had asserted Egyptian sovereignty by nationalizing the Suez Canal. About a year later, Nasser would form the United Arab Republic, the most significant articulation of Arab nationalism at the time, which entailed a union with Syria.

As Kettner noted, this agitation against Eigenheer was inspired by the Egyptian authorities' smear campaign against the "advantages" of foreigners in the country.[68] While we can never know for sure whether that was the case, we do know that the policies of the Nasser-led government emboldened the union to act more assertively than it otherwise may have. Their case for the removal of Eigenheer was based primarily on the fact that he was more than sixty years old and was in violation of the 1955 modification that the government had made to the Company Law of 1947, which required that the government approve the employment of all members of the board over the age of sixty. The law did not impose the same restrictions on employees and workers, but that did not stop the union from leveraging this law for their purposes.

Kettner attempted to mediate the situation by charging Hasan Tawfiq, another Egyptian engineer, with settling the issue. However, Tawfiq's response "sickened" Kettner. When Kettner broached the subject with Tawfiq, he looked at Kettner like "a farmer with a toothache," a Dutch saying meaning that while he listened, he was not that interested in what Kettner had to say. Kettner posited that this reaction was because "the whole affair had been instigated, if not by himself, then by his fellow engineers 'Awad and Nossier."[69] Seeing Tawfiq's response, Kettner believed that Eigenheer's removal was a fait accompli. When he mentioned the events to Wittert van Hoogland, he suggested that Eigenheer was "finished" because he was not a member of the union and that the path of least resistance was to remove Eigenheer by coaxing him to retire.[70] Kettner hoped that he could keep Eigenheer on for a year or two, until he turned sixty-four and could, with repatriation, qualify for a legal base pension in Switzerland.[71] In the end, Eigenheer asked for his own dismissal and left the company in the spring of 1958. Eigenheer's resignation reflected the advantages that some foreign nationals did have. His departure was tied to the very favorable transfer agreements that became available to repatriated Swiss citizens at the time.[72]

Back at Pyramid, Kettner wanted to replace Eigenheer with an Egyptian, Nasser Nusayr, but Emil Natti, his consultant in the workforce, demurred and mentioned that Nusayr had language troubles when he visited Holland because he did not speak enough of any European language to communicate. Kettner thus resolved to leave the issue of a replacement to Natti, Hasan Tawfiq, and Isma'il Hafiz.[73] However, this resolution would not be the end of nationality-based conflicts.[74]

Another power struggle between management and workers would soon arise, for workers had the power not only to agitate against foreign employees whom they found distasteful, but also to demand a greater share of company profits. In June 1957, the union sent a letter to Kettner requesting that he grant them an additional bonus in recognition of their "efforts and sacrifices" in the workplace. Kettner met their demands with a noncommittal response, stating that the management of the company would be delighted to give bonuses to the employees and workers, but that before he could guarantee anything, he had to see the sales results for the year, which would become clear in October.[75] Kettner echoed the sentiment in his meeting with the company management, whose minutes the syndicate could access, adding that his policy on bonuses was "wait and see."

When October came and no further bonuses were forthcoming, the union responded in a strongly worded letter to Kettner:

> Mr. Director, we waited and we saw....We have seen how the Company rewards its workers and its employees for the efforts of a whole season. ...We have seen how the Company appreciates the considerable effort all provided....We have seen how the Company forgets all the sacrifices made by the workers and employees at a price of their nerves and their blood....We have seen how the Company has increased sales but has decreased bonuses.[76]

This infuriated response from the union grew out of the fact that the brewery, under Kettner's leadership, had had a banner year during the first three quarters of 1957 yet decreased bonuses to employees and workers. Sales for the company grew from fifty-one thousand hectoliters between January and September to more than fifty-six thousand hectoliters. This marked nearly a 9 percent increase, and the workers reckoned that by the end of the year it would be nearly 10 percent. In the eyes of the union, these banner profits made an increased bonus a foregone conclusion. They expected to receive a bonus that was more than double what they were paid the year before. However, the bonus in fact represented a 25 percent decrease for employees and salaried workers and a 30 percent decrease for nonsalaried workers from the bonus paid out in October 1956.[77]

The union was obviously not pleased with the bonus and saw this action as another step toward a policy of restricting workers' and employees' payments to only wages and salaries. That year the company did indeed actively try to institute such a policy. The decrease in bonuses followed Kettner's removal of all "special bonuses" to employees and workers, on the pretext that bonuses would cause envy among the company's employees and workers. The union believed that the claims were ridiculous, and they saw the elimination of bonuses as proof that their hopes for improvements were misguided.[78] There was a great deal of bluster in the union's interaction with Kettner, which was emblematic of how disrespected they felt by his actions in general. Emil Natti, Kettner's trusted ally in the fight against "intrigue" in the company, worked hard to calm the tempers on all sides. However, the ultimate solution to the kerfuffle was Kettner's announcement of salary and wage increases for the employees and workers at Pyramid, which, on average, were around 5 to 6 percent.[79] This settlement was a compromise because the money would not come in the form of a bonus, a practice that the management was seeking to curtail, yet it would still allow the employees and workers to enjoy the fruits of Pyramid's excellent profits in 1957.

All of these problems led Kettner to observe to Wittert van Hoogland, "It's like you said to me at the time, you cannot hate these people because hatred has something noble in itself; you can only have the deepest contempt."[80] This remark highlights the deep animus that Kettner and Wittert van Hoogland felt for some Egyptians. The question remains, however, as to how much of Kettner's distaste for Egyptians grew out of their striving against him and how much was imagined. As Robert Vitalis has observed, management's cries about the dangers of nationalism, communism, careerism, and so forth often have roots in antilabor attitudes.[81] Worker solidarity was completely at odds with the ideal workforce of Kettner's imagination. For him, an employee or worker was an independent entity who should follow his rules faithfully and ensure that others did as well. The fact that despite Kettner's very low opinion of him, Nasser and his policies seemed to grow only more popular with the majority of Egyptians, especially his workers, surely amplified Kettner's negative feelings toward those Egyptian workers.

Despite the political volatility of the era from 1952 to 1958, Crown and Pyramid increased profits and cultivated a coherent brand identity that would serve them for the rest of their history. However, as this chapter has shown, this success overlay the internal struggles of a multinational company that existed within a business environment that was increasingly intolerant of any "foreign" presence.

As a result, the activist government of Egypt, besides forcing companies to cater to their demands out of fear of nationalization, soured relationships within companies' management and between management and the workforce through its favoritism toward Muslim Egyptians. Under legislation like the amendments to the Company Law of 1947, ordinary interoffice frictions transformed into pitched nationalist and religious battles. While some may argue that a restructuring of the Egyptian economy to favor the "Egyptian" over the "foreign" was necessary to free it from foreign, imperial control, these policies essentially took a hammer to any productive transreligious and transnational relationships and recast them all in the rhetoric of "us versus them." The management of companies now became a zero-sum game, with foreign nationals, *mutamaṣṣirūn*, and religious minorities seeing every instance of Muslim cooperation as a threat to their endangered status in the company and the country and Muslim Egyptians seeming to believe that they could play by a different set of rules.

# A Pan-Arab Brew

*Stella and the United Arab Republic, 1958–1961*

Do you know the difference between the United States and Egypt?
The U.S.A. have [*sic*] Eisenhower and Bob Hope, whereas the U.A.R.
has Gamal Abdel Nasser and no hope.
— Erick Kettner to Wittert van Hoogland, July 3, 1959

The above joke was making the rounds in Cairo in 1959, according to a letter written by the managing director of Pyramid Brewery at the time, Erick
Kettner. While Kettner's letter did not say any more about the joke, his decision to include it suggests that he enjoyed it and assumed the recipient of his
letter, Wittert van Hoogland, the head of Cobra, would enjoy the joke, too.
The joke probably resonated for the men because the figure of Nasser cast a
dark shadow over their lives. Every one of their interactions with his Egyptian government had resulted in greater difficulties in selling beer in Egypt.
That the reaction of most Egyptians to Nasser's charismatic persona and his
populist policies was overwhelmingly positive only amplified Kettner's dis-
content and his feelings of hopelessness in managing a beer company under
Nasser's regime.

   This chapter examines a set of interactions between the Crown and Pyramid Breweries and the Egyptian government in the period from 1958 to 1961.
As I show, this period of the breweries' history was dominated by a battle between the management and the Nasser government over what constituted a
"model company." For the management of the breweries, a model company
was a profitable one that had the autonomy and the efficient, disciplined, and
obedient workforce to implement Heineken's methods of brewing. For the
Nasser-led government, a model company was one that would make large
profits autonomously but was willing and able to mobilize in support of
Nasser's grand projects, like the United Arab Republic, and his vision for the
Egyptian economy. In the one area where the differing visions overlapped—
namely, in the desire to make profits—the breweries were successful. In the
period from 1957 to 1961, they witnessed unprecedented profits and deep cul-

tural penetration. However, in every other avenue, it was the Nasser-led government and its conception of a model company that won out.

## Young and Fun

During the late 1950s, as beer achieved an unprecedented cultural penetration, Pyramid and Crown were well on their way to reaching their goal of making beer a chief distraction for Egyptians in their social lives. The writings of one of the most popular Arabic authors of the time, Ihsan 'Abd al-Quddus (1919–1991), reflected beer's progress in this regard.[1] 'Abd al-Quddus began his career at one of Egypt's best-known political and cultural magazines, *Ruz al-Yusuf*. The magazine was the brainchild of 'Abd al-Quddus's mother, the retired theater actress Ruz al-Yusuf (Rose el-Yousef). At *Ruz al-Yusuf*, 'Abd al-Quddus became a leading voice of liberal discontentment with the monarchal regime in 1940s Egypt. Indeed, because of his criticism, he spent a short time in prison. While 'Abd al-Quddus initially welcomed the king's ouster, he soon ran afoul of the Free Officers Movement as well, and he served prison time again in 1954.[2]

After 1955 'Abd al-Quddus turned to writing fiction. While his prose never did approach the quality and depth of literary giants like Naguib Mahfouz and Yusuf Idris, his circulation was unparalleled. The relative simplicity of his literary style and lexicon gave his works a mass appeal among the "youth of a modernizing middle class who struggled to free themselves of social and parental constraints, to adapt and adopt changing social and gender roles, and above all to experience and understand the notion of romantic love." It would not be an exaggeration to state that 'Abd al-Quddus gave voice to a generation of young Egyptians growing up in the heady times of post-1952 Egypt. This voice was not one of stolen kisses and furtive rendezvous, but one of "pett[ing] brazenly in the back seat of convertibles, arrang[ing] trysts in plushly furnished bachelor pads, and danc[ing] the night away—with a variety of partners—to the sounds of flowing whiskey and rhythm and blues."[3]

This passage from his collection of short stories *Al-Banat wa al-Sayf* (Girls of the summer) exemplifies this frank modernity:

And she sat at a table that sat next to a window looking out on the sea.
... Sayyid sat in front of her saying:
What would you like to drink?
Whiskey. Whiskey really wakes me up, and I am dead tired, she said.

I have been on my feet all day.

Sayyid got up and ordered a bottle of whiskey from the bar and two glasses. The waiter soon came with two bottles of soda water and a bucket of ice.

Don't give me any soda, just ice, Sharifa said.

I know, said Sayyid.

And then Sharifa drank. She drank three glasses in less than a quarter of an hour, and she felt as if her energy had been replenished to such a point that she was going to explode. She couldn't bear to sit down silently. She wanted to jump, scream, fight, and hit someone.[4]

Ihsan 'Abd al-Quddus's portrayal of this strong female character is particularly noteworthy. According to Joel Gordon, "Ihsan's primary female characters, in one respect or another, are rebels. They may suffer from it, and they may even wind up in seemingly subservient positions they swore they would never occupy," but what they stand against is always wrong. While 'Abd al-Quddus's female characters were the product of a "male pen," they were some of the most complex of the time.[5] They were neither virginal ingenues nor fallen Svengalis but three-dimensional people. Arguably, the prominence of alcohol in this passage and his work in general reflected the reality of this generation rather than merely serving to make his book more exciting.

From 'Abd al-Quddus's writing, we can sense beer's social role among a particular class of Egyptians. His collection of stories *Al-Banat wa al-Sayf* offers further insights into this role. The collection tells the story of five different women's experiences during a summer in Alexandria. This seasonal setting is significant, as it establishes a world frame entirely different from the urban setting of Cairo. In summer many members of a certain Egyptian social class moved out of their houses or apartments and into beach cabins (*al-Kābīn*). One's days were filled not with work and the buzz of everyday life but rather with the relaxation of swimming in the sea (*al-baḥr*) and eating on the beach (*al-bilāj*). Finally, those who summered in cabins would make the pilgrimage from various parts of Egypt to Alexandria, where they could meet with people outside of their typical social circle, although their interactions were still among people of a comparable class.

In this setting, beer was well adapted. In his story "Al-Bint al-Thalith" (The third woman), one character, Isma'il, comments to his friend 'Umar, as he is going out to get food, "When you return your beer will be nice and cold for you." This statement takes on greater significance when we discover that Isma'il is in a romantic relationship with Wafiyya, 'Umar's wife, who is occupying the cabin along with Isma'il and 'Umar. Sending 'Umar out of the cabin is a pretext for Isma'il to spend time with 'Umar's wife. This passage, beyond indicating Isma'il's dastardly behavior, also indicates that the advertising of the beer companies was paying off. The key attribute of the beer here is not its alcoholic content but the fact that it will be a refreshing drink for 'Umar upon his return from running errands. 'Abd al-Quddus's disassociation of drunkenness from beer becomes starker when we examine the way he describes the effects of whiskey in the same story. One powerful description comes when Wafiyya is racked with guilt that her illicit affair is coming to light: "But she drank a cup [of whiskey] and then another and remembered her pain. The alcohol sent a warm feeling through her veins and encouraged her to reformulate her plan."[6] In this instance, whiskey is a useful beverage because of its alcohol content, which can warm one and impart courage.

An even better example of the normalization of beer in Egyptian culture comes from another story in *Al-Banat wa al-Sayf*, "Al-Bint al-Ula" (The first woman). The first mention of beer comes during a party scene:

> The party was at one of the cabins that sat on the rock of Bir Mas'ud and was attended by young men and women between eighteen and twenty-five. Most of the women wore pants . . . and the men wore open shirts revealing sunburned brown skin and necks with gold chains that said "Ma Sha Allah [What God Wants]!" They each had a tuft of hair hanging over their foreheads, which would flap like a black flag when the sea breeze blew. The gramophone sat in the middle of the cabin. . . . There were a lot of bottles of beer and Coca-Cola, Limongo [a local brand of soda], and sandwiches.[7]

This passage attributes three appealing characteristics to beer. First, it presents beer as a drink of the young and the happening, an ideal party beverage that was made for socialization. Second, the passage depicts beer as being, like Coca-Cola and Limongo, a refreshing drink that was ideal for the warm days and nights at the beach. Finally, the passage presents beer as a socially acceptable beverage on par with soft drinks.

The next reference to beer in "Bint al-Ula," which comes when the story's protagonist, Maysa, arrives at the party, again speaks to beer's role as a sociable drink: "Then she entered the cabin and found herself next to Majid. She sat down and crossed her legs. Then Midhat shouted: One rock-and-roll song on account of Maysa. 'Cheers to you,' shouted Nabil, lifting the glass of beer from his lips." This passage is followed by the most significant reference to beer in the story. Maysa, dispirited by the fact that she has partied on the beach so many times before, and presumably has drunk enough beer that it has lost all its fun, bemoans the lack of anything "new" at the party. She is on the lookout for something different, which comes in the form of a mysterious man, Abu Bakr. When Maysa sees him, she wants to talk, but Nabil takes her to dance instead: "She had to dance with Nabil, and when she was done, Abu Bakr was busy talking. He didn't do anything but talk, and his beer remained unfinished in his hand.... The bottles of beer, Coca-Cola, and Limongo eventually ran out. The sandwiches were eaten, the gramophone ran out of juice, and everyone went home. However, she remained, waiting for something new to happen, and Abu Bakr was still there, unfinished beer in his hand."[8] In this instance, the beer and beer bottle represent the potential for sociability. When the beer runs out, it is a signal, like the gramophone running out of power, that the party is over. The beer bottle, specifically the beer bottle of Abu Bakr, also represents Maysa's chances at experiencing something new and exciting. If beer remained in the bottle of Abu Bakr, there was a chance that he would remain and thus fulfill Maysa's desire to find something new. Although Abu Bakr would prove to be a troubling character, eventually involving her in a love triangle, the point here is that Maysa is able to meet this appealing character because his beer remains unfinished.

As Ihsan 'Abd al-Quddus was the son of two actors (his father, Muhammad, had left his engineering career for the stage), it was perhaps natural that he would also find work as a film writer.[9] Even before he wrote specifically for film and television, his prose style made his novels and short stories well suited for adaption to film. Perhaps unsurprisingly, a theme in his films is beer's role as a key to youthful sociability. One excellent example of this theme is in the 1960 film version of *Al-Banat wa al-Sayf*, directed by Izz al-Din Dhu-l-Fiqar, Salah Abu Sayf, and Fatin 'Abd al-Wahab. In one of the movie's first scenes, we discover the secret relationship of Isma'il (Kamal al-Shinawi) and Wafiyya (Magda al-Khatib), which the film portrays as a predatory one, with Isma'il sexually assaulting Wafiyya as he sends 'Umar ('Adil Khayri) out on errands. After assaulting Wafiyya and telling her how much he loves her, Isma'il ends the conversation by saying that he is going to get his beer, which has been chilling. Then, as he sits outside the bedroom where he assaulted Wafiyya, he asks her, "Would you like a glass of beer? It's really hot out, and the beer is so cold." Hearing no answer, he shakes his head and takes a big sip of the foamy glass. As Wafiyya silently refuses her assaulter, 'Umar returns from getting food. When Wafiyya refuses to eat, Isma'il assures 'Umar that Wafiyya's mood is the result of her time out in the sun. He then hands 'Umar a glass of beer and toasts him, as if nothing has happened.

Although the circumstances of this scene are quite gruesome, this adaption of the 'Abd al-Quddus story again emphasizes two important characteristics of beer in Egyptian middle- and upper-class society: first, beer is a refreshing beverage perfectly suited for the warm weather of the beach; second, it is a drink of youthful sociability, a drink for young people looking to party and have fun. There is also a dark undercurrent that links beer to sinful behavior like fornication, a sign that, even in this sunny era, beer could not escape its dark side. Films of this era like *Ana Hurra* (I'm free), another adaption of an early Ihsan 'Abd al-Quddus novel, however, preferred to focus on beer's role as a social lubricant for the youth. This 1959 adaption presents one scene in which beer's essential role in youth sociability is paramount. The scene begins with the party hostess, Vicky (Layla Karim), pouring bottles of beer into glasses. As she passes them out to party patrons, the camera focuses on a couple dancing, the main character Amina (Lubna 'Abd al-'Aziz) and Vicky's brother, Zaki ('Ali Rida), to some Western music. It follows them until they finish, and everyone claps for them. All of this takes place at a celebration for an unnamed non-Muslim holiday, where Amina, a Muslim, consorts with non-Muslims and Muslims alike. The youth from the party then drive to the desert, where they drink more beer and dance. The scene ends with Amina returning after dark to her home in Abbasiyya and her neighbors bemoaning how she was consorting with "foreigners" and "drunks." All of this signals a disconnect between "traditional," "religious" society and the "modern," secular society. Again, beer is the drink of the young and the fun.

This cultural penetration of beer as the summer drink of the young and fun was also seen in the sales of Pyramid and Crown. In 1960 Pyramid sold more than one hundred thousand hectoliters of beer. Of that, most was sold during the summer months of May to August. In these months, the brewery managed to sell more than thirteen thousand hectoliters per month. Even in the months around these summer months, April, September, and October, they sold roughly ten thousand hectoliters per month. The excellent sales were due in large part to the heat wave that hit Egypt in the summer of 1960. In that year, the breweries sold more beer between the months of April and September (roughly seventy-five thousand hectoliters) than in all of 1958 (seventy thousand hectoliters).[10]

However, outside of those months, Pyramid struggled to sell the same volume. Their lowest month that year was January, Egypt's coolest month, when they sold less than two thousand hectoliters. This was in stark contrast to May, when they sold more than fourteen thousand hectoliters.[11] The strong correlation between the cultural and economic had a great deal to do with the fact that the Crown and Pyramid Breweries were the predominant sellers of beer in Egypt in the 1960s. What was good for beer was good for

Crown and Pyramid. In addition, it appears that the advertising work that the two breweries had done in the 1950s to portray beer as the drink of the summer and of youth was paying off.

The hot spell was not the only contributor to increased consumption. Another significant factor was the significant growth and urbanization of the Egyptian population since the 1950s. Between the years 1947 and 1960, the population grew from nineteen million to twenty-six million. Between those same years, 1947 and 1960, more than one million migrants arrived in Cairo. The majority of those migrating were from the rural parts of Egypt, and by 1960 there were nearly seven million rural migrants living in Alexandria and Cairo.[12] However, this growth and urbanization would not have meant as much to the fortunes of the beer industry if not for the policies of Nasser. The social welfare policies that the Nasser government was instituting in the country, i.e., minimum wages, overtime bans to encourage new hires, and forced price cuts, all meant more disposable income for average workers to buy beer. On a cultural level, Nasser's ascendance made the culture of the effendi, which was receptive to beer consumption, the hegemonic cultural discourse in the country.[13]

The two beer companies were doing so well that Pyramid had to make significant changes to meet demand. One way in which Erick Kettner hoped to meet demand was by getting more out of his workers. Prior to the Nasser government's institution of prolabor policies, Kettner was determined to make Pyramid a "model company" by having a docile, efficient, and disciplined Egyptian workforce. As the production manager, Kettner dictated labor relations at the breweries. Kettner was particularly concerned about instilling the ethos of what I call total-control brewing, which entailed applying cutting-edge techniques and technologies to create a standardized and sturdy product for all consumers. Following through on this ethos required not only the best machinery and materials but also an efficient and obedient workforce.

One way that Kettner attempted to bring workers in line with his thinking was through the installation of a system he referred to as the Ten Commandments. These were ten key practices that Kettner believed would produce a better company.[14] They were as follows:

1. Efficiency
2. Organization
3. Training
4. Communications
5. Supervision

6. Discipline
7. Safety
8. Cleanliness, order, and maintenance
9. Human relations
10. Character

Kettner learned these Ten Commandments at lectures he attended at the Central Social Employers Association (Centraal Sociaal Werkgevers Verbond) in the Netherlands. Founded in 1919, this was an organization of employers, among which Heineken was a prominent member—Heineken chief executive officer (CEO) Dirk Stikker served as its head in 1939—that looked to establish standards and practices in the relationship between employers and their employees.[15] Ensuring uniformity in management tactics may have been one of Heineken's secrets to running a successful company. We know that the company had a blue book of guidelines that it distributed to its employees; this book probably contained the Ten Commandments or similar information.[16]

Kettner was very committed to instilling the Ten Commandments among the management and aimed to do so in ways beyond the standard lecture, of which there were many. One particularly interesting method he used was staging a contest among the department heads to see who had the best knowledge of the Ten Commandments. The 'Awad brothers (Ramses and Antoine) ended up winning the contest, and the results were announced at the company cafeteria. While Kettner noted that this contest was "very well received" and that it gave him "an invaluable perspective" on members of the management, one must wonder how well it actually did go over. For example, there were two members of management who chose not to participate.[17]

Kettner's implementation of these commandments went beyond testing the management on them; the commandments framed his very treatment of the workers. He was obsessed with exploiting their working capabilities effectively and efficiently. This desire for exploitation was most obvious in Kettner's treatment of those involved in the most labor-intensive step of beer making, the bottling line. Within Pyramid's bottling plant, there were two bottling lines, the GBGB line and the Benghazi line. The GBGB could bottle roughly 11,500 hectoliters per month. The Benghazi line could produce roughly 4,300 hectoliters a month, and the bottling plant could produce 15,800 hectoliters per month.[18] Kettner was keenly aware of the productive capacity of these lines and was constantly looking to improve their output. Significantly, Kettner could, and did, alter workers' schedules to extract even more work from the bottlers. One year he successfully pushed the bottling plant to produce almost 19,000 hectoliters of beer each month.[19]

But getting more out of workers was not the only thing Kettner was pursuing to meet growing demand. He also, with the help of Heineken, started work in 1958–1959 on a multiyear plant-expansion plan, which would further spur growth and profitability.[20] The Dutch brewer took this opportunity to create a factory optimized for cutting-edge beer making. Heineken not only conducted the feasibility study for the expansion, but also drew up the plans of the factory to best accommodate all the machinery necessary for "modern" brewing.[21] In this modern setup, there were six areas where machinery was updated or replaced: the malting system, cooling system, brew house, filtering system, bottling system, and lager cellar.

The expansion of operations was coupled with a consolidation of their brand portfolio. Although Stella would come to dominate the beer market in Egypt, eventually becoming synonymous with beer in the country, it was not the companies' only brand. One of their most popular brands besides Stella was Märzen. Named after a type of German beer, *märzen bier*, which translates as "March beer," it was a deep amber lager with a full body and moderate bitterness.[22] Originally offered as a seasonal beer sold between October and March, the breweries decided in 1959 to offer it as a full-year beer because the sales were so strong. Wittert van Hoogland was particularly worried that because the name was so tied to a season, it did not make sense to sell it all year. Nevertheless, Kettner resolved that since the name did not carry the same associations in Arabic, it did not really matter.[23]

The breweries also sold a beer they labeled as *Bayrisch*, meaning "Bavarian" in German. Their darkest offering, it was not as successful a brand as Märzen.[24] The name was not accurate, in that it was not brewed in Bavaria, and the Germans protested the use of the name. Germans, like the French with wine, were very keen to protect their beers' reputation. After deliberating over eliminating the brand entirely, they decided to rebrand and indigenize it as Aswan beer, as a nod to the region (Upper Egypt) that they were looking to exploit further. Market growth in the region had driven their excellent sales in the 1950s, as the demand for beer in Upper Egypt increased by 30 percent and 40 percent in the years 1957 and 1958, respectively.[25] The breweries decided to also place it at a different price point than Stella.[26] In 1959 they also debated adding two new types of beer to their portfolio, a higher alcohol-by-volume beer and *bière de menage*, which was a beer and wine mix. They did not proceed on either account out of a desire to protect their established brands.[27]

## The Beer of the United Arab Republic

No matter how successful the breweries were in this period or how much input Heineken sought, they ultimately existed at the whim of the Egyptian government led by Gamal Abdel Nasser. By 1958 the interests of the Egyptian government had become inextricably tied to the interests of its unquestioned leader, Nasser. As the state's ultimate powerbroker, he had the ability to determine the fate of any company, organization, or person in the country with just a few words. To be sure, the breweries' continued operation in Egypt was contingent upon the authorities receiving and approving a yearly application for their continued functioning.[28] Unfortunately for the beer companies and the rest of the private sector, Nasser and his government had not mapped out a clear ideological platform to provide an overarching rationale for his policies. It was unclear, therefore, whether the Nasser-led government's activist policies regarding the economy were intended as a temporary palliative or the beginning of a full-scale takeover of the private sector.

Ideological pragmatism was a key feature of Nasser's ruling style, which can rightly be called self-styled populism, that is, "a predominately middle-class movement that mobilize[d] the lower classes, especially the urban poor, with radical rhetoric against imperialism, foreign capitalism and the political establishment."[29] Nasser placed himself and his charismatic persona, the native-born father (*bābā*) and president to the people (*al-shaʿb*) of Egypt, at the center of this populism. While the businessmen of the private sector could not peg his motives, they recognized that whatever action he took, it would be popularly supported. With his populist policies, like land reform, and his anti-imperialism, Nasser had won massive popularity and legitimacy with the working class, the fellahin, and the *effendiyya*.[30]

Without an explicit agenda from Nasser, the breweries were left to react to the decisions of the president and his government with ad hoc solutions. To see the process in action, one need only look at how Crown and Pyramid dealt with exports in the three years (1958–1961) when Egypt and Syria, supported by Nasser, formed the United Arab Republic. The union was based on political and economic factors. On the political side, it was the full articulation of the Pan-Arabism ideology that was popular in the region and of which Nasser was its most visible champion. As for the economic side, for the Syrians the union shielded them from communism and gave them access to the much-larger Egyptian market. For Egypt and Nasser, Syria was a welcome market for Egypt's industrial products and was the main wheat supplier to Egypt.[31] Nevertheless, the two countries' economies had significant differences, and the work of integrating them became one of the main struggles of this new union.

After September 1958, Nasser's government worked in earnest to create a united Egyptian–Syrian economy. The government created a ten-year economic plan, which calculated expenditures of around 2 billion Syrian pounds. Most of these funds were allocated to the improvement of irrigation and hydroelectric power in the country. The Nasser government also sent a tripartite commission to Syria; called the Higher Ministerial Committee, it was composed of an Egyptian vice president, a Syrian vice president, and the minister of the interior. The committee aimed to "study the obstacles to implementation of projects; to stimulate economic activity; to study the public services program; and to expedite the formation of the National Union."[32]

In that period, the beer companies' exports were divided into three sales zones: exclusive Pyramid zones, exclusive Crown zones, and shared zones. The exclusive Pyramid zone was limited to the Sudan, a region to which exporting full bottles of beer always proved difficult. This difficulty was due in large part to the fact that the Egyptian government's treatment of Egyptian beer in Sudan was paradoxical. Although Egypt had claimed Sudan during the era of the Anglo-Egyptian Condominium in that country (1898-1956), the Egyptian government charged much-higher excise fees and taxes on imported Egyptian beer than foreign beer.[33] After 1956 the beer companies also had to deal with an independent Sudanese government that restricted the import of foreign beer as part of their general protections to encourage local industry.[34] However, Pyramid was still able to profit from the Sudanese market because of their 6 percent ownership stake in a Sudanese brewery, Blue Nile.[35] While Pyramid may not have been able to sell Stella beer directly in Sudan, Blue Nile was a venture that could still make them money. This was due to Pyramid's role as a "colonized colonizer." The term, borrowed from the work of Eve Troutt Powell, refers to the idea that Egypt carried out an imperial project in Sudan as the Ottomans, French, and British pursued their own projects in Egypt. Because of Egypt's dual position, its colonial actions in the Sudan were tied intimately to its efforts to shrug off its own colonial yoke.[36]

The term *colonized colonizer* seems appropriate for Pyramid's venture in the Sudan, too, because Pyramid's relationship to Blue Nile was eerily like Heineken's relationship to Pyramid. Blue Nile could produce its own beer, Camel, but all the raw materials came from abroad. Heineken provided the hops and the yeast, and Pyramid provided the malt; about six hundred metric tons of malt were exported to the company in 1958 alone. The malt was a blend of two- and six-rowed barley that Pyramid itself used when making Stella beer.[37] The brewmaster of Blue Nile, like the brewmaster at Pyramid, was trained outside of the company; specifically, he was trained at Pyramid Brewery rather than Heineken proper. As a "colonized" brewery, Blue Nile was under double surveillance. Erick Kettner, Heineken's representative at Pyramid Brewery, not only monitored the internal happenings of the company but also required that Blue Nile send Camel Beer to Cairo to be tested in their laboratories. Wittert van Hoogland, Kettner's boss, monitored Kettner's work with Blue Nile and the brewery itself.[38]

As for the exclusive Crown zones, they were limited to countries in the Mediterranean basin, including Cyprus, Libya, Syria, and Lebanon. With the formation of the UAR, Syria became the focus of exports for Crown. It would also soon draw the attention of Pyramid. For the breweries, the government's most significant step was the elimination of all custom duties, except nine competitive products, between the two countries.[39] This new free path of trade wedded a market to Egypt that Pyramid and Crown were already looking to tap. In 1957 Kettner and Wittert van Hoogland of Pyramid's Dutch management privately discussed opening a Heineken interest in Syria, with the idea of placing their Dutch brewmaster, Gerardus Hubertus Ulenberg, in charge of it. They chose Ulenberg because of their assumption that Syrians would be more comfortable dealing with a Dutchman than a fellow Middle Easterner.[40] That is, they assumed that the Syrians would rather listen to and follow a foreign, non-Arab expert than an Egyptian, whom they would see as an equal, not a superior.

However, the unification of Egypt and Syria preempted these plans. On the announcement of the union, there was an almost immediate disagreement between the two companies over who should be free to exploit the Syrian market. Although Crown's leaders were amenable to drawing up a new agreement between the two companies, they still argued for their right to be the main exporter to Syria, as before. Pyramid, on the other hand, believed that the situation had changed to such a degree that any prior agreements did not apply.[41]

Pyramid believed it should be exporting the majority of the beer there because it could produce beer cheaper than Crown could.[42] The two companies eventually reached an agreement on the sale of beer in Syria. Crown allowed Pyramid to export to Syria, which was called the Northern Province (Egypt was the Southern Province), if Pyramid agreed to pay a fifty-pound fee on every hectoliter they exported.[43] Crown negotiated only after having difficulty selling its own beer in Syria. Regardless, Pyramid was quite pleased to replace Crown beer, and its beer received a better reception on the market because it was believed to be superior to the Crown-produced Stella in its taste, brilliance, and foam stability.[44]

Nevertheless, the market for Stella beer was not huge. For example, in 1959 Pyramid sold twelve hundred cartons of large bottles (660 ml) and eighteen hundred cartons of small bottles (330 ml), which put sales at around 1,000 hl.[45] The people at Pyramid attributed the lack of demand to the fact that, despite Syrians having greater purchasing power, there were simply fewer of them: Egypt's population was nearly five times larger than Syria's. In addition, Kettner noted that, as compared to Egyptians, Syrian "Muslims were more strict in the interpretation of the Koran."[46] Although this statement comes from a nonexpert on the matter, it still is interesting to note that foreigners perceived Syrians to be somehow more observant than Egyptians in avoiding alcohol. Beyond a smaller population and perhaps a greater religiosity, another reason for the less than stellar sales could have been the presence of a rival beer in Syria called al-Chark. Founded in 1954, this beer came from Aleppo and had already made inroads into the market when Stella arrived in the late 1950s.

The Syrian beer market was small enough that Kettner seriously doubted the utility of exporting there. Unlike Nasser, Kettner was skeptical about possibilities for exports in general. Beyond the risks of shipping beer (bottle breakage, spoilage, etc.), there were significant bureaucratic hurdles, including heavy paperwork, that reduced Pyramid's prospects of a profitable export market. Indeed, exporting to Syria raised a few challenges about doing business in foreign markets. While the gain in visible costs was not huge, the gains in invisible costs (contributions to fixed costs and wages and salaries) were significant.[47] Moreover, the reality of conjoining Egypt with Syria raised practical problems for the breweries. For example, the breweries were unsure whether the UAR's decision to cancel certain import customs meant that those selling Syrian beer in Egypt would have to pay the Egyptian duty of four and a half Egyptian pounds or if the breweries would have to pay the significantly lower Syrian duty.[48] Besides the raised costs of the government's push for exports, the new free trade agreement also inaugurated another possible development, the entrance of another beer onto the Egyptian market. Just as Egyptians could export Stella to Syria, Syrians could now presumably export al-Chark to Egypt.

From the moment the UAR formed in February 1958, al-Chark had its eye on the Egyptian market. In September 1958, the general director of al-Chark, an al-Chark company administrator, and an official from the UAR's Ministry of Agriculture visited Pyramid, where Kettner and Alber Farag received them. Kettner learned that, unlike the brewery in the Sudan, the Syrian brewery was well stocked with malt. One of their administrators was a large landowner who grew barley. The Syrian brewery also put out feelers during the meeting to see whether they could reach an accord with Pyramid.[49] Kettner was willing to listen because the sample of beer they gave him was good, and he was wary of their intentions for the Egyptian market. He was right to be cautious, for, in 1959, this brewery used the port of Alexandria to ship a small amount of beer, 450 cases of large bottles and 150 cases of small bottles, to Egypt.[50]

There were two ways to deal with this new entrant, cooperation and competition. Crown and Pyramid could take the Syrian brewer up on its unofficial offer for partnership in beer distribution, and thus profit from al-Chark's sale while limiting its market penetration. However, Kettner decided against this course for two reasons. First, Kettner was confident that Stella would win out based on quality. While the beer he tasted from al-Chark was good, he felt that it was lacking the brightness and clarity of Stella.[51] More important, Pyramid thought that competition from al-Chark in Egypt would help to make Crown and Pyramid appear not to be a monopoly. This designation was important because at the time the Egyptian government was targeting monopolistic firms to reduce prices.[52] Heineken executives in Amsterdam agreed with Kettner that having an inferior beer on the market would not hurt Stella and would at least give the appearance of a competitive market.[53]

The developments in the Syrian market encouraged Pyramid to reevaluate its entire policy of foreign sales vis-à-vis Crown Brewery. Besides the agreed-upon markets, all other foreign markets, such as Jordan and Aden, remained common markets. This shared responsibility was an issue for Pyramid Brewery. It meant that two varieties of Stella with two different recipes, Crown's version (tailored for the Alexandria market) and Pyramid's version, were entering the same markets. This redundancy was problematic on two counts. First, the two Stellas were competing against each other. For example, in Jordan both Crown and Pyramid had granted concessions to Jordanian traders to sell Stella beer.[54] Second, the different recipes of the beers were confusing consumers on what Stella beer was.[55] In the eyes of Pyramid, this was problematic because they believed strongly that Crown's Stella was inferior and thus was prejudicing consumers from buying the "true" Stella produced by Pyramid.[56]

Pyramid thus laid out both short- and long-term plans to remedy the situation. In the short term, they resolved that Crown and Pyramid would decide, prior to entry, on which company would be the prime distributor in all new markets. As for the markets that Crown controlled, it would keep those that it wanted and immediately offer the others to Pyramid, which would have to pay a fee to sell there. In the long term, this unnecessary competition was another signal that Heineken and Pyramid needed to unify the production of both companies and eliminate any competition in foreign markets.[57]

## A Bid for Unification

The logistical difficulties Heineken faced coordinating exports of Crown and Pyramid in the new United Arab Republic brought to the fore an idea that had been in their minds since their investment in both companies in the 1930s, unification. Although Crown was receiving malt from Pyramid and agreed to sell under the Stella label, they continued to assert their autonomy by putting out a beer in Alexandria that was different from the one in Cairo. When Kettner did some taste tests, he found Crown's beer was lacking in its taste, brilliance, and foam stability. To lack these attributes was a cardinal sin because these were the main selling points of beer on the Egyptian market. Kettner was so distressed at how this nonstandardized beer was affecting the sales of Stella in Egypt that he suggested this failure to adhere to the principle of standardization warranted the replacement of the man in charge of beer production at Crown, Michel Mavroviti.[58] However, an impertinent response, rather than compliance, followed this grandstanding.

Spiro Spiridis, a managing director at Crown, said to Kettner that the difference in quality was merely a matter of appreciation. His customers in Alexandria had never commented on the beer, which fitted perfectly to their taste. Not only that, but these same customers said they preferred beer made in Alexandria to the one made in Cairo, a stab at Kettner and Pyramid. Spiridis noted that they should not dwell on this controversy and that they should have more meetings between the leadership of the two breweries, meetings that had been delayed by the upheaval in the country. He believed that these meetings would lead to slight modifications that would eventually bring the beer formulas more in line.[59] Despite Spiridis's words, the companies were still discussing the issue two years later. In fact, at that point Pyramid had resolved to send a brewmaster trained by Heineken to Crown so that this problem could finally be resolved.[60]

Crown's intransigence was having effects beyond diluting the brand. Kettner noted that during the heat wave, Crown was able to produce only thirty-six thousand bottles of beer per day. This insufficient number was not due to any problems with the bottling machinery or the brew house; rather, the problem was staffing. Crown employed only one team in the brewery, in contrast to the multiple teams working at Pyramid.[61] To try to resolve this problem, Pyramid decided to spend the excess revenue they were stuck with on Crown, infusing it with funds so that they could expand production. The excess at Pyramid was the result of the government's restriction on dividend payouts to stockholders. Although Pyramid was making banner profits, it could not send them out to stockholders, as was typical, in the form of larger dividends. Instead, they were left with a mass of money they could use only to reinvest. With this extra money, Pyramid could help Crown hire new workers and even offer to pay for full control over all exports. Pyramid's proposed takeover of exports, especially to Syria, would be a significant help to Crown, as they had burned through their entire reserves in both 1959 and 1960 trying to export.[62]

However, Zenon and Katerina Pilavachi, who controlled Crown, proved unwilling to forfeit control of a company they had run autonomously for decades. So much was this the case that when Wittert van Hoogland visited Pyramid in March 1961, he decided that instead of investing any more that he should, once again, try to fully incorporate Crown into Pyramid. The plan that Wittert van Hoogland put forth was quite like their first deal that aimed to broker better relations between Crown and Pyramid. In both instances, Heineken, acting through Cobra, encouraged Pyramid to exchange shares they had in an African brewery for shares in Crown. In the 1961 plan, Pyramid was to exchange its 50,000 shares in Blue Nile Brewery in Khartoum for 4,118 shares in Crown. These new Crown shares would bring Pyramid's total to 8,978 and its control in the company to around 30 percent. Pyramid had three reasons for wanting to trade shares with Crown instead of purchasing the shares with cash outright. First, the Egyptian Exchange Control Authorities, the government body that regulated these types of transactions, would most likely object to such a large transfer of cash. Second, Pyramid needed to remain liquid with the cash to pay for its planned expansion. Third, by using shares, this change in control of Blue Nile would have no effect on the export agreement that Pyramid and Blue Nile had vis-à-vis malt.[63]

Although the consolidation with Crown was well thought out and strongly desired by Heineken and Pyramid, it ultimately did not come to pass. This failure was attributable to the tenuous situation of every Egyptian private company in a rapidly changing country. As one illustration, Farghali Pasha never got behind the plan to exchange shares because he believed that if the Exchange Control noticed any irregularities in their accounting, this would lead to immediate nationalization.[64] This hesitation was emblematic of the great trepidation that every Pyramid executive felt about the future of the company. The near-constant threat that the situation was about to radically change prevented anyone from making long-term plans for the companies. It also led Kettner to request that Wittert line up a transfer from Pyramid. It took a great deal of explanation from Wittert to convince Kettner to try to make the best of the situation in which he found himself.[65]


## The President Speaks

The management at Heineken, Pyramid, and Crown was not completely in the dark regarding the plans of the president. Nasser himself shed some light on his plans for the breweries in a 1960 conversation he had with Isma'il Hafiz, a director of Pyramid and the bête noire of Pyramid's managing director, Erick Kettner. This conversation occurred within the framework of an Agricultural and Industrial Production Fair on January 3, 1960. The beer companies, like the rest of the agricultural and industrial firms in the country, had assigned their senior staff to man a stand at the convention. The breweries chose to represent themselves together at the Stella stand.[66] This unanimity exemplifies how powerful a brand Stella had become by this time.

At the Agricultural and Industrial Production Fair, government officials walked around, gathering information on the status of the various companies. Around noon on that day, the president, together with his minister of finance, Dr. 'Abd al-Muni'm al-Qaysuni, and his minister of industry, Dr. 'Aziz Sidqi, stopped at the Stella stand for a twenty-minute conversation. Nasser opened the conversation by asking about the general operations of the company. Hafiz responded that business was good but that the companies paid nearly 400,000 Egyptian pounds in excise taxes.[67] Nasser was quick to remind Hafiz that the excise taxes on exported beer were refunded, and then he turned to al-Qaysuni to confirm this statement. The discussion of excise taxes enabled Nasser to shift the conversation to the topic that interested him, namely, the export of beer.

Nasser posed, "How are exports?" Hafiz could answer only that, besides the malt that the companies sent to the Sudan, exports were rather limited. Troubled by this answer, Nasser called over 'Aziz Sidqi and had Hafiz repeat the same information to the minister of industry. Sidqi's response was that the Egyptian government had limited the production of the company by withholding export licenses. Sidqi pointed out that recently, a new export license had been issued to allow Stella to bolster its exports. Hafiz agreed and noted that the companies had been doing all they could to increase exports. As Nasser perused photographs of the factories and their latest installments, Hafiz stated that the larger issue was that the empty bottles necessary for bottling the beer were not produced locally. Although a local company, Yasin Glass, had attempted to do so, they had proved incapable of the task. Nasser pointed out, quite astutely, that Yasin Glass's failure was due in part to their inability to produce colored glass.[68]

Colored glass was a vital innovation in beer-bottling because hops, one of the main ingredients of beer, are light sensitive. When hops are exposed to light, a process of photooxidation occurs, and a compound known as 3-methyl-2-butene-thiol is produced. MBT is a powerful substance that can provide both a pungent odor and an off flavor to beer.[69] Thus, while glass bottles proved to be an excellent and reproducible container that created an impermeable boundary between beer and most outside forces, unless colored they provided no protection against the damaging sun. Moreover, not all colored bottles were created equal. Brown glass bottles provided the optimal amount of protection against the sun, although Pyramid and Crown chose green bottles for Stella beer.[70] Green bottles were in fact quite poor at keeping the light out, but the choice was driven by marketing: green bottles gave a better sense of the crisp and clear beer contained within.

Back at the Stella stand, Hafiz noted the president's correct assessment of the bottle situation, but added that part of the issue was also that these local factories preferred to make bottles manually rather than automatically. The fact that this choice was an issue for Pyramid and Crown communicates how mechanized the beer-making process had become. Not only was Stella beer made using automated machinery, but the filling of the bottles occurred through a mechanized process as well. Thus, a factory that was handmaking glass bottles was unable to fill the needs of Crown and Pyramid; handmade bottles, even those made by the best craftsmen, were never the same size. The bottling machines were calibrated to a specific bottle size and thus could not accommodate bottles of varying sizes. "Of course that is correct," Nasser noted to Hafiz, and then turned to Sidqi and repeated the same phrase.[71]

Next, Nasser wondered from where and for how much the breweries were getting the bottles. Hafiz responded that they were imported from East Germany and Czechoslovakia at the price of eighteen to twenty milliemes for the 630 ml bottles and twelve to fifteen milliemes for the 330 ml bottles. Hafiz added that the breweries had faced difficulties in importing these bottles due to the Ministry of Industry refusing their import requests. What happened next was an illustration of how fully power was concentrated in Nasser's hands and of how intensely personal—and one might say micromanagerial—his rule truly was. The president turned to the minister of industry and said, "Give them the license agreement." Speaking then to

Hafiz, he said, "Send the request off tomorrow and it will be immediately approved."[72]

Why was Nasser so quick to offer to fix this bottle-import problem? The answer must surely be that he believed sincerely that exports were an essential part of Egypt's economic restructuring—and because he was amenable to beer production. In particular, exporting products like Stella beer abroad was a way to achieve a favorable trade balance and restore the currency reserves that had been completely depleted by the Nasser government's spending. The year that this fair took place was the same year that Egypt's Ministry of Planning issued its first comprehensive five-year plan, which "intended to raise national income from £E 100 million to £E 184 million." Key goals of this five-year plan included the restoration of a favorable trade balance, the balancing of economic growth, the expansion of employment, and the ensuring of greater social justice.[73] Also, in the same month that this fair was taking place, January 1960, the Nasser regime began its work on the Aswan High Dam, an edifice that represented Egypt's new, empowered economic direction. It was funded in part by revenues from the nationalized Suez Canal.

There at the Stella stand at the Agricultural and Industrial Production Fair, Nasser's sincere belief in the power of exports led him to begin lecturing Hafiz on the matter. He believed that Stella could be a part of his effort because it had a good reputation at home, especially among tourists, and abroad. After pontificating for several minutes, he suggested, again showing his awareness of the positive aspects of the beer industry, that the breweries should look further into their exports in Ghana and the other countries of Southeast Africa, where there was a good market for their products. He closed his speech to Hafiz by saying that because Stella produced good beer and had a good reputation on the market, there was no reason for the government to interfere with its processes.[74]

This interaction between Nasser and the upper management of Crown and Pyramid, while short, is packed with significance for the story of the beer industry in Egypt. The most noteworthy facet of the conversation was Nasser's awareness of the particularities of beer making in Egypt and of the strength of the Stella brand in both domestic and foreign markets. Nasser's frank and knowledgeable discussion of beer shows openness to the product and a desire to support its growth, a stance that would become unthinkable for an Egyptian president after the 1970s. The conversation also shows that like the industrialists working at the breweries, Nasser was just as committed, if not more so, to making the Egyptian economy, including the beer industry, strong and expansive. He saw Stella, and specifically its export to other countries in the Third World, as a way to collect currency and even out Egypt's trade balance. Even if we view Nasser's words as idle promises, they are still evidence of the charisma and political acumen that allowed Nasser to reach the highest echelons of the Egyptian government.

The policies of the Nasser government exerted a dramatic impact on Pyramid and Crown Breweries in the prenationalization period from 1958 to 1961. While earlier chapters in this book discussed how the Nasser-led government defined and favored the "Egyptian" over the "foreign," this chapter examined how the government, as well as the beer industry itself, defined a "model company" in the private sector in the period from 1957 to 1960. The government wanted a company that was autonomous but ultimately subservient, a company whose growth would support Nasser's grand projects, including the United Arab Republic. Just as the beer companies had resisted Nasser's policies regarding foreigners, so too they did not meet with passivity the legislation aimed at making them model companies. The companies' resistance was especially important, as their leadership had their own ideas about what a model company should be. Kettner wanted a company in which Heineken's executives would prevail over a docile, loyal, and exploitable workforce. Despite this strong vision, the beer companies in this period would ultimately recognize their tenuous position. They would work to keep the government happy, doing mostly as they were asked and dutifully maintaining profitability. Meanwhile, throughout the period from 1957 to 1961, profits and sales were rising, and beer was enjoying a firm place in Egyptian culture.

# Getting the Dutch Out

*How Stella Became the Beer of the Egyptian Regime, 1961–1972*

But to return to my office roles these are, as mentioned, minimal. The only regular contact I have takes place during weekly management meetings. Beyond that, [Ismail Omar] Foda never consults me, and I do not give unsolicited advice except during said meetings in the general discussions. Neither does [Alber] Farag come to me to ask for my opinion.

—Erick Kettner to Wittert van Hoogland, January 8, 1962

As the above passage indicates, the actual experience of nationalization proved to be a deeply personal one for the executives and workers of the companies involved. From 1956 onward, the fear of nationalization was a persistent reality for the Crown and Pyramid Breweries. This fear drove the companies to be ever mindful of the government's demands, even as they worked to pursue the paths that would be most profitable. This balancing act shaped not only the interactions between the companies and the government, but also the relationships between the companies' executives and management and between their management and workforce. In 1960 the government pursued a new round of nationalizations that shattered any hope that the beer companies could remain independent.

To be sure, the Dutch, Greek, and Egyptian people involved in the beer industry had been expecting the takeover for some time; nevertheless, they responded to the government's measures not with resignation but rather by struggling to hold on to what they believed to be theirs. Some individuals fought against the regime, while others collaborated. However, as shown by the case of the Egyptian who came to head both companies, Dr. Ismail Omar Foda (commonly referred to as Dr. Omar Foda and the author's grandfather), the only thing that mattered to the government was how useful any given person or entity could be to them. The business of commandeering a private-sector enterprise was a messy one, and very few in the beer industry were left unscathed.

The nationalization or Egyptianization of the beer industry went beyond ensuring that everyone who worked in the companies had Egyptian citizenship. It also entailed excising all elements of the industry that the government deemed "foreign," including all foreign nationals, some indigenous Coptic Christians, and *mutamaṣṣirūn*, those "people of foreign origin who had become permanent residents" and whose language and habits had become "Egyptianized."[1] Nationalization also meant the removal of some Muslim Egyptians, who, in the eyes of the government, had used their financial position to exploit the country and stifle its growth. Although these people had the key feature of true Egyptians—adherence to Islam—they could never be "authentic" Egyptians in the eyes of the government because they had come from the elite classes. Beyond that, Egyptianizing meant closing the power and wealth gaps among the executives, the management, and the workforce. Most important, it meant placing the entire industry under the government's control.

The beer itself, as previous chapters have shown, needed no Egyptianizing. Thanks to the work of influential Dutchmen and of the Egyptian entrepreneurs against whom the Nasser-led regime would rally, Stella beer had become the beverage of choice for young Egyptians looking for fun. Recall that by the 1950s, Egyptians had unprecedented access to Stella beer. As Stella had become *the* beer of Egypt, it had lost some of its "foreign" allure and veneer. Along the way, many Egyptians had come to regard beer as not merely an "evil" drink or a "fun" drink, but as something in between: part of an everyday culture of leisure.

## Nationalizations

In 1960 the government shook the Egyptian business world with a new round of nationalizations, inspiring deep fear among the beer companies that they could be next. Nasser's government struck the first blow against Egypt's national banks, Bank Misr and the National Bank of Egypt, in February. The government followed by nationalizing major daily newspapers, such as *al-Ahram*, *Akhbar al-Youm*, and *Ruz al-Yusuf*. Next, it took over the bus companies. Although the specter of government involvement had hung over Erick Kettner's head for nearly five years, as the managing director of Pyramid Brewery, he was still shocked by these events. When Kettner reported the events to Wittert van Hoogland, he could barely contain his disdain: "These [nationalizations] are justified by the claim that they are done to ensure the freedom of the press (seriously)." For Kettner, this reasoning was farcical, as he believed these nationalizations had both economic and political motives, including the suppression of free speech. He noted that it was a poorly kept secret that the nationalized newspapers were going to have no say in what was printed.[2]

Kettner's negative reaction to these nationalizations grew out of his distaste for Nasser and his government. Kettner had little faith in the populism of Nasser and saw it only as trouble for the Egyptian economy. Kettner's feelings were only exacerbated by the fact that with each passing month, the star of Nasser shone only brighter for most Egyptians. Nasser's populist policies—land reforms, support for workers and peasants rights, and the push for greater social equality, all infused by a strong anti-imperialism and jingoism—had won him massive support among the *effendiyya* (the liminal class composed of students, professionals, teachers, civil servants, and small businessmen), workers, and peasants. The nationalization of the newspapers, which turned a relatively free press into one aimed solely to "justify, support and flatter" the increasingly authoritarian Nasser regime, only confirmed to Kettner that his skepticism of the regime was justified.[3]

The nationalization of three vital sectors in quick succession—banks, transport, and newspapers—set the entire private sector on alert. The businessmen of the private sector assumed that the cotton firms would be the next target and that their nationalization would be accompanied by a potential modification of the Agrarian Land Reform of 1952, reducing the number of *feddans* one could own from two hundred to fifty. After that, perhaps even a larger round of nationalizations would follow. Businessmen were worried that even if they managed to avoid nationalization, the government would still destroy their profits with the restrictive policies that accompanied these nationalizations.[4]

The businessmen of the private sector proved prescient in their worries over the renewed activist streak of the government. In the summer of 1960, the government nationalized "import houses and wholesalers of pharmaceutical products simultaneously with the tea packers." In the winter, the government nationalized all institutions that had significant investments of Belgian capital. This included the Tramways du Caire, the Rolin Group (to which Pyramid used to belong), and the Banque Belge. This last bit of government business was quite troubling to Pyramid because Banque Belge was their primary bank. Kettner had a trusted contact in the bank, Mr. Ashkar, who had aided the brewery in the numerous transfer issues it faced as a multinational functioning in Nasser's Egypt.[5] Kettner trusted this man to such an extent that, even after the bank had been nationalized, he wanted to maintain the relationship.

This round of nationalizations reverberated beyond Pyramid's relations with the Banque Belge. The Egyptian stock market took a significant hit, as economic volatility deleteriously affected domestic and foreign sales of one of Egypt's biggest products, cotton. Prices dropped, and in the first quarter of 1960, cotton sellers were able to sell only three-fifths of what they had sold the previous year. The dip in the stock market would not have been so bad if it had been met by new capital from foreign investors looking to profit by "buying low." However, the Egyptian government severely limited foreign investment, claiming to fear "predatory" foreign capitalists. The government, in fact, promulgated a law that required President Nasser to approve all foreign investment in the country.[6] The limiting of foreign capital coupled with the government's nationalizations of companies supported by large amounts of foreign capital struck fear in the hearts of those working at the Heineken-backed Crown and Pyramid Breweries. They could not help but dread what the future held for them.

## The First Salvo

In July 1961, the political mood in Egypt quickly changed. Nasser's distaste for the private sector had become clear to journalists and industrialists alike by 1960, but the decrees he issued in July 1961 went beyond what either group had imagined.[7] Nasser's moves sent a clear signal that he no longer believed the private sector could lead Egypt to the economic resurgence that he desired.[8] Not coincidentally, these decrees occurred on the ninth anniversary of the Free Officers Movement. The regime portrayed the decrees as a revolution against "the dictatorship of capital."[9] Although the regime did not express it in these exact terms, these actions were an open declaration of war on those "compradorial" elements within Egypt that had stifled the development of the country.[10] A comprador is defined in the traditional study of political economy as the "native agents or partners of foreign investors who operate in some form in the local economy."[11] While Robert Vitalis has shown that this term was ill-suited to Egyptian businessmen, like 'Abbud Pasha, who would come under attack by the Nasser regime, the term does reasonably encapsulate the Egyptian government's view of capitalists like Farghali Pasha, the president of Pyramid Brewery.[12] In their eyes, he was using his foreign business links to enrich himself at the expense of "regular" Egyptians. For the government, men like Farghali were part of the group of "exploiters" ("only 5 percent") who need to be vanquished in order to free the exploited ("95 percent").[13]

What this fight against the exploiters meant in practice was the modification of the land law, which limited property owners to one hundred *fed-*

*dans* per person, as well as the enactment of a series of laws that nationalized the great majority of the corporate sector.[14] These laws allowed the government to take full control of 149 companies, which included all banks, insurance companies, and cement factories, all of which were central to the Nasser-led government's plans for a rapid industrialization of Egypt.[15] The Socialist Laws of 1961 and 1962 also allowed Nasser's government to take 50 percent of the shares of 91 other companies, in exchange for government bonds with 4 percent interest. The laws limited the holdings of one person in one of 159 more companies to 10,000 pounds worth of shares. A purported goal of these laws was to improve the working conditions of Egyptians. They legislated that workers must be represented on every corporate board in the country and that boards could have only seven members. All corporate dividends were abolished, and the government legislated that companies had to allocate 10 percent of net profits to workers, another 10 percent to a central service fund, and 5 percent to social services. The laws limited working hours to seven hours per day and restricted every person to working just one job. They also limited remuneration to 5,000 pounds. Finally, the laws increased tax revenues and closed the stock exchange for two months.[16]

Despite the passage of this legislation, both Pyramid and Crown were initially able to avoid the fate of nationalization. Incidentally, Gianaclis wine and Société Nationale de Levure (yeast) were left out of the purview of the nationalization legislation as well. Farghali Pasha saw this as more than a coincidence, believing it inconceivable that the state would get involved in the alcohol business because of the traditional Islamic disapproval of wine. He was so sure of it that he assured Kettner to ignore Isma'il Hafiz, who was claiming that the day of reckoning was coming for the breweries.[17] Kettner needed no convincing, as he believed Farghali Pasha's claims were merely wishful thinking. Kettner could not imagine that the government would leave only the alcohol producers unaffected by the nationalization, that they would give special treatment to a "forbidden" product. Kettner figured that the delay was only because it would take some time to persuade the "preachers of the Quran," probably meaning the shaykhs of al-Azhar, that it was lawful for the government to nationalize the companies.[18]

Kettner did not have to wait long to find out. On August 7, 1961, the process of nationalization began, innocuously enough, with an article published in *Journal Officiel*, the French-language government gazette, stating that the government had sequestrated Pyramid, which entailed freezing all of the company's assets and placing them under the control of a sequestrator. When Kettner told Farghali Pasha the news, he was shocked. So was Isma'il Hafiz, although he was more upset that the government did not appoint him as the chief sequestrator of the company.[19] Hafiz, utterly bewildered by the decision, took a trip to Alexandria to save face. Kettner was not surprised by the move, but he was confused and a bit suspicious about the circumstances that surrounded it. He was not sure why they were sequestrated rather than nationalized. He imagined that this maneuver was a way for the government to gather information on the company and its finances before it decided to which of the three nationalization operations it would subject the company.[20]

While Kettner was unsure about the reasons the government decided to sequester and not nationalize them, he was reasonably certain that the decision for sequestration was the result of intrigues by an Egyptian within the company. He had reason to suspect someone because, at the time, it appeared that the government sequestered only those companies suspected of irregularity. The possibility became even more probable when Crown escaped being sequestered.[21] Considering the long history between Kettner and Hafiz, as well as the latter's well-known desire to be the chief sequestrator, it was no wonder that Kettner suspected Hafiz of turning the keys of the company over to the government. Kettner also came upon information that seemed to support the idea that it was Hafiz who had sold out the company. In discussions with the executives at Philips, the Dutch technology giant, one remarked to Kettner that an Egyptian was selling them out, just like "Ismail Hafiz did at another Dutch company."[22]

For Kettner, this theory of treachery could explain why Hafiz was so upset when he was not appointed sequestrator of the company. It also explained why Hafiz delayed his departure to Holland until around the time of the company's sequestration. In addition to these hints, before sequestration, Hafiz was a vocal proponent of a government plan to incorporate Pyramid in a newly created body for consumer products, of which one of his friends was in charge.[23] Of course, Hafiz pinned the blame on Abu al-'Aynayn al-Salim, another member of the board of directors.[24] This was not such an unreasonable statement, as Kettner suspected Salim as well. Kettner noted that during the board meeting on July 21, 1961, Salim "behaved very strangely and made, in Arabic, all kinds of threats." Then on August 3, he threatened Kettner that he was going to write to the government ministers about the "intolerable state of affairs" within the company. When Kettner informed Farghali Pasha of Salim's odd behavior, Farghali Pasha told him in French, "Salim is crazy and he is a moron."[25] Regardless of who was responsible for sequestration, Kettner decided on discretion—as he termed it, "waiting for the ulcer to burst"—because the company was still under investigation by the government, and he had no intention of bringing unneeded attention to the issue.[26]

Part of his unwillingness to pursue the issue further may have derived from the fact that, from the beginning, Kettner had assumed government interference was inevitable. It would have been exceptional if the alcohol industry had avoided a reality that most of the private sector had suffered. In the case of Pyramid, avoiding sequestration would have been especially noteworthy because of the strong association the company had with Farghali Pasha. He was the embodiment of the exploitative comprador that the Nasser government held up as the bane to the development of a self-sufficient Egypt. Exemplary of this fact is that Farghali Pasha contravened every regulation that the Nasser government passed on the private sector and executives. For example, after 1955, when the government modified the Company Law requiring anyone who sat on the board of companies as an *administrateur*, or trustee, to be under the age of sixty and to be a director at only one company, Farghali Pasha was over the age of sixty and sat on the boards of twenty-nine different companies. When the Nasser-led government put forth its July Decrees in 1961, Farghali Pasha, as the largest stockholder in Pyramid, was in clear violation of the law that one's stake in the company was not to exceed 10,000 Egyptian pounds.[27]

When the Egyptian government arrested individuals "planning to overthrow the regime," Farghali Pasha was among them. These arrests came in the aftermath of the secession of Syria from the United Arab Republic, which was a blow to Nasser's prestige in the Arab world as the head of Arab nationalism.[28] His crackdown on these supposed antiregime forces was a way to prove the continuing vibrancy and effectiveness of his message in the wake of a diplomatic defeat. Striking out against his enemies in response to foreign policy issues was not a new policy. As Kettner stated, "Nasser becomes more dangerous as he has less success with his foreign policy."[29] These "antiregime" forces were in fact "three different strains of the old regime: politicians, remnants of the old landed elite like the Badrawi Ashur Family; and a mixed group of merchants and industrialists, a few of Egyptian nationality and many more of foreign descent."[30]

The arrest of Farghali Pasha and his ilk represented the Nasser regime's further expansion of those classified as enemies of the state. Despite all the legislation working against Farghali Pasha, he was able to maintain his position after 1956 for the same reason that he was able to reach his position in the first place, namely, he had strong international business connections and claimed an identity as a Muslim Egyptian. Farghali Pasha's arrest and subsequent expulsion from the corporate sector represents the Nasser-led government's full enunciation that, like "foreign" forces, predatory "Egyptian" Muslim capitalists like Farghali Pasha had stifled Egypt's economic development, too. For so long, Farghali Pasha, and to a lesser extent Hafiz and other Muslim Egyptians such as Abu al-'Aynayn al-Salim, had relied on the fact that they were the "good guys," who could use their privileged position to avoid the fates of "foreign" entities. These arrests marked the end of that era.

After this point, Farghali Pasha, like many of the business elites associated with the old regime, was broken and marginalized. Farghali Pasha reportedly disappeared from Cairo, not even returning when the government confiscated his horses at the Sporting Club. In that same Sporting Club, the Nasser-led government carried out another symbolic act. They transformed the polo fields, the staging ground for a game of the wealthy, into football pitches, the staging ground for the popular (sha'bi) game of the people. The golfers of the club, displaying a bit of tone deafness, were upset that this transformation also eliminated the main course on which they practiced.[31] Nevertheless, Farghali Pasha did not disappear completely. Kettner later met him by chance at the upscale Semiramis Hotel, where he was eating with a "belle," and reported that Farghali Pasha seemed pleased to see him and even inquired about the company. Farghali Pasha expressed his regret that Hafiz was so unwise as to refuse to cooperate with the new sequestrator, Dr. Omar Foda.[32] Under the watch of Dr. Foda, the company would accelerate down the path to full "Egyptianization."

## A New Boss

In Omar Foda's capacity as, at first, the government's sequestrator, he ran the beer industry in Egypt and indeed led it for the next twenty-four years.[33] This next section will look at what sequestration under Foda meant for the beer companies in practice. Specifically, it will look at how Foda dealt with key people like Kettner, Hafiz, the Pilavachis, and the workers and how the beer companies fared under his tenure in their activities, including domestic and foreign sales.

The regime's first choice for sequestrator had in fact been Dr. 'Abd al-'Aziz Husayn. But after Dr. Husayn recused himself for the position and recommended Foda instead, Foda assumed the position. With a PhD in microbiology from the University of California–Berkeley, Dr. Omar Foda certainly claimed educational credentials and a degree of technical expertise that was unmatched among Egyptians. While hiring someone with such expertise was certainly a boon for Pyramid, it must also have been a difficult decision for the regime members who appointed him. Foda came from a family of landed elite, one of the main targets of the Nasser-led regime. In the view of Nasser ideologues, these feudalist property owners (*al-iqtāʿūn*) had done to the country's land what the compradors had done to the economy. Dr. Foda was the grandson of a large landowner from Sinballawein in the Dahqaliyya province in the Delta, and his father was a member of the Chamber of Deputies (Majlis al-Nuwab). Emblematic of how Foda came from one of the targeted groups of the regime, the government had confiscated thousands of *feddans* of lands from his father, Hussein Foda, in the agrarian reform acts, and also frozen the assets of his brother, Daoud, while placing him under house arrest in 1961. In other words, and perhaps ironically, Dr. Foda had direct familial experience with the kind of socialist takeover that had struck out against the beer companies—albeit, in his own case, with regard to landed and not corporate property.

While the regime may have had difficulty in appointing Foda, he also had difficulty in accepting. The government's land reforms had hit his family hard, and many of his relatives privately maintained that the reforms had sent their paterfamilias, Hussein Foda, his father, to an early grave. Yet with his father gone and his brother incapacitated, Dr. Foda had responsibility for supporting his mother and five sisters as they struggled with their new reality. He had been supporting his family by serving in the Department of Food Technology at the College of Agriculture at Cairo University, but the government position—despite being objectionable on philosophical grounds—offered the possibility of government leniency in any other future dealings with the family. Indeed, Dr. Foda's appointment had elements of mutual convenience on both sides. For Dr. Foda, accepting the government's offer was done out of necessity and not out of fondness, while the government officials were motivated by a pragmatic recognition that Dr. Foda was exceptionally qualified for the position.

Foda was cordially received by the Dutch contingent of Pyramid, despite being the physical embodiment of the government's takeover. Kettner and the Dutch brewmaster, Gerardus Ulenberg, were well disposed to him. Foda's intrusion was surely softened by the fact that he paid all respects to Heineken and their operations. He also was quite forthcoming with Kettner on the reasons that precipitated the sequestration. As he made clear to Kettner as well, the underlying reason for the sequestration was the regime's fear that the Egyptian board members would manipulate the company's finances to extract even more money from the country. The government was also worried that "reactionaries" could use profits to prevent the realization of a socialist state by funding a counterrevolution.[34]

Not everyone was so cordial with Dr. Foda. Hafiz admitted spontaneously to Kettner that his relationship with Foda was extremely negative.[35] Nevertheless, despite Foda's power to remove Hafiz, Foda kept him on as his assistant sequestrator. This relationship, like Foda's with the government, was defined by a need for convenience that overcame the enmity at its heart. For Foda, Hafiz was one of the longest-tenured executives left who remained "acceptable" in the eyes of the government. As a Muslim Egyptian whom the government had not designated as persona non grata, he was a definite asset as well. He had the benefit of years of experience with the company, which Foda lacked.

Hafiz did not face the same fate as Farghali because, for one, he had not reached the high position of Farghali Pasha. Another reason he may have been acceptable to the government was that he was an alleged government collaborator. Beyond the previously discussed allegations, which are all but confirmed by the archival record, Hafiz had also served as an informant to the government on Pyramid, reporting that the Dutch were moving a large amount of money outside of Egypt in a form of capital flight. Hafiz, who had wanted to be chief sequestrator himself and who therefore harbored ill will toward Foda, benefited from his contacts with the regime. He was able to become directing manager at Pyramid, the position that Kettner once held and that Hafiz had always wanted. Nevertheless, Hafiz did not make life easy for Foda. For example, Hafiz almost caused mutiny among the staff by publicly proposing a plan that would replace all of them.[36] Foda was aware of Hafiz's plans and his scheming, but they ultimately led to very little.[37] Foda kept him on regardless, to maintain continuity.

The whole history of the relationship between Pyramid and Crown was characterized by dueling forces, as economic forces pushed the companies together and executives pulled them apart, so it is perhaps not surprising that the two companies did not enter sequestration in unison. While Pyramid was sequestered in August 1961, Crown remained free from government control. However, everyone involved in both Crown and Pyramid recognized that this situation was temporary. Isma'il Hafiz, in particular, had his eyes on Crown and pushed hard for its sequestration. He hoped that if he led the charge, he could serve as the main sequestrator of the company, a position he failed to secure at Pyramid. Hafiz was so set on this plan that he fabricated an elaborate lie that there was a "Hafiz Period" at Pyramid Brewery, where he ruled supreme.[38]

Hafiz was not the only one preparing for the eventuality of Crown's sequestration. The Pilavachis, Zenon and Katerina, were likewise preparing for imminent change. As Greek citizens, they realized that their stake in the company was in danger. This danger was made more fully manifest by the fact that the government had nationalized Zenon Pilavachi's interest in

Abu Zabal and Kafr al-Zayat Fertiliser.[39] When sequestration hit individual members of Crown's board Samih Musa and Mahmud ʿAbd al-Sidqi, in 1961, Crown took the opportunity to reorganize. Katerina Pilavachi resigned from the board, as did Spiro Spiridis, who had served as managing director of the brewery, and Muhammad Wathiq Abaza, a relative of ʿAziz Abaza.[40] Beyond this reorganization, the Pilavachis also followed a plan to limit the damage from Crown's eventual sequestration. They sold a small amount of their shares to reduce their holding in Crown to four thousand shares. The purpose of the sale was not to end their relationship, but rather, they believed, to establish a reasonable price for the shares. By establishing this price, they hoped that when the government did sequester the company, it would pay the established price for their shares.[41]

The Pilavachis, who were ethnic Greeks born and raised in Egypt, anticipated the entrance of the Greek government into the matter. As they saw it, if the Greeks in Egypt voluntarily liquidated their assets, then the odds of Greek government intervention on their behalf would be quite low. The odds were much better if their property was forcibly confiscated. The Pilavachis based this assumption on the fact that the Greek government partially compensated those Greeks who had lost their possessions in the communist takeover of Bulgaria in 1946.[42] Kettner was confident that if the Pilavachis had not expected Greek intervention, they would have redone their entire business portfolio.[43]

However, all the Pilavachis' planning was for naught, as they never received a response from the Egyptian government. Instead, when the Egyptian government informed Crown and Pyramid that it would levy an excise tax on beer, they were left sitting on the stock. News of the tax spread, the stock tumbled, and the Pilavachis faced a significant loss. Meanwhile, the position of Greeks within Egypt was becoming even more tenuous.[44] News spread of state security forces capturing fourteen Egyptian-born Greeks carrying out espionage for Israel.[45] Because it was a matter of espionage, it is difficult to determine whether the accusations are true, especially because the government did not aggressively pursue it and the papers remain closed to researchers, but in any case, the mere allegation was damaging enough. These events, coupled with the Greek government's membership in the North Atlantic Treaty Organization, meant that the situation for Greeks in Egypt was becoming increasingly awkward.[46]

In December 1961, the government sequestered Crown Brewery. This sequestration was accompanied by the sequestration of the Central Bureau, the shared depot where both Pyramid and Crown sold their beer. Despite Ismaʿil Hafiz's machinations, he was not awarded the position of head sequestrator, as that position was once again given to Omar Foda. The government also passed over Hafiz for the position of subsequestrator. In a case similar to that of Pyramid Brewery, the government gave no reason for the sequestration. Alber Farag speculated that the government targeted Crown because the Pilavachis did not offer enough of their shares up for sale.[47]

Kettner believed that the Pilavachis' actions could have been part of the reason the government targeted Crown, but he believed a more significant reason was the reorganization of what he called *Organismes Publiques*. These were the structures through which the Nasser regime aimed to organize the growing public sector. Prior to December 1961, formerly private assets that the government absorbed went into three public holding companies: the Economic Organization, the Misr Organization, and the Nasr Organization. The Economic Organization was the first structure that the government created, and it came in response to the nationalization of British and French assets in 1957. The government created the Misr Organization to handle the assets of the Misr Group, which included Bank Misr and its assets, which "accounted for 60 percent of all textile production and 53 percent of employment in the textile sector." Finally, the Nasr Organization, which was composed of twenty-four companies capitalized at 40 million pounds, covered the state enterprises that arose from the first five-year plan laid out by Minister of the Economy 'Abd al-Mun'im al-Qaysuni in 1960.[48]

However, as Crown was being sequestered, the Egyptian government was rethinking its organization of the public sector. An upshot of their latest rounds of nationalization was that the public sector was outgrowing these three ad hoc organizations. On December 16, 1961, the government, through decree number 1899, "effectively abolished the three existing General Organizations."[49] In their place, the government grouped 438 companies, including the newly sequestered Crown Brewery, into thirty-nine General Organizations organized along sectoral lines. Each of these General Organizations was attached to the ministry that was most relevant. In the case of Pyramid Brewery, Crown Brewery, and the Central Bureau, all of their stock was nationalized, and the government placed them under the auspices of the newly formed General Corporation for Food Industries (al-Mu'assasa al-Misriyya al-'Amma li-l-Sina'at al-Ghidha'iyya), headed by Dr. Hasan Muhammad 'Ashmawi.[50]

The General Organizations' full integration into the Egyptian economic system had a great deal to do with how highly the Egyptian government valued beer exports. The government saw these exports as an easy way to bring foreign currency into the country. It was not coincidental, then, that one of the first directives the government assigned Foda as the head of the beer companies was to export ten thousand hectoliters of beer to Romania.[51] This trade relationship proved to be one of the most fruitful for the company. Foda was even able to sign a trade agreement with Romania in 1968 that guaranteed the export of forty thousand hectoliters of beer in exchange for nearly $1 million from the Romanian government.[52] In a similar vein, the government also forced the company to start exporting to Aden.[53] Perhaps the greatest example of the use of the beer company to expand foreign trade is that by 1966, the beer company had even expanded into the Jordanian market, owning 40 percent of a company there.[54]

After Crown's sequestration in 1961, the government resolved that both it and Pyramid would be officially nationalized, which meant being conglomerated into al-Ahram (Arabic: "Pyramid") Brewing Company. This welding together of the two companies would occur in a multistep process, and Foda was tasked with overseeing it. The July Decrees required the new conglomerated board of directors to reserve spots for a representative of the workers (ʿummāl) and a representative employee (muwazzafīn). This requirement forced a radical change in the board of the newly amalgamated company. Besides Foda, who occupied the position of delegated member (ʿuḍū al-muntadab) on the board of directors, the board was composed of appointed and elected members. In the case of appointed members, again, it appears that Foda preferred continuity under his tenure. He chose Egyptian workers, who had trained and worked under the watch of Dutch managers.

This board represented the culmination of the government-led takeover of the beer industry. Not only did a handpicked representative sit at the top of the company, but the board also embodied the government's demographic vision for the country. The entire board was composed of Egyptians. Perhaps unsurprisingly considering the regime's rhetoric, only two out of the nine members of the new executive board, Alber Farag and Ghattas Hanna Ghattas, were Christians. The rest, and the overwhelming seven-out-of-nine majority, were Muslims. Not only were all the "foreign" elements eliminated or outnumbered, but the Egyptian collaborators were sidelined as well. Even masters of industry like Farghali Pasha were absent from the board. And again, for personal reasons relating to the government's prior treatment of his family's property, the board's most powerful member, Foda, was subservient to the government as well. Thus, the nationalization and consolidation created a board loyal to the regime. The board's subservience derived from the fact their continued employment was entirely reliant on the whims of the government and its leader, Nasser.

## Dealing with the Dutch

Although the "foreign" elements had all been purged from the executive, the nationalization of the breweries did not mark the end of the relationship between Dutch and Egyptian brewing. Due to both Dutch desire and the Egyptian government's prodding, the relationship between the two countries' brewing industries lasted until the mid-1970s. The government's sequestration of Pyramid in 1961 signaled a new era in Egyptian brewing, but it was the government's sequestration of Crown later that year that confirmed that the situation would never be the same. When the news of Crown's sequestration reached Holland, Wittert van Hoogland conceded that Cobra and Heineken's influence beyond the technical level was "0.0."[55] As was true of all developments in the beer industry in Egypt after 1957, there was no better observer of this than Kettner.

Despite Kettner's long track record with the company, upon the sequestration of Pyramid, he was immediately marginalized. He was removed from his post as managing director and assigned the role of consultant.[56] This total marginalization was quite a change from the elevated position to which Kettner was accustomed. Nevertheless, the Nasser-led government's policy initiatives meant there was no other way for the business to operate. Despite his well-demonstrated expertise, Kettner was the embodiment of the foreign capitalist exploiting Egypt. As for the other major Dutch force on the ground, Gerardus Ulenberg, the head brewmaster, it initially appeared that the government would allow Ulenberg to stay on after nationalization as the director of brewing in Egypt. This made sense, as he was much less visible than Kettner and much more central to the brewing operations.[57]

Eventually, however, the departures of these last two vestiges were all but decided by March 1962. Kettner and Ulenberg did not leave Egypt until May 1962, since even in the act of resignation, the Egyptian government held control. Specifically, all departures had to be approved by Dr. Foda. In addition, all outstanding debts and payments had to be settled with the Egyptian authorities. Only then did the government grant an exit visa. Although it took Kettner a significant amount of time to settle his account with the Egyptian government, Dr. Foda eventually accepted his resignation and departure.

However, Dr. Foda was not as conciliatory with Ulenberg, as his departure from Egypt became a serious bone of contention between the Dutch and the Egyptian. This turn of events came as a shock to the Dutch, because it appeared initially that Foda was fully behind the move. Foda had even committed to paying the full travel expenses for Ulenberg's departure. However, after the initial appearance of support, Dr. Foda made "an about-face."[58]

Heineken could not figure out why Dr. Foda had taken this position because it appeared to go against the interests of the breweries and the Egyptian government. If it was an attempt at intimidation, Heineken believed that they could take a strong stand. First, they understood that the breweries and the Egyptian government would like the technical support of Heineken to continue "at all costs." In addition, Egypt was looking for international loans. Thus, any international incident could possibly endanger their chances of receiving help from other Western countries. Heineken conjectured that Dr. Foda was acting on his own accord. In their eyes, his actions were a poor attempt to make sure that the relationship between the breweries and Heineken continued when they became part of the General Corporation for Food Industries.[59] Regardless, Heineken, through some heavy prodding, was able to extract Ulenberg and Kettner from the country in the summer of 1962.

For Ulenberg, this was the end of his tenure in Egypt, but not his relationship with the brewery. In 1964 he would visit the brewery as a representative for Cobra/Heineken to make a technical assessment of the brewery. This visit was part of a larger tour of breweries he made for Cobra. For example, he would also carry out a technical evaluation of a brewery in Australian New Guinea.[60] Thus, Ulenberg slid from his position in Egypt back into the world beer empire of Heineken/Cobra. Kettner, however, did not reintegrate so easily back into the Heineken/Cobra world. Heineken wrote him in January 1963, stating that they were unable to find a "suitable" position for him within the company. The board expressed regret, but affirmed that they had tried as hard as they could to find a position that would be in some way connected to what he did in Cairo. Unfortunately, no position existed for him. Thus, his years of work in Egypt ensured him nothing except a generous severance package of $50,000. One wonders whether Heineken's failure to find a position for Kettner had anything to do with his difficult, imperious personality.

Although the last vestiges of their control on the ground had disappeared, Heineken and Cobra's relationship continued with the breweries and the Egyptian government. In 1964 they signed a new technical contract for a period of five years. As part of the agreement, the conglomerated breweries could request a technical adviser from Heineken. However, they never took the Dutch brewery up on that provision. Rather, the relationship was much more distant than during the time of Kettner. The most probable reason for the distance was the heated debate among the entities over the remuneration for the nationalization of Heineken's interest in the two companies.

The dispute between Heineken and the Egyptian government—Heineken referred to this issue as the Delenda affair, after a Crown shareholder who was likewise unhappy with the remuneration—was over what stock price should be used when calculating what the Egyptian government owed foreign investors. Should they pay the price of the shares on the day of sequestration in 1961 or the price on the day of nationalization in 1963? Heineken asserted that the Egyptian government's sequestration of the beer companies' assets had cratered the price of the stock, and thus, the price at nationalization, the price the Egyptian government was willing to pay, was not an accurate reflection of their investment in the company. Only the sequestration price would do. The feud would simmer until the middle of the 1970s and would embroil the foreign ministries of both countries.[61] At one point, Heineken even reached out to the International Monetary Fund (IMF).[62] The two sides would finally come to an agreement when the Egyptian government agreed to pay Heineken 7 Egyptian pounds per Pyramid share and 10 Egyptian pounds per Crown share, for a total of more than 514,000 Egyptian pounds.[63]

## A Lasting Impact

As chapter 5 showed, by the 1960s advertising campaigns had helped to make beer the young Egyptian's choice for a party beverage, perfect for warm days and nights on summer vacations. The image Stella beer exuded was one of youth, sociability, and refreshment. This image continued during and after nationalization and sequestration. One particularly notable example comes, again, from a cinematic adaption of an Ihsan 'Abd al-Quddus story, *Al-Nazzara al-Sawda'* (The dark glasses [1963]). The film revolves around another "bad" girl, Madiha, nicknamed Maddy (played by Nadia Lutfi), and her relationship with 'Umar (Ahmad Mazhar) as they both struggle with finding love and happiness in Nasserite Cairo. Beer makes a cameo in their love affair when Maddy brings 'Umar to the pool of the social club that she frequents. As she introduces 'Umar to all her friends using their nicknames, we see the young crowd wearing bathing suits and sitting around a table with beer bottles on it.

'Umar, who is a conscientious and serious factory manager, is visibly put off by the lighthearted attitudes of her friends. This dichotomy between the serious and the trivial is a major theme in the film, one with which both Maddy and 'Umar struggle. In the pool scene, the beer bottles, like the nicknames and the pool, are part and parcel of the fun and triviality of Maddy's life. They sit in opposition to the classicist literature that 'Umar reads— Balzac, Shaw, Checkov, Ahmad Shawqi, and Taha Husayn—and the social consciousness he shows by visiting infirm factory workers.[64] Nevertheless, beer still carried the same association: youth, fun, and refreshment.

That is not to say, however, that nationalization and sequestration did not change the place of Stella beer in Egyptian culture. One significant index of that change comes from an English novel published in 1964, *Beer in the Snooker Club*. Written by a previously unknown Anglophone Copt named Waguih Ghali, it tells the story of Ram, "a Francophone, British-educated Copt," as he struggles with his transcultural identity.[65] As should be obvious from the title, beer has some role to play in his internal struggle. The clearest example of this role relates to a concoction, a sort of cocktail, that Ram makes and calls "Draught Bass." While its name was taken from the English beer Bass, it had very little in common with that beer, as is obvious from Ram's recipe for it: "I opened two bottles of Egyptian Stella beer and poured them into a large tumbler, then beat the liquid until all the gas had escaped. I then added a drop of vodka and some whiskey. It was the nearest we could get to Draught Bass."[66] This cocktail, one literary critic has suggested, was "as much a symbol of Nasser's Egypt, as of the characters' divided sympathies." Further, Ram's mixing of constituent alcohols represents his desire to eschew "the English brew and the prefabricated cultural hegemony it represents" to produce "a more complex construction of himself influenced by, but not a product of, England."[67] However, Ram's use of Stella goes beyond merely its identification as an Egyptian beer. The violence he performs on it, as well as its centrality to his concoction, represents his complicated relationship with this product.

This novel came out at a time when Stella was the only beer that an Egyptian could buy on the open market. As *the* beer of Egypt, it did not hold the same allure that a drink like Bass did. It was a semiluxury product, one that was easily accessible but, because of its long cultural history, not devoid of meaning. The beer was not as luxurious as Bass, and its consumption did not connect its drinker to another world of the imagination, namely, "the world of intellectuals and underground metros and cobbled streets and a green countryside … [t]he world where students had rooms, and typists for girlfriends, and sang songs and drank beer in large mugs … [a] whole imaginary world." Nevertheless, Stella had such hegemony over the beer market in Egypt that it was still central to the life that Ram wanted to live. For example, when he goes to a club to swim at the pool, he drinks a cold Egyptian beer with lunch. Then, another time at the club in Egypt, he gets the urge for a beer: "I felt like having a cold beer and eating salted peanuts; then a cigarette and another beer and more peanuts. I could do it, of course, even though I had no money. But I knew the pattern too well, the depression afterward and the self-disgust."[68] In both instances, the temperature of the beer is central to its description. This description shows how as much as he would like to transcend it, both Ram and Ghali were attuned to the pleasures of a cold Stella on a warm Egyptian day by the pool or in the club.

The relationship that the fictional character Ram had with Stella paralleled the one that the author Waguih Ghali had with the Nasser regime. Ghali was conflicted: he supported the socialist, anticolonial platform of Nasser, but he was also a strong opponent of its repressive policies, including its curtailment of political expression.[69] Stella beer was an ideal commodity to embody this dilemma: the regime produced it after the beer companies' nationalization, yet it had become so central to the lives of a certain class of Egyptians that its cultural value was able, in many respects, to transcend this or any regime.

The changing role of beer was also on display in the film adaption of another Ihsan 'Abd al-Quddus story, *Abi Fawq al-Shajara* (Father's up a tree [1968]). The last film to feature one of Egypt's most famous singers and actors, 'Abd al-Halim Hafiz, *Abi Fawq al-Shajara* tells the story of the moral rise and fall of 'Adil ('Abd al-Halim Hafiz), a young Egyptian male student. The main driver of the story is 'Adil's love for a girl named Amal (Mervet Amin). Although she reciprocates the feeling, she is unwilling to spend time alone with 'Adil out of her own sense of propriety. Amal's repeated rebuffing of 'Adil's demands for alone time of the kind that, he claims, a lot of other young men and women were having leads 'Adil to fall in with the "wrong" crowd.

'Adil first meets the "wrong" crowd—where else?—on the beach. Beer plays a central role in this critical moment of the film. As 'Adil jogs out of the water onto the beach, the camera frames him and an unidentified hand, its owner otherwise obscured by a beach umbrella, emptying a green bottle into a glass embossed with the famous Stella star. Signaling the imminent danger, the music shifts from playful to ominous as we watch the hand perfectly pour the beer. When 'Adil reaches the umbrella, the camera reveals a group of four young men drinking and having fun. After exchanging English "hellos," one of the young men asks 'Adil if he would like a sip. He says, "No, thank you. I don't drink." They all burst out laughing when they hear his response. They invite 'Adil out to party with them, but he turns them down.

The short conversation is filled with laughter and jokes. After 'Adil excuses himself from their presence, they make fun of him for not coming out. 'Adil then meets one of his friends, who asks him how he knows the group of "guys," a leading question meant to signal that the friend does not trust the group. ʿAdil assures his friend that the men have *damm khafīf* (Arabic: "a sense of humor," literally "light blood"). He states that they meet everything in the world with a sense of humor and are willing to try anything. His friend warns ʿAdil to stay away from them, as it is obvious to him that they are not good people.

After a couple of encounters between ʿAdil and Amal, where ʿAdil lays out what he wants from Amal and meets only rejection, ʿAdil decides to make a change. Instead of going to the beach where ʿAmal and the rest of his social group (*al-shilla*) hang out, he joins the "wrong" crowd for a party on another beach. Their beach party is rowdy and alcohol infused. The scene opens with the leader of the gang, Ashraf (Samir Sabri), guzzling a whole large bottle of beer as the beer spills all over his chest and face. There are music and dancing, and beer is central to the party. One partygoer dips his sandwich in his beer and then eats it. Another couple dances while they balance a beer bottle between their foreheads. At first, ʿAdil observes on the sidelines, but then Ashraf comes over and pours him a beer. ʿAdil asks him what he is pouring, and when Ashraf responds, "Beer," ʿAdil states, again, that he does not drink. Ashraf goads him to "just try it." When he does, he immediately spits it out. Ashraf encourages him to try it again and pours him some more. While he pours, he says to ʿAdil, "Look, this here [points at the beer] *fātḥa shahiyya* [awakens your appetite], and when you drink it you will have a night that you will never forget."

True to Ashraf's words, the group transitions from the wild beach scene to a cabaret. There they continue to drink beer and have a wild night watching the dancer Fardos (Nadia Lutfi). ʿAdil meets Fardos, who has taken a liking to him, and they eventually start drinking whiskey together. From here, the plot takes ʿAdil and Fardos, now lovers, to Beirut. ʿAdil's father, worried by his son's actions, travels to Lebanon, only to fall into the "libertine charms of Beirut." Eventually, son and father meet, come to their senses, and leave Beirut together. The movie ends with ʿAdil reuniting with Amal, who has abandoned her "old ways." The film ends with the two "running then embracing and kissing numerous times, silhouetted by the setting sun."[70]

This film, which was a "smash success," tells us a great deal about Stella beer's role after nationalization. In this film, beer still carried its association with youth, refreshment, beaches, and summer. It also had achieved an association with the medicinal properties that advertisers had been attributing to it. As Ashraf noted, it really "awakens your appetite." However, this phrase, like beer itself, had a double meaning. It was an appetite not only for food but for sex as well. In this movie, it was a straight line from ʿAdil tasting a beer on the beach to cavorting with a dancer in Beirut. Thus, postnationalization, beer regained its sense of danger. Yes, it could refresh, but it could also lead to intoxication and poor decision making. Still, it was only a "gateway" drink. When 'Adil really starts to veer off the righteous path, he eschews beer for hard liquor. This positioning of beer as a gateway drug for friends gathering on a public beach is a reflection of how deeply beer had penetrated Egyptian society, but it was also a sign that beer was developing a more ominous reputation and that attitudes toward it were shifting. After nearly eighty years in the country, beer was no longer a generic and unambiguously negative beverage grouped with all the other alcoholic drinks in the category of "alcohol." Nor was it the harmless and refreshing soft drink that advertisers tried to portray it as. By the end of the 1960s, there was a full enunciation of a cultural valuation that grappled with beer's complex reality. It was something that could refresh *and* intoxicate, something that could be fun *and* dangerous.

Through the nationalization of the Crown and Pyramid Breweries, a process that the business sector was powerless to stop, the Egyptian government achieved the indisputable "Egyptianization" of the country's beer industry. What this Egyptianization meant in practice was a company devoid of both "foreign" elements and rich indigenous Egyptians who had ties to the business order of the former regime and in which operations were ultimately controlled by a Nasser-led government.

    The nationalization of companies occurred not by means of police raids and arrests, but through polite letters and high-level negotiations. These outward expressions of decorum masked the forceful maneuverings of a government that was determined to wrest control over the economic system by pushing individuals like Kettner and Farghali Pasha out of the way. Yet Heineken, the multinational beer conglomerate, pushed back to the extent that it could, fighting into the 1970s for the value of its nationalized shares—a fact that suggests, again, how protracted nationalization was in practice. The beer industry that remained after that process found itself docile, beholden to Nasser's regime and its quest for a self-sufficient and self-assured Egypt. Nevertheless, the continuing high demand for Stella in Egypt testified to the cultural history of beer in Egypt, which had been shaped by the work of Dutchmen and their associates in Egypt.

# Opening Up Stella

*The Infitah and the Beer Business in Egypt, 1973–1985*

After giving up the job of prime minister, President Sadat is expected
to appoint a new cabinet any day now, with the economic expert Mr. ʿAbd
al-ʿAziz Hegazi as prime minister. Mr. Hegazi's confirmation in the job
would symbolize and accelerate Egypt's drive to dismantle President
Nasser's Arab socialism. He is no believer in total state control of banks,
basic industry and other large firms, nationalisation of most foreign
investment and economic links mainly with the Soviet block [*sic*].
Instead, he will be looking for Arab money and western know-how.
So far Arab money has been choked off by Egypt's perennial payments
weakness, and by memory of Nasser's nationalisations in which Arab
banks were nationalised along with the rest.
—"De-Nasserising," *Economist* (January 26, 1974)

I found the above quote not in the *Economist*'s archive of past issues but in
Heineken's records of its time in Egypt. It was sent by H. A. Meijer of Heineken to E. J. de Vries, who worked at Philips, the Dutch technology giant. Meijer sent the article to de Vries because it mentioned Philips, which he assumed would be of interest to de Vries, and to ask about the situation in
Egypt. Since Philips was still on the ground in Egypt, Heineken wanted
"some further information about the current developments in Egypt."[1] As I
have discussed in previous chapters, Heineken was interested because they
were looking for compensation for the nationalization of their shares in the
Crown and Pyramid Breweries.

One can read the paragraph as proof of the new era in Egypt under Anwar
Sadat (1970–1981). Coming off the claimed victory in the October War of
1973, which included reclaiming the Sinai, Anwar Sadat embarked on an ambitious economic "open-door policy" in Egypt called the Infitah (Opening
Up). In many ways, Anwar Sadat's Infitah fundamentally changed Egypt and
its economy. But was Sadat, as the *Economist* claimed and Heineken hoped,
"De-Nasserizing" Egypt? The answer to this question is more complex. An

analysis of the fortunes of al-Ahram Brewing Company in the period from 1973 to 1985 can help us answer this question. There was, no doubt, a significant change in the amount of foreign investment, imports, and money that entered the country under Sadat. However, the underlying structures, including a heavily bureaucratic public sector, would remain intact until Egypt embarked on a program of Economic Reform and Structural Adjustment (ERSAP) in the 1990s, nearly ten years into the reign of Hosni Mubarak (1981–2011). The economic fate of al-Ahram displays this reality. The period from 1973 to 1985 was one of profitable stability.

On the social level, the Infitah's impact was more transformational. Egypt's 1967 defeat in the Six-Day War struck a huge blow to the ideology of Nasserism and Pan-Arabism. As Nasserism faded, so did its greatest champions, the effendi middle class. Their cultural place was taken by two new groups: the nouveau riche (the *infitahi*), created by the money flowing into the country under Sadat, and the Islamists. Each offered their answers to Egypt's problems. The *infitahi* believed the consumption of foreign products and foreign knowledge would save Egypt. The Islamists viewed the return of Egypt to its Islamic roots as the solution to the structural problems. These two groups were not mutually exclusive, and in fact the connection could be quite strong, as many of these *infitahis* had made their money in the Gulf countries, which were strong supporters of Islamism. Most important for this study, neither of these groups championed Stella beer. For the *infitahi*, Stella beer was a decidedly common drink not fit for new lifestyles centered on Marlboro Reds, jeans, fancy watches, and expensive cars. As for the Islamists, Stella, like the rest of the alcohol in the country, was an example of Egypt's deviation from its proud Islamic roots. Although sales of Stella beer would reach their highest point in this era, the roots of a future downturn were taking hold.

## An Unwieldy Public Sector Company

The Infitah was meant as a tonic for an Egyptian economy that was suffering from the "gross inefficiencies of a public sector called upon to do too many things." It was tasked with selling products, absorbing excesses of the labor force, generating foreign exchange, and meeting local demand.[2] An overstressed public sector coupled with an overtaxed, outmoded, and underperforming agricultural sector produced an economic malaise, which, coupled with the failure in the 1967 war, augured the end of Nasserism. Despite its rhetoric, the Infitah was meant as a step toward a more mixed economy, not a wholesale economic restructuring. What this meant in practice was the unrestrained welcoming of foreign investment coupled with little attempt to curb the dominant public sector.

The government set the tenor for foreign investment with the 1971 issuance of Law 65. The law called for a "five-year corporate tax grace period, the establishment of free zones, and stated that joint ventures between foreign investors and public sector units would be considered autonomous." This was superseded by Law 43, which represented "a major easing of certain preexisting priorities," including making no sector off-limits for foreign investing and ending the public sector's control of banks.[3] The effects of these regulations were immediately apparent. Between 1973 and 1975, consumption grew from 63 percent of gross domestic product to 75 percent, and imports almost quadrupled, growing from 10 percent of GDP to 30 percent. This consumption-focused mind-set, bolstered by the oil boom and influx of remittances, meant that much of Egypt's foreign exchange earnings were going toward luxury imported goods rather than investment in the country and its industries.[4]

Private-sector growth did not mark the fall of the public sector. Rather, the influx of imported consumer goods and foreign investment was paired with the expansion of the already large public sector that Nasser's regime had built. By 1981 the public sector accounted for "40 percent of total employment, 54 percent of value-added, over 60 percent of total expenditure, and 70 percent of total investment." The growth was not of a healthy variety, as these public institutions were structured as untouchable monopolies, free to ignore market forces and their debts to the government or banks. There was simply no incentive to increase efficiency, which led to a very low ratio of productivity to capital used.[5] In addition, private companies were more likely to be coconspirators, looking for the easy money of monopolistic public institutions, than competitors.[6]

It was not as if those in charge, Sadat and his economic ministers, did not recognize the problems that these developments would cause. There were discussions within the government to institute restrictions to make the increase in consumption more gradual and to strike at the ever-expanding private sector. However, neither party was interested in the sacrifice necessary to pursue unpopular economic policy. On Sadat's part, he did not have the political capital to weather threats to extremely popular policies like guaranteed government employment for college graduates and subsidies on daily staples. For the ministers, they had no interest in attaching their names to austerity measures with long-term payoffs, as they had a rather short shelf life.[7] These were not idle concerns but rather legitimate worries when considered in the context of the 1977 bread riots.

The riots started January 17 when 'Abd al-Muni'm al-Qaysuni, the deputy prime minister for financial and economic affairs, "presented a budget that entailed cutting subsidies on sugar, tea, flour, rice, and cooking oil, thus increasing their price by 25–50 percent." The evening of the announcement, workers' protests broke out in Helwan and Alexandria. They continued the next morning, expanding to urban centers and growing to include students, Islamists, and the general population. The Islamists led attacks on the nightclubs and casinos of Pyramids Road in Cairo, places noted for their gambling, prostitution, and alcohol consumption. Clashes between government security forces and protesters killed seventy-three, injured eight hundred, and led to 1,270 arrests.[8] The violent riots led to a rollback of the proposed changes and ingrained an attitude of "once bitten, twice shy" among the government vis-à-vis austerity measures.

The almost schizophrenic policies of the Infitah had a deleterious effect on many monopolistic public firms in Egypt. Without the existential threat of market-led annihilation, these firms grew bloated with unneeded workers, outdated technology, and poor management.[9] Al-Ahram suffered from some of these maladies, especially employee bloat. Nasser's 1961 and 1962 socialist decrees as well as Sadat's modification of them in 1971 and 1972 empowered the Egyptian workforce. The decrees limited working hours to seven hours per day and eliminated overtime. Likewise, companies could not use any seasonal workers; anyone who worked for the company had to be a full-time employee. These regulations plus the ruling that a person could hold only one job at a time aimed at not only lessening the burden of workers, but also opening up more jobs. In addition to regulations on who could work for a company and for how long, the decrees also sought to close the wage gap. They eliminated all dividends and required each company to use 25 percent of its profit for its workers, in the form of wage increases and increased social service.[10]

This legislation had a serious effect on al-Ahram, undercutting many of the policies Heineken had put in place to create a modern, total-control brewery. These new laws eliminated their shift system and the ability to keep the brewery open continuously with three teams of workers. The company also lost the ability to take advantage of temporary workers, who used to fill in when needed with minimal commitment.[11] Besides increasing the operating costs of the company, this legislation also limited al-Ahram's ability to shape its work staff. All hiring and firing, even for the lowest-paid worker, had to be approved by the government. This made it extremely difficult for managers to make changes.[12] The government also forced al-Ahram, and other public companies, to accept the college graduates they guaranteed employment.[13]

Even al-Ahram's ability to evaluate their employees was limited by the government. The evaluation of employees, which had to be reviewed by the government, was based upon a rigid grading system. There were three general classes, ḍaʿīf (weak), kafʾ (adequate), and mumtāz (excellent). Workers were evaluated yearly and could move up and down in rank. In the case of al-Ahram's Alexandria factory in 1979, there were 27 workers who achieved excellence, 168 who achieved adequacy, and only 1 that was weak. Those who achieved a higher rank were given a bonus and a letter thanking them for their hard work. Those who received the rank of weak were given a note on their status, explaining the danger of having a weak status.[14] The "danger" was not real, as it was only the government who could act on the evaluations. The result of all this legislation was ever-expanding employment rolls. By the 1990s, it was estimated that out of the 3,200 working at the company, only 10 percent were really needed.[15]

Given these system inefficiencies, the most astounding thing is that the period of the Infitah (1973–1987) was one of tremendous growth for al-Ahram. Between the years of 1963 and 1987, beer production nearly tripled. It grew from 190,000 hectoliters in 1962–1963 to 510,000 hectoliters in 1987–1988.[16] This was, without a doubt, al-Ahram's most successful period. By 1974 an estimated five million of the thirty-five million Muslims in Egypt consumed beer, most of which was sold by the al-Ahram.[17] While we cannot be sure of the veracity of these numbers, it surely gives a sense of how significant beer's presence was in Egypt, a presence built on a local market monopoly and continued protection from the government through high tariffs on imported foreign brands.[18]

Stella comprised the great majority of al-Ahram's sales. Sold either in large (660 ml) or small bottles (330 ml), it would make up, at least in Alexandria and the rest of Lower Egypt, roughly 90 percent of sales.[19] The remaining 10 percent was made up of two alternate brands: al-Ahram's German-style *märzen* beer, simply called Märzen, and their dark-beer offering, called Aswan.

There was a third beer in al-Ahram's portfolio, but it was not technically on the Egyptian market. Stella Export was a premium brand directed at the export market. It was sold only outside of the country or in duty-free shops and could be bought using only foreign currency. Although it carried a premium label, its recipe was not significantly different from the Stella that al-Ahram was presenting to the home market.[20]

## A Successful Formula

What can explain this tremendous success despite forces pushing al-Ahram to settle into a period of profitable stagnation? The first explanation is the residual effect of Heineken control. As I have shown, Heineken worked its hardest to make Stella a world-class beer. Although the Dutch staff, investors, and advisers were unceremoniously removed, their work both structurally and intellectually did not disappear.

One of the beer giant's last major initiatives was work on a multiyear plant-expansion plan for Pyramid Brewery.[21] Heineken saw the record sales of Pyramid in 1960 and resolved to expand Pyramid factory production. Heineken created a five-year plan that added even more construction to an already planned expansion. In this modern setup, there were six areas where machinery was updated or replaced: the malting system, cooling system, brew house, filtering system, bottling system, and lager cellar. With each of these changes in place, the maximum monthly capacity of the brewery was raised from around seventeen thousand hectoliters to sixty-two thousand hectoliters.[22]

For all the machines built in Egypt, Heineken provided detailed diagrams to ensure their proper construction and installation. For the machinery that needed to be brought from abroad, they provided the pro forma invoices to aid the purchase and transport and did their best to examine the machinery before it arrived in Cairo.[23] They even sent engineers to Egypt to ensure the work was progressing according to plan. Finally, Heineken offered fully subsidized internships in Holland for engineers and managers from Pyramid who wanted to learn Heineken's best practices. For example, in 1961 Heineken hosted two agricultural and beer technicians, Muhammad Ramses ʿAwad and Ihab al-Shammaʿ; the chief accountant, Munir Tadrus; and Pyramid's commercial director, Alber Farag.[24] When Heineken left, they left behind a world-class facility.

These technical advantages would not have had the same impact if not for the fact that the man who took control of al-Ahram was the ideal candidate for the job. With a PhD in microbiology from the University of California–Berkeley, Dr. Omar Foda certainly claimed educational credentials and a degree of technical expertise that was unmatched among Egyptians. His doctoral work at Berkeley focused on the nutrition and metabolism of a strain of bacteria, *Acetobacter melanogenum*.[25] Specifically, he had examined *Acetobacter*'s use of maltose as a nutrient, a process that would result in the production of "gluconic and 5-ketogluconic acids."[26] This research expertise proved relevant to his work for al-Ahram because many *Acetobacters* can convert ethanol, the alcohol in beer and wine, into acetic acid. Likewise, because *Acetobacters* "are acid- and ethanol-tolerant and not inhibited by hop compounds, they grow rapidly in beer, producing acid off-flavors and turbidity." This process had a negative impact on the flavor of beer; however, if brewers properly stored the beer and kept its exposure to oxygen low, they could avoid the problem of *Acetobacter* altogether.[27] Put quite simply, he had the academic grounding to become exactly what al-Ahram needed as its head, a beer scientist.

Besides his academic interest in beer, Foda was also a lover of beer. During his winters in Cairo (he and his family would relocate to Alexandria in the summer), beer was an axis around which his life spun. He and his brother, Daoud, spent every Friday afternoon in the garden of the Hilton Hotel drinking Stella and discussing business and life. The rest of the family—their wives, their children, and their five sisters—knew the Foda brothers would be there and stopped in throughout the day to catch up, give greetings, or just enjoy the weather.[28] The combination of personal belief in his product and academic interest made Foda a constant striver for the best beer possible.

As part of this commitment, he worked hard to maintain the intellectual investment Heineken had made in the company. He relied heavily on Egyptian managers and workers, who had trained and worked under the watch of Dutch managers. His director of factories, Hasan Tawfiq, served as the head of garages under Heineken. His business director, Alber Farag, previously headed Pyramid's communications department. Foda also elevated the assistant brewmaster, Fathi al-Malt, to the new directorship of malt making and made Muhammad Ramses 'Awad, who had overseen the brewery's cellars, the director of beer making.[29] With these appointments, Foda elevated the Egyptians who had served as the heads of old departments under the Dutch to new directorships in the nationalized al-Ahram. These directorships also had a seat on the executive board.

Having experienced people on the board was a counterbalance against the other four members on the board, who, according to Nasser-era regulations, sat in positions elected by the members of the company union. This action was necessary, as only one of the four elected board members, Ihab al-Shamma', had served in any leadership position previously. Prior to being elected as the assistant director of beer making, he had served as the head of fermentation under Ulenberg. As for the other three, Ghattas Hanna Ghattas was elected to the board as the head of the warehouses, Husayn Ahmad

Muhammad Mani was elected as the head of the car workshop in Giza, and Jalal Ahmad Rutan was elected as the head machinist at the factory in Alexandria.[30]

But Nasser-era policies also granted Foda stability not seen by any other head in the history of the company; he sat in his position from 1961 to 1985. His more than twenty-year period of leadership would make him the second-longest-tenured executive in the company's history after Farghali Pasha. In comparison to the frequent reorganization prior to the arrival of Heineken and the turbulent times under Nasser, al-Ahram under Foda settled into a stable reality where his position was not questioned and his desired company structure was not radically altered.

Emblematic of the positive effects of this continuity is the career of Muhammad Ramses 'Awad. He started working with the company in 1945. He worked under both Wittert van Hoogland and Kettner and made trips to Amsterdam to learn about the beer trade from the source. Prior to nationalization, he worked his way up to the head of cellars. With the Dutch exit, he became the head of beer making and achieved a place on the al-Ahram board. He would serve in that position until his retirement on November 23, 1979. In 'Awad's thirty-four years at the company, as Foda said, he had "participated more than once in the advancement of beer making in developing countries."[31]

Nevertheless, the barriers to worker movement could be a double-edged sword. Every significant personnel change had to be approved by the government. For example, to give a raise to an employee or to change positions, the company had to put those decisions through the governmental approval process. This process involved sending letters to the appropriate government department explaining why a certain decision needed to be made.[32] It was then in the government's hands to decide how a company could proceed.

The heavily bureaucratized employment system proved to be a problem during Muhammad Ramses 'Awad's retirement. As he had been such a useful employee to the company, his retirement was a major loss; filling his position required two people. On the administrative side, it was Antoine 'Abd al-Karim 'Awad, his brother, that would fill his spot on the board. This 'Awad had also worked for the company for more than thirty years. He started in 1950 after graduating from the University of Cairo with a degree in mechanical engineering.[33] On his elevation to the board, he served as the head of engineering for the company. As for Ramses 'Awad's replacement as head of beer making, it was 'Abd al-Rahman 'Abd al-Mun'im Salama, a chemist who had been with the company since 1958. After joining from Eastman Kodak, he had worked his way up first to head of the workshops and then to director of malt making.[34]

However, Foda and al-Ahram were keen on an extension of their relationship with 'Awad after he reached the mandatory retirement age of sixty.[35] They hoped to appoint him technical adviser for a period of six months and provide him with a monthly stipend of 150 Egyptian pounds. Although the requirement for retirement at age sixty was relatively ironclad, the government would make exceptions in the extreme case where the employee had incredible rare and valuable experience or knowledge that no other employee could replicate. Foda and al-Ahram believed that 'Awad had that and pushed hard to keep him. The government, specifically the Ministry of Industry, Petrol, and Mining, however, did not see the need to extend his employment and did not grant the request.[36] Foda wrote back to the ministry, noting the extraordinary nature of 'Awad's work and the necessity of his advice, but to no avail.[37]

Al-Ahram and Foda were so keen on extending 'Awad's contract because they, with the support of the government, were pursuing an expansion of al-Ahram's facilities at roughly the same time. They aimed to build two new factories, one in the village Kafr El-Azazy in Sharqiyya Province and one in Dishna in Qena Province. These two new factories were meant not only to address the growing demand for beer, but also to produce carbonated beverages. They were to be financed by four parties. Al-Ahram would provide 4 million Egyptian pounds of equity for each brewery issued "against their expenses for the project and the balance to be offered to investors against cash."[38] Another 6 million would come from the Bank of Alexandria, the Egyptian American bank, and a foreign brewer picked by al-Ahram and the government.[39] These factory ventures were also meant to build relations with foreign beverage makers, an example of the symbiosis between the public sector and the foreign investment newly allowed in the country.

Unsurprisingly, this process was also slave to government bureaucracy. In this instance, it was the interactions with the potential foreign investors that were of most interest to the government. Foda met with representatives of Stella Artois, Carlsberg/Turborg, Allied Brewers of the United Kingdom (whose dominant brand was Skol), and Heineken, and each offered a prospectus, which was then relayed to the Egyptian government. The government eventually went forward with only one location, in Sharqiyya Province, and went with their old friend Heineken.[40]

The Sharqiyya brewery was a step into al-Ahram's nonalcoholic future. Besides beer, Sharqiyya was equipped to manufacture nonalcoholic beer and soft drinks. Producing soft drinks—made of sugar, carbonated water, and flavorings—did not require a great deal of new machinery. Nonalcoholic beer, however, required the installation of an evaporator for removing alcohol from beer before it was bottled.[41] Besides outfitting a new facility to make these nonalcoholic beverages, al-Ahram also started to work with the nationalized Coca-Cola and Pepsi ventures. Having seen the strong work Foda did with al-Ahram, the government tasked him with turning around the two nationalized beverage makers, who were suffering during the Infitah. From the 1970s onward, he would successfully help El Nasr Bottling Company (previously owned by Coca-Cola) and the Egyptian Bottling Company (previously owned by Pepsi) become profitable companies.[42]

### Infitahis

The growing production of Stella beer was not solely due to internal factors. There were concomitant social changes occurring in Egypt that also led to the growth. Sadat's pursuit of an unrestrained opening of Egypt did not fix Egypt's underlying economic problems. Nor did it eliminate many of the import substitution tenets that sat at the base of the economy. Sadat's Infitah did, however, mark a "fortuitous inflow of resources" into the economy. The three main sources of this inflow were an increase in price and the volume of Egypt's oil export from the reclaimed Suez, a growth in remittances from Egyptians working abroad in the oil-enriched Gulf countries, and a significant increase in foreign aid from Gulf countries, Japan, and Western countries, especially the United States. On a country-wide scale, Egypt did well. Between 1975 and 1986, Egypt had an average GDP of more than 9 percent. Real per capita income levels also increased an average of 6 percent over the same period.[43]

Egypt was thus a richer country under Sadat and the early years of Mubarak than under Nasser. It was also a country where consumption was taking on an even more prominent role. The most significant signal of this new social reality was cultural commentators' fear of a new specter, the *infitahi*. This imagined nouveau riche group, in opposition to the effendi, made their money from either working abroad in one of the newly rich Gulf countries or in burgeoning consumer goods markets. Like the effendi, consumption was a key identifier of the *infitahi*. In fact, cultural commentators deemed their consumption diametrically opposed to that of the *effendiyya*. Whereas the effendis' consumption was tied heavily to national products that signaled their Egyptianness and framed by the deprivation of the import substitution of the Nasser economy, *infitahi* consumption was inextricably tied to the mass consumption of imported goods. It was, for these commentators, a battle between those defined by what they produced and those defined by what they consumed.[44]

Cultural commentators and creators, often self-proclaimed effendis, depicted a coherent group of consumer goods synonymous with this new *infitahi* lifestyle. Foreign cars, suits, fancy watches, and imported cigarettes were the stereotyped outfit of the *infitahi*.[45] The drink of choice for these *infitahi*? Imported liquors that carried the image of refinement, such as Johnnie Walker and other scotches, champagnes, and other luxe drinks. It was decidedly not Stella beer.

But was this group really a new cultural force? And for the purposes of this book, did it affect Stella consumption? On the first account, we do not have proper ethnographic data to answer this complex question. We can, however, at least glean the cultural association between the *infitahi* and Stella from media at the time. Movies, as opposed to television where depictions of alcohol were banned, provide the best view.

To get a grasp on the imagined social place of beer, it is useful to turn to the works of Husayn Kamal (1934–2003). Focusing on one director allows us a laser focus on the artistic uses of a substance across time. Kamal is useful because he frequently used beer as a prop and provided the most accurate depiction of its use in his films. As discussed in the previous chapter, his film *Abi Fawq al-Shajara* provided an excellent snapshot of the beer drinker in the 1960s. If we look at five movies of Kamal taken from the period 1972–1992 — *Anf wa Thalath ʿUyun* (A nose and three eyes [1972]), *Imbaraturiyyat Mim* (Empire of M [1972]), *Ehna bitu al autobis* (We are the bus people [1979]), *Arjuka Iʿtini Hadha al-Dawa* (Please give me this medicine [1984]), and *Al-Masatil* (The stoners [1992]) — we can craft an image of the beer drinker in the post-Infitah Egypt.

When the depiction of beer in these movies is viewed holistically, the best way to describe it is the alcoholic beverage of leisure for urbanized Egyptians. It was not the beverage of choice when you wanted to impress a date or guests, show your wealth, or get intoxicated. In these cases, it would be a liquor, primarily scotch whiskey or brandy.[46] Stella was absent from nightclub scenes and rarely seen as a way to entertain guests. Stella appeared during lunch on a Nile boat, a house party, a beach party, or playing cards. It was also not the intoxicant of choice for the rural populations. When the fellahin were depicted consuming something besides tea, it was hashish. It was smoked in the traditional *gūza* (Egyptian Arabic: "waterpipe") and its consumption came during a *jalsa* (Arabic: "a sitting") as men passed around the pipe and the news, gossip, or idle talk of the day.

These appearances can be attributed to two points of differentiation between Stella and other substances: its price and its availability. It was a comparatively cheap alcoholic beverage. Significantly cheaper than liquors and wines, it was an excellent choice of beverage for those who needed alcohol at an affordable price. With Stella, young people and urban subalterns, groups with limited means, could still ply their parties with alcohol. Its price, however, made it a less than ideal choice of beverage for the *infitahi*. As it was affordable enough to be accessed by most social groups, it simply did not carry the social power of the more expensive and more exclusive foreign liquors. Nevertheless, the *infitahi* still drank Stella. They merely did so in more informal settings. For example, in the movie *Arjuka I'tini Hadha al-Dawa*, Refaat (Mahmud 'Abd al-'Aziz) drinks Stella as he sits for lunch with his paramour, Mervet (Sahar Hamdi), discussing how they will continue their infidelities after her husband has returned early from his business trip.

Although it was relatively cheap, Stella beer was still not more affordable than hashish and the *gūza*, which could be easily grown and made in the countryside. It was easy to place a hashish plant between a tall growing crop in the field, and the *gūza* could be made from spare parts found around a farm. It was not only Stella's price that was a deterrent for the rural consumer but also its availability. Stella was primarily an urban and semi-urban product distributed through shops and bars, which were less plentiful in rural locales. The one time we see the fellahin consume beer in Kamal's movies is at a party hosted by a college-age student, Mustafa (Sayf abu al-Naja), in the movie *Imbaraturiyyat Mim*. The party is meant to be a celebration of the equality between the rural fellahin and the urban youth, a signal to Mustafa's political leanings. The fellahin are invited, offered beer, and encouraged to dance to show how Mustafa hopes to smash the boundary between urban and rural Egyptians.[47]

Moreover, the consumption of Stella beer was gendered. Those depicted consuming Stella are overwhelmingly male. Women are depicted in scenes of beer consumption—for example, in *Anf wa Thalath 'Uyun, Imbaraturiyyat Mim, Arjuka I'tini Hadha al-Dawa*, and *Ehna bitu al autobis*—but are typically beer adjacent; they are there, but rarely caught on film drinking. The one significant exception is the character of Zuzu (Magda al-Khatib) in *Arjuka I'tini Hadha al-Dawa*.

Beer plays an important role in Zuzu's lifestyle, which for Egypt at the time could be called nontraditional. Zuzu's love life is composed of relationships of varying length with younger men. She provides them money, food, and clothes in exchange for them fulfilling her needs. When she is done with her "boy toys," she throws them away "like a pack of cigarettes."[48] We first see the synergy of this lifestyle and beer when Zuzu spots a new target in a bar. She raises her glass to him across the room, a signal by the director of a new relationship. Later in Zuzu's apartment, as we witness her dumping one paramour for his replacement, a beer sits half poured on the bedside table. It, like many other beers, the audience can assume, is witness to Zuzu's illicit relationship. In this instance, it also serves as Zuzu's tonic. She drinks heavily from the glass after she ends the relationship with her lover and pays him for his services. The depiction of beer is not a normative one. Zuzu's lifestyle is framed as an amoral oddity practiced by a Western-leaning woman. Her beer drinking is fully part of that.

The negative association of women with beer is not limited only to this Kamal film. Even in the films where women are merely beer adjacent, they carry a negative image. Women spotted in scenes with beer, even though they are not drinking, are depicted as licentious, foreign, low-class, or boundary transgressors. The message is clear from Husayn Kamal's films: beer drinking is for men and for nontraditional women. The idealized woman of Egyptian society can drink alcohol, but only champagne or other "high-class" alcohols and always in moderation.

Husayn Kamal's depiction of the Stella drinker is consistent with the cultural image present in Egypt since the 1960s. It was the alcohol beverage of choice for those urban classes of limited means, the youth, and the poor. For those urbanites who sat above them, the effendi and *infitahi*, it was one in their arsenal of alcohol beverages. It was not appropriate for "classier" situations—e.g., the nightclub, the evening soiree—but Stella had its place in casual and relaxed settings. It was also primarily a male drink. It held such gender associations because it held ambiguous value. It was something that could refresh *and* intoxicate, something that could be fun *and* dangerous.

This cultural consistency can, in part, explain the persistent growth in sales. With an established place in Egyptian culture, sales would naturally grow with the growing wealth and population of the country. The Infitah brought cultural change, but it did not mean the sidelining of Stella. In fact, a consumer product like Stella, which had a monopoly over the market, years of building brand loyalty with customers, and the full support of the government, was in a prime position to succeed. There were simply more people who could afford and wanted to drink Stella in the 1970s and 1980s than in the 1950s.

## Islamic Revival

It was not all good news for Stella. The changes that the Infitah brought also helped bolster a movement that was completely inimical to the consumption of beer, Egypt's Islamic Revival. The constituent parts of what could be called the Islamic Revival can trace their origins to the Islamic modernist movement.

In using the term *Islamic modernists*, I am referring to those Egyptians who believed that Islam was an inseparable part of Egyptian modernity. As I have discussed previously, modernity was a performative act that involved the use of new media, new social spaces, and new consumer goods to make "being modern observable and reproducible."[49] Modernity was performed through the consumption of new materials and through the absorption and appropriation of Western technoscientific ideas and concepts, which reshaped the temporal frame of the country.[50] Internalizing this new time frame, Egyptian thinkers of this period came to view their country as "delayed" in the linear and inexorable progress of civilizations toward modernity.

Modernity in Egypt was particularly important to the *effendiyya*. As we have seen, alcohol played a role in the performance of modernity, but the *effendiyya* were not monolithic. For some, modernity was found at the bottom of a bottle of beer as they chatted with their friends and colleagues at the bar or brasserie.[51] For others, modernity had a more Islamic bent. The main progenitors of this Islamic modernity were two of the Middle East's most influential thinkers, Jamal al-Din al-Afghani (1838–1897) and Muhammad 'Abduh (1849–1905). Both men were deeply concerned with the Islamic world's response to the ever-expanding colonial enterprise. Al-Afghani believed that Muslims' response to colonialism should be primarily political, with an Islamic revival serving as a main force to repel the colonial interlopers. 'Abduh, one of al-Afghani's students, took a longer view, believing that the reformation of the Islamic populace through education and legal renewal was the path forward for the Islamic world.[52] 'Abduh's greatest legacy was to inspire a generation of scholars, including Muhammad Rashid Rida and Mustafa 'Abd al-Raziq, who took up his Islamic modernism while nevertheless interpreting it in very different ways. Rida is particularly important; as we saw in chapter 2, he made common cause with Ahmad Ghalwash and the Egyptian Temperance Association, who were likewise inspired by 'Abduh. He was also a spiritual adviser to Hasan al-Banna, who founded the Muslim Brotherhood in 1928.

However, this strain of thought took a backseat when Egypt entered the

Nasser era, as its greatest proponents, the leadership of the Muslim Brother-hood, were executed or jailed. The relationship between the Revolutionary Command Council and the Muslim Brotherhood was a multifaceted one. It included common causes (the fight against foreign power in Egypt, political corruption, and Palestine), conflicting personalities, and struggles over who controlled the country. Interactions were generally tense, but they reached a breaking point when a member of the Muslim Brotherhood attempted to as-sassinate Nasser in 1954. The president arrested and executed the perpetra-tors, outlawed the organization, and arrested much of its leadership. From that point until at least 1967, the Egyptian state apparatus did everything in its power to prevent the Muslim Brotherhood from providing any challenge, armed or ideological, to the regime. The clearest example of this determi-nation was the execution of the movement's main ideologue in this period, Sayyid Qutb, for his intellectual support of a supposed coup.[53]

This would have been the death knell for the Muslim Brotherhood, and may have marked the Egyptian state's assumption as the main arbiter of Islam in the country, were it not for the events of the 1967 (Six-Day) War, or as it is known in the Arab world, the *Naksa*, the Setback. As once scholar put it, "There are few events in contemporary Middle East history that can be said to have single-handedly transformed the course of the region's future as did the Six Day War of June 1967."[54] One of its biggest effects is that the mili-tary defeat deflated the persuasive message of Nasserism that had captivated the region. In Egypt it robbed the ruling regime, first under Nasser and then Sadat after 1970, of its ideological underpinning. It left the government as a movement without a message. From that point forward, the Egyptian gov-ernment was in a struggle with movements across the political spectrum to claim the ideological upper hand.

Having a strong message was particularly important, as the reforms of the Nasser era had created a volatile legacy. Nasser's promise of free college education and guaranteed employment in the government after graduation made the state the primary guarantor of a middle-class lifestyle for lower-class Egyptians. This role became a heavy burden under Sadat and led to "over-expansion and dilution that diminished the system's incorporating power." The quality of the education degraded, the wages for civil service declined, and the time between graduation and employment dragged on longer and longer.[55] Sadat was faced with a population that was more highly educated and had greater demands of the state, but was not armed with the powerful messages, tools, or charisma that Nasser had.

The first response to the regime's ideological emptiness was the student movement of the late 1960s. This movement was an ideologically unified front of students dissatisfied with the general university atmosphere, future job prospects, and general political repression. From this student movement would grow the three major ideological trends of Sadat's Egypt: secular liberal, radical socialist, and Islamist.[56] It was the first two groups who would initially be the strongest opposition to Sadat. Thus, Sadat found it prudent to style himself as "the believer president," imbuing his words, actions, and policy with Islam. This move was not necessarily an innovation in the office of the president. Despite Nasser's calls for secularism, he worked hard to make the government the legitimate arbiter of religion in Egypt. As it relates to beer, the Nasser-led government, in a bid to gain greater revenue from Crown and Pyramid, and perhaps also to atone for the government's ownership of the beer companies, raised the excise tax on beer to six Egyptian pounds per hectoliter in 1962.[57]

On Sadat's part, his state speeches contained Quranic verses, his acts of piety (e.g., listening to sermons) were broadcast across state television, and he helped pass a new constitution that placed the sharia as a source of legislation.[58] He believed that his state should be built upon the idea of "Science and Faith" (al-'Ilm wa-l-'Imān) and that the two could work symphonically to produce a better Egypt.[59] As part of this push, he reopened space in Egyptian society for Islamist organizations, especially the Muslim Brotherhood. He released many of its members from prison and tried to welcome former Muslim Brotherhood members who had taken up residence in the Gulf back to Egypt.[60] As it relates to beer, his regime passed Law 63, in 1976, which stated, "It is prohibited to offer or consume spirits or alcohol in public places or shops excluded from this provision: (A) hotels and tourist facilities specified in accordance with the provisions of Law 1/1973 . . . and (B) clubs characterised by tourism as determined by a decision of the Minister of Tourism in accordance with Law 77/1975."[61]

Although it is impossible to know the sincerity of Sadat's Islamic turn, the political expediency of these moves was obvious. This turn helped weaken leftist political power by offering another pole unto which power could coalesce. In addition, this Islamic turn helped Sadat push Egypt away from the leftist policies of Nasserism, which favored the Soviets, toward the West and their liberal economic policies. Another strike in the column of viewing Sadat's Islamization as political maneuvering is his courting of the Muslim Brotherhood affiliates in the Gulf countries. This action accomplished three goals. One, it warmed relations with a group that had given a great deal of money to Egypt. Two, it served as a bridge to stronger relations between

Egypt and the newly rich Gulf countries. Finally, it placed these actors, who sat on the periphery of the Muslim Brotherhood, as a counterweight to the Muslim Brothers he was releasing from prison, who were generally the ideological heavyweights of the movement.[62]

The processes that Sadat started accelerated under the Infitah. The rapid opening of the country to foreign goods, services, and money made the market an undeniably more attractive option than state employment. Nevertheless, access to these markets required marketable skills or social connections that most of these college-educated graduates did not have.[63] They were left with either their poor-paying government job or the possibility of taking a better-paying job below their education level.

The sum result of Sadat's actions was that Egypt was primed for the resurgence of the Muslim Brotherhood and other Islamic movements. There thus arose a battle between the regime and these movements for legitimate claim to Islam.[64] This was a battle that was hard fought through the 1970s and one that Sadat lost; an adherent of one of the Islamist groups that grew under his government's watch assassinated him. From that point forward, the country experienced an Islamic revival. This revival is best described as follows:

> "Islamic Revival" is a term that refers not only to the activities of state-oriented political groups but more broadly to a religious ethos or sensibility that has developed within contemporary Muslim societies. This sensibility has a palpable public presence in Egypt, manifest in the vast proliferation of neighborhood mosques and other institutions of Islamic learning and social welfare, in a dramatic increase in attendance at mosques by both women and men, and in marked displays of religious sociability. Examples of the latter include the adoption of the veil (hijab), a brisk consumption and production of religious media and literature, and a growing circle of intellectuals who write and comment upon contemporary affairs in the popular press from a self-described Islamic point of view.[65]

The Islamization of the sociocultural landscape of Egyptian society was built upon the concept of *da'wa*. *Da'wa* was an Islamic precept that required "all adult members of the Islamic community to urge fellow Muslims to greater piety, and to teach one another correct Islamic conduct."[66] An obvious target for this *da'wa*, as seen in the actions of the Bread Riots of 1977, was the licentious habits of Egyptians that included gambling, prostitution, and alcohol consumption. To understand the centrality of temperance to *da'wa* in this period, one need only to look at the words of the grand imam of al-Azhar,

Egypt's leading religious university, 'Abd al-Halim Mahmud (1910–1978). He believed it was ridiculous that Egypt still produced beer for morally corrupt tourists.[67]

The rhetoric surrounding Anwar Sadat's Infitah promised a new era for Egypt. The opening of Egypt up to the world economy was meant to shake Egypt out of the post-1967 doldrums. It offered a new direction that would bring new investment, new goods, and new hope to the country. When viewed through this very wide lens, it did those things. Nevertheless, it did not fundamentally alter the realities of the country. This is best seen in Stella beer and the company that sold it. The period from 1973 to 1985 was a massively successful one, as sales grew to unprecedented levels. More people were drinking Stella than ever before. But that success should not be attributed primarily to the change the Infitah brought but rather credited to the stasis of the company and the product in this period. In this era, the company witnessed one of its most stable periods, with an unchanged leadership and workforce. This permanence was a boon to the company, as its director, Omar Foda, had the desire and technical capability to produce a good-quality beer for Egyptians. Stella as a brand was also quite stable in this period, maintaining its cultural position in Egypt.

While stability was a distinguishing feature of Stella and the company that sold it, the Infitah and the Sadat presidency did augur a change that would ultimately undercut them both. As Stella was reaching great heights, Egypt was undergoing an Islamic revival. Due to a mix of government support, growing cultural contact with conservative Gulf regimes, and the power of the message of political Islam, more middle-class Egyptians came to believe that Islam was the essential feature of Egyptian identity. This change was matched with growing public religiosity, which made Stella's presence in Egyptian culture uncomfortable. The true results of this change would not be seen in the company's bottom line until the end of the 1980s, a time when they were particularly vulnerable, having lost their leader Omar Foda. How Stella and al-Ahram survived this new challenge is the story of the next chapter.

# An American Pharaoh and the Egyptian Star
*Stella, 1985–2003*

This is a highly profitable company. But the amount of waste and
the amount of corruption is beyond my wildest imagination.
—Ahmed Zayat, quoted in Mark Huband, "Waste and Corruption
  'Beyond Imagination,'" *Financial Times*, May 13, 1997

The above words from the American Egyptian entrepreneur Ahmed Zayat
(a.k.a. Ahmed El-Zayyat) to the *Financial Times* encapsulate the reality of al-
Ahram after the end of the tenure of Omar Foda in 1985 and before privatization in 1997. It was still a profitable company, but its underlying realities were
troubling. Its payroll was bloated, its machinery was out of date, and it was
losing money as Stella went straight from the factory to the black market.
But it was not only internal issues that were threatening the company. The
Egyptian economy was suffering after the collapse of the oil boom and from
its own structural weaknesses. Poor management and technical deficiencies
had severely hurt the beer's reputation in the market. Finally, Egypt's public
society was undergoing a strong Islamization, which made the position of an
alcoholic beverage company tenuous.

Al-Ahram's savior would come in the form of a multinational investment
group, the Luxor Group. With the aid of a desperate government and the
dynamism of its mysterious leader, Ahmed Zayat, Luxor was able to pursue the hard steps needed to turn around the company. Despite Luxor's use
of the rhetoric of neoliberalism, which deemed the history of the company
superfluous and in some ways damaging, much of this turnaround can be
attributed to a return to the realities of the company during its most successful periods. Zayat helped to turn the company from a distressed asset to
one that Heineken would pay millions for. The change was not without its
victims, though; the company's institutional memory and its once flagship
brand, Stella, were pushed aside to ensure brighter days for al-Ahram.

## Issues, Internal and External

The year 1987 was a banner time for beer production in Egypt. That year al-Ahram produced 510,000 hectoliters of beer, a number the company has yet to reach again in the thirty years since. The fact that 1987 was the apotheosis rather than the beginning of a new era for al-Ahram and Stella comes down to three factors: a lack of leadership, a general financial downturn, and the Islamization of Egyptian public culture. Only two years prior they had lost their CEO, Omar Foda, to mandatory retirement. As a state-run company, the impact of one man was outsize. Without strong leadership, there was no force preventing the company from falling into complacency and desuetude, and that is exactly what happened.

The sources we have for the internal workings of the company are limited, and, since they are primarily from the Luxor Group, which had a vested interest in emphasizing their triumph, they may purposely play up the negatives. Nevertheless, they can provide some sense of the poor shape the company was in. Al-Ahram after 1985 was a poorly run company. Its management was bloated. It had twenty-seven sector heads and seventy-two general managers. Likewise, it had an overstaffed and inefficient sales force. There were markets in the Delta, Alexandria, and Upper Egypt that were not being properly served.[1] One investor, who was part of Luxor Group, which would take the company over from the government in the 1990s, estimated that out of the thirty-two hundred working at the company, only 10 percent were really needed.[2] Despite the overemployment, the company had no real marketing department. The lack makes some sense considering the monopoly the company had, but it was still a rather jarring absence for a consumer-product seller.[3] This type of bloat was endemic to the entire Egyptian public sector at the time, as it was forced to incorporate all the college-educated Egyptians guaranteed government employment after graduation.

The surplus of useless workers opened the company up to another stark reality of business in post-Nasser Egypt: corruption. For many, the goal was not doing a good job but personal enrichment, achieved by skimming profits or selling products on the black market. Many of the worst offenders were concentrated in a group of managers the Luxor Group called the Golden Island (*Jazirat al-Dahab*). As their name indicated, they viewed the company as their golden goose.[4] Local bureaucrats and police were in on it, too, preventing the sale and distribution of the beer if they did not receive payment.[5] As Ahmed Zayat, the man who would head Luxor Group, stated: "A case of Stella beer is E£54, but it doesn't leave our warehouse until E£60 has been paid. The kick-backs are high. The money that is being paid for each case is shared almost from the top to the bottom of the company."[6]

Beyond the bloat and corruption, the technical side of the equation had degraded without strong leadership. The three beer plants—in Cairo, Alexandria, and Sharqiyya—were all in bad shape, having been allowed to become completely run-down. The breweries were still using open fermentation tanks, an outdated method that led to a less consistent product and possible foreign contamination. Other equipment, like the storage tanks, had degraded to the point of unsuitability; their enamel had chipped off, putting beer in direct contact with untreated metal, which corroded the metal and negatively flavored the beer. In the case of the two urban factories (the very heart of al-Ahram for nearly a century), the sprawl of the surrounding cities had completely overtaken them.[7] The only aspect of the beer operations that had remained suitable was the distribution system centered around depots and truck deliveries.

A piece in the *New York Times* captures the general atmosphere around al-Ahram after 1985: "Workers lounged around reading newspapers or napping while grimy, ancient machines gushed foaming beer into dirty green bottles, often along with insects, twigs and clumps of dirt."[8] One member of Luxor Group remembers walking through the Cairo factory on an exploratory investor mission dodging debris from the ceiling as they stepped through unidentified pools of liquid.[9]

While we should be careful not to believe these stories unreservedly, there is no doubt that the reputation of Stella in the Egyptian market, at the time, was suffering. It was no longer a desirable and clean product but another example of an Egyptian-made product deserving of derision. The damage from this period remains to this day. There is a joke that still floats among the Egyptian beer drinkers that goes something like this: "An Egyptian wants to test out the quality of his local beer, Stella. So, he sends a sample to a laboratory. He soon receives the results from the lab and they read: Congratulations! Your camel is pregnant!"[10]

It was not only this joke, and ones like it, that represented Stella's degraded position in the Egyptian market. For example, in the late 2000s you could still buy a shirt in the Khan al-Khalili market that had the Stella symbol on the front and the phrase "What doesn't kill us makes us stronger" on the back.[11] If that did not fit your fancy, you could buy a shirt emblazoned with the catchy slogan "Buy a Stella: 10 million cockroaches can't be wrong."[12]

These internal issues were compounded by external forces. The whole of the Egyptian economy was suffering under a confluence of factors. An unsurprising result of the ever-growing public sector, which began under Nasser and continued unabated under Sadat and Mubarak, was that the Egyptian government was racking up a huge amount of debt to employ its citizens and subsidize foodstuffs, petrol, and other commodities. At the same time, Egypt was taking a hit in its revenue inflows. Between the years 1982 and 1988, government revenues declined from 40 percent of gross domestic product to 24 percent. Nearly half of this loss could be attributed to the oil bust of the 1980s, which hit at major revenue sources for the government.[13] By the years 1989–1990, "the government budget deficit soared to over 21 percent of GDP, inflation reached 25 percent, foreign exchange levels were critically low, and the total foreign debt was nearly $50 billion—about 150 percent of GDP, perhaps the highest ratio in the world."[14]

Egypt was on the verge of an economic disaster and had to turn to international financial organizations, the IMF and World Bank, to extricate itself from a continually worsening situation. In 1991 the Egyptian government secured debt relief from these organizations in exchange for pursuing an Economic Reform and Structural Adjustment Program. As it applied to Egypt, one of its biggest steps was the privatization of state-owned enterprises like al-Ahram. As we will see in the next section, this privatization ushered in a new era for Stella and al-Ahram, one that tried to undo the damage of the era that preceded it.

Another external factor that made 1987–1988 a false dawn for Stella and al-Ahram was the expanding Islamic Revival. The movement that was taking shape in the Sadat era reached its full form in Mubarak's Egypt. While the outlines of this trend go beyond this book, it suffices to note that the net result was the Islamization of Egyptian public culture.[15]

This Islamization led to the rise of what I term the *Islamiyyun*. Whereas it was the effendis who were the imagined middle stratum of Egyptian society from the 1920s through the 1960s, and who were threatened and marginalized by the *infitahis* in the 1970s and 1980s, from the 1990s onward it has been the *Islamis* who have come to dominate Egypt. The choice of the word *Islami* is a way to reconcile the fact that the Egyptians of pre-1980 who wore miniskirts or shorts, drank alcohol, had unsupervised time with the opposite sex, fitted their prayer schedule around their lives, and so on were Muslims just like those who after the 1980s demanded a more pious Egyptian public domain. The difference between them was performance of their Muslim identity. For many of the pre-1980 Egyptians, their Muslim identity fitted around the world they lived in. For the *Islami*, it is rather the world that must be shaped to fit their Islamic identity.

One of the best examples of the *Islami* reality is the battle between the Egyptian government and government employees over praying the afternoon prayer. Whereas previously the workers who wanted to pray would, according to Islamic tradition, pray their midafternoon prayer during cessation of their work schedule, in the 1970s workers started to demand that they be allowed to pray as soon as the call to prayer was sounded. As Aaron Rock-Singer argues, this effort was Egyptians trying to practice their pietism within the confines of state structures.[16] They were pushing not for an alternative reality but for one shaped by their piety.

## Privatization

Stella and al-Ahram faced the nineties without one of their greatest advocates, the country in deep economic trouble, and a public increasingly unwelcoming to alcohol. The company's precarious situation was evident in its production numbers. After its high point in 1987–1988, production tabled off in 1989–1990 at 500,000 hectoliters and then began a steady decline. By 1995 production had slipped to just 380,000.[17] Stella, and the company that sold it, was a "distressed" asset. It is appropriate to conceptualize the fate of Stella in the terms of neoliberal capitalism, because with the Egyptian government embarking on ERSAP in 1990, neoliberal capitalism became the dominant ideology of the day. As it concerned al-Ahram, and the rest of the state-owned enterprises, ERSAP meant privatization.

Like every economic transition that al-Ahram witnessed in its history, the transition from public to private was stop-start. In the case of privatization, the most significant point of friction was the institutional inertia that had been built up in state-owned enterprises over thirty years of public ownership. The Egyptian government was hesitant to shake the foundations of its support, which was its role as the country's largest employer and subsidizer. "The Egyptian government had to weigh the merits of selling rapidly and reforming thoroughly ... versus holding out for higher sale prices, cultivating domestic property ownership, and maintaining the cooperation of numerous interest groups." As a result, from 1990 to 1995 the privatization of the public sector proceeded glacially. The government had pledged to sell 105 state-owned enterprises by 1995, but ended up with only "ten majority sales to employee shareholder associations (ESA's), and a limited number of liquidations and minority offerings." In the case of al-Ahram, there was very little change between 1990 and 1995, except al-Ahram broke off from the General

Corporation of Food Industries and came under the control of the Holding Company for Housing, Tourism, and Cinema.[18] It also took on a new name, al-Ahram Beverage Company.

The pacing of privatization was so slow that the IMF decided to postpone $4 billion of debt forgiveness and withhold the third and final part of the $10 billion agreed upon in 1990.[19] The threat proved an effective one and pushed the Egyptian government to a greater commitment to privatization. The privatization of al-Ahram was meant to be part of this renewed effort. Even still, the sale of the company was a convoluted process that led to the government agreeing to a less than favorable deal.

The government first put al-Ahram up for sale in 1994 but rejected more than twenty bids, as it spent the next two years "prevaricating between various direct sale and share issue schemes."[20] The government's indecisiveness was a feature of most of its privatizations and pushed away many investors hoping for profitable returns.[21] In 1996, under the pressure of international financial institutions, such as the World Bank and the IMF, the government ramped up its efforts to sell ABC and other companies. They received one serious offer from a partnership of the Egyptian Finance Company and al-Ahly for Development & Investment, but deemed the bid undervalued.[22]

In response, they decided to proceed with a 60 percent public offering of the company on the Egyptian Bourse, the stock market. In this instance, ABC was hurt by being an alcohol company in an Islamizing country. The public offering was undersubscribed, there was not enough of the Egyptian population willing to buy stock in an alcohol company, and the government eventually had to settle on selling "5 percent of the company on the stock exchange, and at an offering price of $4.925 . . . rather than a hoped-for $6.25." It also sold two other 5 percent blocks to "two big Egyptian institutional investors and gave another 10 percent to employees."[23]

The lead investor of a New York–based investment group, called the Luxor Group, would use the tepid response to the public sale of the company to acquire the remaining 75 percent of the company in a sweetheart deal. Ahmed Zayat, an Egyptian American entrepreneur, used some dogged determination—negotiations stretched over eighteen months and included twenty-two separate negotiation sessions—to acquire al-Ahram at LE 68.50 a share, which was less than half of what the government was hoping to receive. Zayat reached this agreement with the government even though he did not have the money to pay for it. He thus had to sell the idea of selling beer to Muslims to international investors. "He lined up a public offering of global depository receipts in London and set off on a road show across Europe and the United States that yielded Mr. Zayat not only enough money to pay the government but even more to pocket himself."[24]

In addition to the huge windfall from the purchase, the government also agreed to two other significant concessions. The first was selling five parcels of land in the developing industrial city thirty-five miles north of Cairo, called El-Obour, under market value to ABC. Likewise, they granted a ten-year tax concession to ABC on the land in El-Obour.[25] Overall, the deal was a bad one for the government.[26]

## Moving Past Stella

One of the key ways in which Zayat and the Luxor Group could negotiate such a favorable deal with the government was by ignoring one of the most important parts of al-Ahram's history, its two breweries in Giza, Cairo, and Ibrahimiyya, Alexandria. The government believed that the location of these breweries, on prime downtown real estate, should significantly inflate the price of the company. Zayat was not interested in owning the land the factories were on and rather agreed to a nominal five-year lease of the land.[27]

The reason he was so willing to abandon these significant historical artifacts, and possible financial boons, was that he had no plans for them in the future. As mentioned above, the factories were in poor shape at the time of the sale. Luxor had outside confirmation of their inadequacy when, as part of the takeover, they contracted with Danbrew, a Danish brewer, to perform a technical assessment of the breweries.

The technical management team that arrived from Denmark included a brewmaster, a laboratory and quality specialist, and a utilities and management specialist. All of them were highly qualified and beer lovers. Much to the shock of everyone at ABC, during their time at the company, they would sample the breweries' product every day at lunch.[28] The situation that brewmaster Jens Erik Holmsgaard faced was quite bad. In words that echoed the problems faced by Erick Kettner, he found that the three breweries each used their own recipe to produce the same beer, and workers followed no specifications. There was little communication between the factories and the laboratories at each of the breweries, a critical deficiency in producing high-quality beer. Finally, the equipment was either in bad shape or completely run-down.[29]

The great majority of the beers that he sampled tasted from "bad to awful," as they had been infected by foreign bodies, were flat, or had not been pasteurized properly. This was anathema to Holmsgaard, as the impermeable boundary between the environment and the beer had been compromised at three critical points. First, the beer-making process was not sterile, allowing the environment to encroach on the beer. Second, the containers for the beer were not protecting the beer and its appealing carbonation. Finally, the last defense against foul-tasting organisms, the pasteurization process, was not being carried out to its full potential.[30]

After their assessment, Luxor and Danbrew agreed upon a two-step plan for resurrecting the beer industry in Egypt. First, they would send a technical management team who would oversee the improvement of the products and the efficiency of the two old factories as well as the factory in Sharqiyya. Second, Danbrew would provide a "turnkey" brewery, that is, a brewery that was ready to make beer the day it opened, in El-Obour. Luxor Group also reached a licensing agreement with Carlsberg, the Danish brewery, to produce their beer at El-Obour.[31]

Holmsgaard, who was part of the technical team and would become vice president, technical, at ABC, had to institute a great deal of change to produce a high-quality beer at the three breweries. Holmsgaard approached the problem in several ways. He drafted action plans for each of the breweries, which corresponded to all the deficiencies laid out in the technical reports. He then held weekly meetings to follow up on the progress of goals. He also implemented Danbrew's specific quality management system, which was meant to ensure sanitary and efficient beer production.[32]

As for personnel, with the privatization agreement the government removed all the top management, including the Golden Island. Luxor replaced them with local management from other industries, Egyptians born and trained abroad, and a few expatriates. Most of the new management had no experience in brewing.[33] The middle management and below had the power of the union backing them, and thus the government let them remain. Nevertheless, ABC made strong efforts to reduce their numbers and the general bloat of the company.[34] These measures took the form of "better-defined responsibilities, the setting of objectives and performance measures, retraining, [and] voluntary employee buyouts." Abandoning its factories may also have allowed for easier pruning of the problematic workforce. The aim was to remove up to one hundred employees annually from 1997 until 2003 at an annual cost of about LE 2 million (LE 20,000 per employee).[35]

Of those who remained at al-Ahram, Luxor aimed to educate and discipline them. That is not to say they were without education. The production directors were typically agricultural engineers trained in food technology. As for the utilities department, it was composed of mechanical and electrical engineers.[36] Nevertheless, the new hires and remaining employees needed education in cutting-edge brewing. This education entailed not only learning from the Danbrew staff present, but also trips to other Mediterranean breweries and attending lessons at the Scandinavian School of Brewing and the Carlsberg Brewing Academy in Copenhagen.[37]

As for discipline, the main target of the effort was the corruption that was sapping the company's profits. Addressing this problem was difficult because it was so endemic to government-owned enterprises in Egypt. Luxor pursued a four-part program to try to stamp out the problem. They first displayed the seriousness of the issue by reporting perpetrators to the authorities and filing criminal charges against some employees. They then worked with the workers' union to create a united front against the problem. Once their desires were known to all workers, they changed the security personnel, which involved removing old security employees and retraining some of the excess workers for the security detail. Finally, they implemented new systems for monitoring inventory. These maneuvers had a noticeable and immediate financial impact on the company.[38]

Both sets of actions were generally met with little resistance. The surprising result can be attributed to the fact that Luxor was careful to couple any painful changes with worthwhile incentives for their workers. Some of the most noteworthy rewards they provided were new uniforms, a new cafeteria, and a revamped health care system (in terms of both quality and affordability). Most significantly, they restructured the compensation plan, with the approval of the union, on an incentive-based system. As part of the compensation plan, employees were given a stake in the company. On average, the stake was worth roughly LE 30,000.[39]

The culmination of this work, and, as Holmsgaard termed it, a "Trojan horse" for these changes, was the launching of another brand, named Stella Premium. There was already a two-tiered system of Stellas prior to privatization. There was Stella Local, which used only Egyptian-manufactured bottles and caps, and Stella Export, which was intended for export and could be bought in Egypt only with foreign currency at certain retailers. The upshot of this foreign exclusivity meant that al-Ahram could import the caps, which unlike local caps fitted perfectly, for Stella Premium and thus provide a more expensive and more consistent product. In the dark period of 1985 until 1996, the difference between the two shrank to a point that they were indistinguishable.[40]

Stella Premium was meant to again create a luxe offering for the company. It also was a nonconfrontational way of introducing Danbrew's quality management system and bringing the products of the three breweries in line. This last goal was something that had never been achieved in the history of al-Ahram. The Danes were quite successful, and within a half year of privatization they launched Stella Premium. It was a 5.0 alcohol-by-volume beer and was sold in 330 ml bottles emblazoned with a silver label.

Besides Stella's signature star that sat atop the label, there was the picture of Tutankhamen's mask, front and center. This iconic Egyptian image was surrounded by pictures of barley and hops. The great majority of the text on the label was written in Arabic. The top of the label read: "Produced by al-Ahram Beverage Company/Stella Beer Premium/Made in Egypt—Good for Six Months." As for the bottom of the label, it read: "Contents: Malt, Water, and Barley/Alcohol by volume 5 +/− .2%/330 ml+/− 10ml/ Keep far from light and heat." Immediately under the Tutankhamen, there were three bits of English: the name, Stella; underneath that the words *Premium* and *Lager*; and underneath that the last bit of English, matched by an Arabic translation below it, "Produced in September 1997."

The extensive description of the label is useful because it was Luxor's first statement to Egypt on its intentions for Stella and al-Ahram. Their message had two major pushes. First, Stella was Egypt's beer. We see this in both words and images. The choice of Arabic was one signal of Egyptianness, as was the use of the phrase "Made in Egypt." These choices work well with the image of Tutankhamen's mask surrounded by barley and hops, an on-point declaration of the beer's Egyptianness.

The other push of the label is subtler. Through the inclusion of information like the contents, the alcohol volume, the production date, and directions like "keep far from heat and sunlight" and "good for six months," ABC was declaring that it was using science to ensure Stella's quality. This label made a great deal of sense in the context of the situation Luxor confronted when they took over al-Ahram. The push to emphasize Egyptianness was a way to fight against the Islamization of Egypt that grouped Stella with the rest of alcohol as foreign impositions despoiling Egypt. Likewise, the turn to the scientific support of quality was an attempt to counter the poor experiences many Stella drinkers had with the beer in the years prior.

Stella Premium was just the first shot in the salvo to rebrand al-Ahram as a "modern" beverage company deserving of the trust of customers, the government, and investors. Stella Premium was followed with the production of canned and draft beers. ABC then introduced a new brand of beer, called Meister, in 1998 to celebrate the one-year anniversary of privatization and the centennial of the breweries' founding. It was a rather strong, highly fermented beer with "low color and low bitterness."[41]

## A New Brewery

The most significant move that al-Ahram took under the leadership of Luxor was the establishment of a brewery in El-Obour. The turnkey brewery Danbrew was building was meant not as a supplement but rather as a replacement for the Giza and Ibrahimiyya breweries. The measures that Holmsgaard took to improve the old breweries were meant only to keep production going while they were slowly phased out. As part of Luxor's radical restructuring of ABC, the Cairo and Alexandria breweries were to be shuttered.

Production stopped at the Giza and Alexandria plants in the summer of 2000. However, both retained some function in the company. The brewery in Giza held the company's administration, until a new administration could be built in El-Obour. As for the Alexandria brewery, it would continue to be used a distribution center for the company, a role that it had played since the 1960s.[42]

The El-Obour brewery covered fifty-one thousand square meters and was built in a depression in the desert. Based on al-Ahram's output of 350,000 hectoliters yearly during privatization, all the machinery was designed to produce 500,000 hectoliters with the ability to expand to 1 million. The entire complex was outfitted to produce Carlsberg beer but still could produce Stella and Stella Premium. There were three building complexes contained within the brewery area: one contained the raw materials handling plant, another contained the various brewing and packaging plants, and the third contained the waste-treatment plant.[43]

The main building complex contained a brew-house plant, tank farm, beer-processing plant, bottling line, water-treatment plant, cooling plant, $CO_2$ recovery plant, and compressed-air plant. Each of these plants had a function essential to cutting-edge beer making. For example, the brew house was where the raw materials of malt and rice were turned into cold wort, which was the cold, unfermented, sugary liquid produced from steeping or decocting a cereal (rice or malt) in water.[44] This area could put out eight brews a day. The brew house was the main differentiation point between Carlsberg beer and Stella. Carlsberg beer was made only with malt and hops, while Stella was made with a mix of malt, rice, sugar, and other adjuncts, depending on the type they were making.[45]

The El-Obour brewery was a state-of-the-art facility, staffed with a well-trained workforce, all of which signaled the Luxor Group's desire to turn a new page for al-Ahram. It was fully outfitted with the equipment to ensure that the beer leaving was up to the chemical, microbiological, and packaging standards of Carlsberg.[46] As for Stella, they also aimed to raise its quality. They did so gradually, however, out of fear that a too quick change would scare off customers accustomed to the lesser brew.[47]

But that was not the only transformation that Luxor and Zayat had in store for the company. They sought to bring change to almost every other aspect of it. For example, when they arrived there were "four telephones," which they increased to sixteen hundred. Luxor also raised the number of desktop computers "from four to more than 300, and fax machines, from one to dozens."[48] E-mail and voice messages became a key way in which messages were communicated from the board to the management and the workforce.[49]

Perhaps their largest contribution was bringing their knowledge of Western sales and brand management to the country. In service of their sales goals, they hired thirty-five sales executives, most coming from Pepsico and Schweppes.[50] They also added more than a hundred trucks to their fleet of three hundred to deliver beer to a larger section of the country. But it was not only personnel changes they brought but also changes in their sales system. One significant innovation was to start offering home delivery. This move was a way to circumvent patrons' hesitation in buying alcohol in public and the limited number of liquor licenses the government had for retailers.[51] In addition to home delivery, Luxor rebranded the *mustawda'*, the depots that were so central to selling beer in the 1970s and 1980s, as Drinkies-branded stores while expanding their numbers.

The move to Drinkies represented the general push of the company to take control of their brand. Every move of the company, under Luxor, was either in conjunction with or publicized by al-Ahram's new marketing department. For example, the brewery spent nearly $2 million on an advertising and marketing plan to celebrate the breweries' hundred-year anniversary.[52] One of the most significant hurdles of this effort to brand and market their product was the government's prohibition on public advertisement of alcohol, a policy that grew out of the government's attempt to claim the dominant religious voice. The way ABC attempted to navigate this problem was quite ingenious. In the same way that Stella Premium was a Trojan horse for new management methods, advertisements for nonalcoholic beer were meant to raise brand awareness of ABC's offerings, including Stella.[53]

## Nonalcoholic Beer

The al-Ahram company had first discussed the possibility of producing a nonalcoholic drink in 1949. In that year, Pieter Feith, an intermediary between Heineken and al-Ahram (also called Pyramid), had brought a nonalcoholic flavored malt drink to the executive board meeting. The drink had been made in Heineken's Rotterdam lab and could be flavored with various fruit essences. Wittert van Hoogland, the Heineken-trained Dutch managing director of al-Ahram Brewery, had tested it and deemed it worthy to be presented. The board at that time was quite pleased with the sample. One of the main selling points for them was that it, being nonalcoholic, would not be taxed, and their profit margin would be high. Heineken also seemed to believe in the project, because it was willing to launch a pilot campaign in 1950. The pilot campaign did not happen, and nonalcoholic drinks did not make another real appearance in the company's plans until the 1970s.

A report on the meeting indicates why this campaign was not pursued. As Feith warned, the profits, even though it was a nontaxed product, would not be as significant as the board imagined. The money signs in their eyes distracted them from the fact that there were already companies selling nonalcoholic drinks in Egypt with better sales and distribution systems. Carbonated beverages with natural flavors, as this malt drink was, were already the province of international companies, such as Coca-Cola and Pepsi-Cola. Al-Ahram held no market advantage over these companies when it came to selling nonalcoholic drinks — quite the opposite in fact.

Al-Ahram would stay out of the nonalcoholic drink business until they were forced into it by the government. There were overtures by the government to invite al-Ahram to get involved in the soft-drink business during its nationalization. After taking over King Farouk's shares in the primary Pepsi bottler, the Egyptian government was looking for Heineken's technical aid in the soda business. Wittert van Hoogland, however, warned Erick Kettner from getting involved, stating bluntly: "Apart from the first years of its existence, Pepsi-Cola always worked in Egypt with a great loss." Coca-Cola bottlers, Wittert added, were able to profit only because Coca-Cola sold synthetic syrups.[54]

Although they avoided direct collaboration, as part of the nationalization process al-Ahram was placed in the General Corporation of Food Industries, where they sat with the nationalized companies that produced Coca-Cola, Pespi-Cola, Sinalco (a local variant), and Spathis Soda. Due to the nature of beer and soft-drink making, there was overlap in the processes and machinery of their operations. The overlap would not have been a significant issue, as inefficiency was not uncommon in government-owned enterprises, except for the fact that after nationalization the soda companies were losing a good deal of money.

To turn around the carbonated-beverage companies, the Egyptian government turned to Omar Foda. He had flirted with the idea of al-Ahram offering nonalcoholic beverages. In the early days after nationalization, Foda purchased a lemonade-making machine with this possibility in mind, but nothing came of it.[55] That changed in the late 1970s, when the government enlisted his help in turning around Coke and Pepsi. From that point onward, he worked to help El Nasr Bottling Company (previously owned by Coca-Cola) and the Egyptian Bottling Company (previously owned by Pepsi) to turn around their fortunes.[56] How he succeeded is less important than the fact that from that point forward, al-Ahram's fate was intertwined with that of soft drinks in Egypt. The clearest example of this linkage was that when building the Sharqiyya brewery, al-Ahram wanted it outfitted to make beer and nonalcoholic drinks. For example, one of the proposals for building the brewery they received from Britvic Beverage Company was built around the company's experience in both beverage types.[57]

But it was not only desires of improving performance that turned al-Ahram's eyes toward nonalcoholic drinks. By the 1970s, there was a growing market for nonalcoholic beer. To address this want, al-Ahram ran a 1972 advertisement for nonalcoholic Stella that read:

> Stella Beer
> Nonalcoholic
> Refreshing and Reinvigorating
> Always Fresh and Pure.[58]

This advertisement (fig. 08.01) shows that the message of refreshment that the company tied to Stella in the 1950s continued to have relevance after nationalization. As the company branched out into nonalcoholic beers, they held firmly to the fresh and refreshing aspects of their beer. In fact, there is very little in the advertisement to suggest that the beer was nonalcoholic outside of the bottle, which had the words *bidūn kaḥūl* (nonalcoholic) on the label beneath the Stella name. The image of the frothy glass of beer on the left side of the advertisement could easily have been lifted from an advertisement for regular Stella.[59] As I have discussed above, this repurposing would not have been difficult, as Stella in the 1960s had transcended its position as solely an alcoholic beverage and had come to be seen, especially among middle- and upper-class Egyptians, as a refreshing summertime beverage.

This continuity not only speaks to how deeply Stella had become associated with summertime refreshment, but also shows how demand for nonalcoholic beer was tied to the alcoholic variety. Although Pyramid had discussed producing a nonalcoholic beer in 1949, al-Ahram started production of it only in the 1970s, in response to the rising tide of Islamic religiosity in

Figure 08.01. Stella nonalcoholic beer (*Ruz al-Yusuf*, July 17, 1972)

the country.[60] As discussed above, a central part of the *Islami* identity was shaping the contemporary world (read: secular) around themselves to fit a new pious lifestyle. Like demanding that the work schedule accommodate prayer times, drinking a nonalcoholic beer was taking a feature of the secular contemporary world, convivial alcohol consumption, and shaping it to one's sense of piety.

This demand was a post–Islamic Revival phenomenon. There was no market for a nonalcoholic beer in the 1940s, because for Egyptians in that period, drinking beer was an either-or proposition. You either drank beer as a reflection of your acceptance and participation in modern secular culture or rejected it totally, as it was part of the corrupting influence of Western culture on Egypt. There was no need to try to capture that aspect of modern life in a more pious manner.

We see this dichotomy if we turn to a fatwa published by the famed Islamic modernist Muhammad Rashid Rida. In the 1929 fatwa "*al-Ji'a* [beer] is *Khamr* and drinking it is Illicit," he uses a hadith that states that even a little bit of something that can intoxicate a great deal is illicit (*ḥarām*) to establish the illicitness of beer. Having made this point, Rida goes on to discuss a worrying trend he had seen in Egypt: people making nonalcoholic beer for improving urination. Rida believed that the drink in and of itself was acceptable if it was like the *nabīdh* that the Prophet and the companions of the Prophet used to drink, a liquid made from dates and grapes steeped in water *but not fermented*. This last bit about fermentation is quite vital when understood in the context of how nonalcoholic beer is made.

The process for making nonalcoholic beer is almost identical to making standard beer except that after it has fermented, and before it is bottled, the alcohol is removed through one of several processes.[61] So, when Rida says nonalcoholic beer is allowed if it is not fermented, he is essentially saying it is not allowed. For Rida, the only acceptable drink would be a cereal steeped in water, the wort. This interpretation makes sense considering in the text that he also warns that *nabīdh* was used by licentious kings, princes, elites, and scholars to justify the drinking of alcoholic beverages.[62]

By the 1970s, this mind-set had changed, not only because of the rise of the *Islamiyyun*, but also because of the change in Stella's role in Egypt. As I have documented, between the 1940s and the 1970s, Stella beer became a cultural institution in Egypt. It was Egypt's beer, if not Egypt's alcoholic beverage, of choice. As public culture Islamized in the 1970s and 1980s, there appeared a new group of Egyptians: those who desired Stella beer for its taste and its cultural associations but did not want its religiously troubling alcohol.[63] The change is noticeable when we consider the actions of Yusuf al-Qardawi, an intellectual descendant of Rida and one of the most significant scholars of the *Islami* movement, who produced a controversial fatwa saying nonalcoholic beer was religiously acceptable.[64]

The main avenue for addressing this growing need was the new brewery in Sharqiyya. There, the al-Ahram Brewery housed an evaporator for removing alcohol from Stella.[65] However, the demand in the 1970s was not significant enough to be more than a low-level concern for al-Ahram. Nonalcoholic beer only really took off in the 1980s. This was also the time when al-Ahram made a real commitment to the nonalcoholic beer market, presenting a new brand to consumers, Birell. This was a very low-alcoholic beer that was brewed under the license of the Swiss brewer Hürlimann (later part of the Carlsberg Group).[66] In 1986, the first year of Birell sales, al-Ahram sold 21,080 hectoliters of nonalcoholic beer and 470,000 hectoliters of regular beer.[67] From this point on, it would be nonalcoholic beer that would be the growth leader for the company. While Stella reached its peak in 1987–1988, Birell and Fayrouz, al-Ahram's flavored malt beverage line also launched in 1985, would be only starting their ascents.

By the time Luxor had secured control of al-Ahram, beer sales had declined from a peak of 510,000 hectoliters of beer in 1987–1988 to 380,000 in 1995–1996. In that same period, nonalcoholic beer production had grown from 21,000 hectoliters in 1987–1988 to 96,160 hectoliters in 1995–1996.[68] Seeing this trend, it was no wonder that the Sharqiyya brewery was spared the same fate of the Giza and Ibrahimmiyya breweries. In fact, after taking control, Luxor made Sharqiyya its flagship brewery, becoming ABC's center of nonalcoholic beverage production.[69] Luxor, under the supervision of Danbrew, replaced the outdated nonalcoholic machinery with a new German rectification plant and expanded the brewery to meet the new demand for nonalcoholic beer.[70] They also contracted with Guinness to produce their nonalcoholic offering, Kaliber. Beer would be trucked from Giza and Ibrahimiyya, at first, and then later the El-Obour brewery, to Sharqiyya for alcohol removal and canning.[71] As Jens Holmsgaard noted: "In the greater perspective, the brewery in the delta [sic], the Sharkia Brewery, shall not be over looked. We did not only brew beer here, more importantly was the production of Feyruz (non-alcoholic malt beverage with fruit flavors), Birell … and the non-alcoholic Caliber [sic] beer from which the alcohol had been distilled off. It was made under license from Guinness. It was actually exported to the G[u]lf area."[72]

The renewed focus on Sharqiyya marked Luxor's full-on press to make nonalcoholic beer happen in Egypt. Within two years of their takeover, they had grown the amount of nonalcoholic beer produced from nearly 100,000 hectoliters to 367,000 hectoliters. That made up nearly 48 percent of their beer production in 1999. This was a stark shift from even a year prior, when nonalcoholic beer made up only 37 percent of their beer production.[73] This turn to nonalcoholic was rapid, but as I have shown it did not come out of nowhere. As ABC's new marketing director, Fatenn Mostafa, stated, it was the only way to proceed: "'It [nonalcoholic beer]'s our future.' … 'We will never succeed in getting every Egyptian to drink beer,' Ms. Mostafa said. 'It will always be a Muslim country. But nonalcoholic beer has all the elements to succeed. It's very healthy. It doesn't have caffeine. It looks like beer. It tastes like beer. But it's religiously accepted.'"[74]

### A New Era?

The ease with which Luxor closed the two-hundred-year-old factories should not be too shocking considering the dilapidated shape they were in when they were acquired. Likewise, the de-emphasizing of Stella beer makes sense when considering market trends (the rise of the *Islami* identity) and its own diminished standing in the eyes of consumers. When taken together, however, it is somewhat jarring how quickly Luxor sidelined the pillars upon which the Egyptian beer industry had been built since its inception. Although there were some attempts to reclaim that history—the centennial celebration and a retro-style advertisement campaign for Stella beer are two examples—there was no real effort to document the history of one of Egypt's longest-running companies. In fact, despite what might have been said, it was actually to the benefit of the company to move past its history. As a publicly traded company, especially one courting foreign investment, it was essential to craft a narrative of progress, change, and growth.

To do this, al-Ahram's history, which was heavily entwined with government ownership, needed to be presented not as an asset but as an anchor. As Luxor told it, they were freeing al-Ahram from the shackles of government ownership. It was neoliberalism at its best; the market was saving al-Ahram in the way the international monetary institutions (such as the IMF and World Bank) were saving Egypt. But how much of what Luxor was doing was new?

When we consider many of their actions in the context of the entire company's history, it is less than they claimed. One of the most significant examples is in the leadership of the company. Before nationalization in 1963, the boards of the Crown and Pyramid Breweries (the breweries that would become al-Ahram) were transnational affairs. For example, in 1907, the directorate of both companies was split between Alexandria and Brussels, where the head offices were located. Two members of the five-person board for Crown Brewery and three members of the seven-person board for Pyramid lived in Brussels, while the rest, who were a mix of Egyptian citizens and foreign protégés, maintained operations in Egypt.[75]

Transnationalism was a persistent feature of the executives for both companies from 1907 until 1963, even as the Egyptian government worked to push more Egyptians into executive positions in private-sector companies after the 1940s. For example, in 1954 the Pyramid Brewery board contained three Egyptian citizens and four non-Egyptians.[76] Meanwhile, Crown Brewery had a similar percentage of Egyptian citizens on its board.[77] Between 1963 and 1997, the trend of transnationalism was sidelined, as the entire board was Egyptian and under the control of the Egyptian government.

The Luxor board after the takeover renewed the transnational character of al-Ahram's executive. This character started at the top with the executive chairman and CEO, Ahmed Zayat. Born in the Maadi district of Cairo, he attended Victoria College in Cairo and then went to the United States for college. From there he worked as "senior vice president, focusing on mergers, acquisitions and New York real estate transactions for various entities controlled by Zev Wolfson."[78] He then worked as a consultant for AT&T and Fitch Investor Services before launching his bid for al-Ahram. Of the seven other members of the board in 1999, four were heavily tied to the Egyptian business community, and three came from abroad. Of the four Egyptian entrepreneurs, one was Ahmad's brother Sherif, who received his undergraduate degree in mechanical engineering from the American University in Cairo and sat in management positions at Watania Company for nonwoven textiles and the Horse Foam company. Another, 'Alaa' 'Awn, Zayat's uncle, received his undergraduate and graduate degrees from Ain Shams University and a PhD in mechanical engineering from Imperial College, University of London, before serving in executive positions in several Egypt-based cold-storage companies. The remaining two Egyptians, Muhammad Anwar Gamal 'Awn and Muhammad al-Tayr, received all their schooling in Egypt and were heavily involved in the Egyptian business community.

Of the three non-Egyptians on the board, two of them, Andrew Capitman and Steve Keefer, were Americans from the Fieldstone Private Capital Group, "an international investment banking firm headquartered in New York." Capitman, with a bachelor's degree from Yale and a master's in economics from the University of Miami, had extensive investment-banking experience before taking on a non–executive director position on the ABC board. Keefer, who served as a US Army ranger after receiving degrees from the University of Pennsylvania, took on a larger role in the company. He became the chief of staff to the chairman and investor and press-relations director. In this role, he was the company's spokesperson and coordinated "investor, press, and public relations."[79]

The third non-Egyptian was Dan Bibro, a German who had thirty-six years' experience in brewing and wine making. Before coming to ABC, he had worked as a managing director for Tempo Industries.[80] The parallels between Tempo and what ABC would become were quite striking. Tempo was founded in 1953 by Moshe Bernstein as a soft-drink company selling their signature lemon-lime-flavored drink. In 1985 it bought Eretz Israel Beer Industries, the first brewery established in Palestine in 1934, which produced Nesher, Goldstar, and Maccabee beers. Coupled with its control of one of Israel's biggest winemakers, Barkan winery, and other agreements to produce foreign spirits, such as Beefeater Gin, and soft drinks, including Pepsi, it had a strong presence in the Israeli beverage market. Heineken saw this strength and bought 40 percent of the company in 2005.[81]

The involvement of an industrialist with Israeli connections was both groundbreaking—it was a sure signal of the improved relations between Egypt and Israel due to the Camp David Accords—and a return to the multireligious history of al-Ahram. As discussed above, throughout most of the companies' history, Crown and Pyramid had a good mix of Muslims, Christians, and Jews. This changed only in the 1960s, when the Egyptian Jewish community as well as most expatriate communities were thinned out under the policies of Gamal Abdel Nasser. But it was not only Bibro that showed the return of a truly multifaith al-Ahram, but the CEO himself as well, Ahmed Zayat.

From his name (his first name has the same root as the name of the Prophet Muhammad), one would guess Ahmed Zayat is Muslim. Likewise, he has said nothing to counter that perception. When asked about his religion, he has said, "Why is it relevant, and why does it matter? It's personal." Yet the *New York Times* had this to say about him: "In fact, Mr. Zayat, who graduated from Yeshiva University, has given amply to Jewish causes. He lives with his wife and four children in a largely modern Orthodox neighborhood of Tudor and Victorian houses known as West Englewood in Teaneck, N.J. They keep kosher, arranging menus in advance at racetracks and, if they cannot locate a hotel close by, they stay in an R.V. and walk to the track, as they did at the Preakness Stakes, to avoid driving on the Sabbath." The *New York Times* even cites a quote from his rabbi in Teaneck. A simple Google search finds sources of various repute claiming his Judaism. The truth is not particularly important to this study; rather, the story around it is. His evasiveness in this regard can fit with two narratives. The first is that Zayat prefers to craft his own life story. We see this desire in his claimed graduation from Harvard. He maintained for decades that he graduated from the university, yet the *New York Times* and the university itself found no record of it. Further proof of his desire for control is the story of his unreported bankruptcy under the name Ephraim David Zayat.[82]

The second narrative is that his faith would have been a problem for the Egyptian government. One of the cudgels the Golden Island and other al-Ahram employees used to fight privatization was smearing Luxor as a Zionist-American plot to steal one of Egypt's jewels.[83] Beyond the possibility of discrimination affecting his business relations in Egypt, there is also the possibility he is a convert from Islam. This would also make dissimulation preferable, due to the strong social and cultural taboo against leaving Islam. According to Islamic law, "The punishment for the one who leaves Islam, an apostate, is death."[84]

It was not only the executive board of the company that echoed the transnational history of the company, but also the chief beer maker. Jens Holmsgaard, the head brewmaster at ABC under Luxor, had extensive microbiological training at Western institutions. He received his master's degree in biology and microbiology from the University of Copenhagen in 1976. He then spent a few years working in a food-ingredient company "as marine biologist, prospecting and studying the companies' [sic] raw materials—red seaweeds." He then entered the Scandinavian School of Brewing, graduating in 1982. After graduating he ran his own biotech consultancy for five years and then joined Danbrew, where he was approached by the CEO to establish the Process Consultancy Division in the company.[85]

His profile fits well with most of the other brewmasters in the history of al-Ahram. Outside of the period under government control, 1963–1997, the brewmaster was traditionally a European. For example, Crown before World War II employed a German as its brewmaster.[86] The most prominent and well-documented example is Gerardus Ulenberg, who served as Pyramid's brewmaster from 1952 to 1963. Like Holmsgaard, he received extensive training in the art of brewing with a private organization. Unlike Holmsgaard, Ulenberg never attained a bachelor's degree, which proved to be an issue for the Egyptian government as they tightened control of the company in the 1950s.[87] Despite this lack of the diploma, he had an outsize impact on beer making in Egypt. It is arguable that he may have perfected it.

Beyond personnel, many of the directives that Luxor carried out find echoes in the long history of the company. Every new owner or director embarked on a mission to update machinery. For example, Pyramid, with the help of Heineken, began work in 1958 and 1959 on a multiyear plant-expansion plan, which would further spur growth and profitability.[88] Products like nonalcoholic beer and canned beer, supposed innovations of Luxor, had been discussed and tried previously. For example, soon after taking over, Omar Foda had written to "Continental Can in Illinois, to issue tender for a canning line." After the Dutch exit, the company did not pursue the canning issue further. That was in part due to the technical difficulties and partly due to the fact that Foda was not really convinced of the usefulness of canned beer.[89]

Even Stella Premium and Meister, which Luxor positioned as its flagship brews, had their precedents in the company's history. Stella Premium was a revival of the Stella Export brand. As for Meister, which Luxor positioned as a "European-style dark lager," it had its precedent in one of al-Ahram's most popular brands besides Stella, Märzen. Named after a type of German beer, *märzen bier*, which translates as "March beer," it was a deep amber lager with a full body and moderate bitterness.[90] Originally offered as a seasonal beer sold between October and March, the breweries decided in 1959 to offer it as a full-year beer because the sales were so strong.[91] A similar process occurred with the Drinkies establishments, cornerstones of Luxor's new sales efforts; they were often repurposed *mustadaw'* depots.

Perhaps the most startling resonance between the activities of Luxor and the history of the company is its dealings with Nile Brewery. In June 1947, Muhammad Sirri Bey founded a competing beer company, Nile Brewery, that differentiated itself from Pyramid and Crown by touting its Egyptianness. This domestic challenger to the Pyramid-Crown conglomerate not only sought to distance itself from its competitor with its Egyptianness, but also aimed to capitalize on the rising economic nationalism of the period. Besides its Egyptian name, which evoked the image of beer brewed with Nile water, its leadership and workforce comprised mostly Egyptians. Of the original board, five of the seven members were Egyptian. Likewise, of the thirty-two employees listed in the records for 1954, twenty-nine of them were Egyptian, with twenty-one being Muslim.[92] Despite Nile Brewery's nationalist credentials, it proved no match for the embedded Pyramid–Crown partnership. It was out of business by 1956.

In 1999, having failed in their bid to take over al-Ahram, Mohamed Nusayr and Farid Sa'ad "sought and received a license to start a new beer company, to be known as Nile Brewery." Their challenge to al-Ahram was even less successful than their 1950s namesakes, as they did not even get off the ground. Their company was absorbed by al-Ahram before they even entered the market.[93]

This takeover is emblematic of how hard ABC fought to maintain another historical reality of al-Ahram, its monopoly of the Egyptian market. We see this in ABC's dealings with El-Gouna Brewery and Gianaclis Vineries. The entry of El-Gouna Brewery, funded by one of Egypt's richest families, the Sawiris, would prove a bit more of a challenge. Founded in 1999, its flagship brand was Sakkara beer (named after a pyramid complex in Egypt). The sales from this beer and the company's own privatization of the Egypt government's spirits business helped it stage a real challenge to al-Ahram. In 2000 it made roughly LE 63 million in revenue.[94] Nevertheless, al-Ahram again proved too imbedded to be challenged, and El-Gouna was bought out in 2001. El-Gouna was added to Nile and Gianaclis, the government-owned wine business that was as old as al-Ahram and was sold by the government to ABC in 1999. As a result, from 2001 onward, ABC has had a monopoly over the Egyptian beer and wine markets. The ease with which al-Ahram maintained its monopolistic market control, and the few barriers the government erected to stop it, signals how the government prioritized the success of Egyptian firms over any attempts to create a competitive market.

That is even more evident in the Gianaclis sale, which, like the al-Ahram deal, was a sweetheart deal for Luxor. It was sold at a very favorable price for Luxor and went to them despite other competitive offers. This was in line with the government's very favorable treatment of Luxor. For example, the government transferred the tax holidays granted to Nile and El-Gouna to ABC when they acquired the assets, which added to their own ten-year tax holiday on the El-Obour facility. Their agreement to allow them to supply Safi-brand water to the army also demonstrates where the government's allegiances laid. Even the tariff schedule the government pursued vis-à-vis foreign alcohol benefited ABC. "Around the time of the ABC privatization the government had actually enacted a broad reduction in tariffs, yet it left those on alcohol intact. . . . As of 2010, average duties for beer stood at 1,200%, wine 1,800%, and spirits 3,000%, while the 300% rate still applied for tourist outlets."[95]

The benefits of this favorable government treatment went beyond the balance sheets. They allowed Luxor to push through many of its desired reforms. For example, Luxor had greater success dealing with its workforce because of government support. Unlike Heineken, which battled an Egyptian workforce empowered by a government that prioritized Muslim Egyptians above all others, Holmsgaard could mold a receptive workforce who knew they were up against the company and the government.

This ability to change quickly without the fear of a government or workforce slowing down the process was the vital difference between ABC after Luxor took over and the era that preceded it. This agility combined with its total market dominance made it an attractive asset. It was so attractive, in fact, that an old friend, Heineken, reentered the picture. They would buy the company in 2002 for 1.3 billion Egyptian pounds. The purchase would push ABC into the era in which it remains today, an outpost in Heineken's ever-expanding global empire.

One constant feature of the privatization of al-Ahram was the heavy involvement of the government. Between its two sales, from the government to Luxor and from Luxor to Heineken, it was obvious that the government was heavily invested in the success of the privatization. So was it a success? The massive sale of the company to Heineken in 2002, which brought in nearly half of the country's net foreign direct investment for that year, makes it hard to say it was not for the government.[96]

Privatization also appears to have been a success for al-Ahram. As laid out at the beginning of the chapter, the company was facing an uncertain, if not troubling, future. It had lost one of its biggest advocates, its reputation in the market was suffering because of technological obsolescence and employee bloat, and it was facing a shrinking market due to the dual forces of the rising *Islami* mind-set and the overall stagnation of the Egyptian economy. In the period between 1997 and 2002, Luxor would turn a company that was bought for LE 230 million into one they sold for LE 1.3 billion. The turnaround needs several caveats. First, the situation was not as dire as it seemed, and al-Ahram was undervalued. Second, the government did everything in its power to provide a favorable atmosphere for Luxor to be successful. Finally, Luxor and Zayat were not as innovative as they imagined or portrayed. Even still, the work they did was overall positive. We need only to look at the fact that Heineken, as part of their purchase agreement, kept Ahmed Zayat on as the managing director for another three years to see the value Luxor's leadership added to the company.[97]

The story of success continues if we move to the people who made up the company. Outside of the leadership of al-Ahram who were immediately removed upon privatization, it worked out well for most others. The Luxor members who took over al-Ahram all made out quite well. Zayat was last seen as one of his horses, American Pharaoh, won the three most famous horse races in the world, the Triple Crown. As for the rest, they were extremely well compensated for their work, as were the investors, who very quickly made a nice return on their investment. Besides the bad actors who had been supplying the black market with Stella, the employees who remained and received stock in the company profited with the Heineken buyout.

There were only two losers in this whole transition, the company's history and the brand of Stella. As noted above, in almost every capacity, Luxor's takeover severed the ties of the company to its history. Losing the factories in Giza and Ibrahimiyya marked the end of one hundred years of history. Further, every name in the company's history, especially those that immediately preceded Luxor, was lost to the narrative of triumphant neoliberalism. As for Stella, its days as the flagship brand of al-Ahram were closed. As Luxor recognized, the winds of change were coming, and instead of looking to valiantly, and perhaps fruitlessly, fight to keep Stella its star product, it pivoted to different formulas (Stella Premium, Meister), other internationally known brands (Carlsberg), and nonalcoholic beverages (Birell, Fayrouz). Economically, this was the right choice. One of the reasons ABC was so attractive to Heineken was its pivot to nonalcoholic beer. The Dutch brewers saw huge growth potential in the nonalcoholic beer market in the region and believed that ABC could be a center of this operation. It would be too cynical to say that it did not come without a cost. The triumphant history of Stella was, for all intents and purposes, over.

During my research for this book, I made several trips to the copy room of Egypt's national library (Dar al-Kutub) in Cairo. The room is truly an awe-inspiring place, endlessly engrossing for a student of the country's history. Besides being filled with the comforting smell of toner and the persistent hum of laser scanners and printers, the place is a nexus of past and present, where millennia of Egyptian history are accessed, copied, and distributed to the contemporary world. The sight of a manuscript, yellowed by the centuries, being laboriously scanned and reproduced by the latest digital scanner is a stark and compelling juxtaposition. This room is more striking in that it functions in a distinctly Egyptian way. You hand your copy-request slip to an employee at a desk at the end of the room, and he tells you to sit in a row of chairs with the other researchers. Then you wait until your name is called by one of the employees working at the machines. If it is microfilm you are here for, you then sit with the employee at the microfilm copier, telling him the pages that you want copied as he brusquely flips through the film. The man does all of this with the patience of one who has tens of thousands of pages to copy before the end of the day and for whom your pages constitute a mere one hundred.

I was quite taken aback when, one day in that copy room, the employee who was so graciously helping me, having noticed a pattern in my copy requests, asked, "Does Stella beer still exist in Egypt?" The question shocked me at first because, for me, Stella and Egypt have long been inextricably linked. I do not think there has ever been a time when I have been in Egypt and *not* seen something related to Stella, whether the distinctive green bottle or a chance bit of paraphernalia such as a coaster, mug, or ashtray. Moreover, Egypt is the only place in the world where I have been that a person can buy Stella. Everywhere else in the world, when you ask for a Stella, you receive its Belgian cousin, Stella Artois. Therefore, I had assumed, foolishly, that this was the case for all Egyptians living in the country's urban centers—that even if they did not drink Stella due to personal taste or religious objections, they at least knew of its continued presence within Egypt.

However, the more I thought it over, the more I realized that without seeking Stella out or having a preestablished connection to it, an Egyptian could live his or her entire life without ever becoming aware of this important cultural artifact. As a product, Stella is not nearly as culturally pervasive as Budweiser, Miller, or Coors in the United States. No billboards announce it, no newspapers or televisions advertise it, and no sports teams or stadia bear its name. As this book has shown, this absence is not accidental. Since the 1970s, Egyptian public society has become increasingly intolerant of anything that could be deemed religiously suspect. But it was not only external forces that forced Stella out of the minds of Egyptians; it was also concessions by the company that sold it, al-Ahram Beverage Company.

There is very little evidence that what Ahmed Zayat and his Luxor Group did for the company was detrimental. In fact, in almost every way their management moves were a success and exactly what the company needed. Nevertheless, the one area where they failed, an area that means a great deal to a historian, was preserving the institutional memory of Stella. They made some token gestures to the beer's history—celebrating the anniversary, etc.—but in general they quickly abandoned it. Names, dates, even buildings were summarily discarded. Yes, there is some sentimentality here that may not jive with the cold reality of capitalism, but there is also the sense of a missed opportunity to own one's history. If you look at successful legacy companies like Coca-Cola, Heineken, and Pepsi, they not only own their history but carefully control it to bolster their reputation and their product.

This drive is arguably more important for a product that is slowly disappearing from society. Coca-Cola does not need to present a strong, historically supported argument that it is a vital part of American society. That battle has been won. That is not the case for Stella. Since the 1980s, it has struggled to maintain its place in a culture that grows more inimical to it by the year. That is why Luxor's moves are so jarring in hindsight. With Luxor's willingness to abandon Stella's history, the battle is probably already lost. If Egypt's beer company will not claim its rightful place in the historical memory of Egypt, there are very few who care enough to do so in their stead.

That was one aim of this book: fighting the battle to preserve a part of Egyptian history that many today would care to forget or may not even know to begin with. This book began with a quote: "You know, without doubt, every group of people needs a distraction. For example, there's *arak* in Turkey and Lebanon. We wish for beer to become the popular drink in Egypt. It is my pleasure to inform you that it was the ancient Egyptians who first manufactured beer."[1] I came back to that quote many times as I wrote this book because it is a snapshot of a time when someone could imagine beer becoming Egypt's popular drink. It has been a gentle reminder to not let the present situation of Stella in Egypt guide the writing of its history. Rather, it is the words and actions of those who worked to sell Stella beer as well as its social, political, economic, and technological realities that should lead that history. When viewed through this prism, it appears that not only was Isma'il Hafiz not delusional, but he was also quite prescient. As I have shown, for at least a short time, Stella did become the popular pastime of Egyptians. There was no denying Stella was the beer of Egypt.

## A Social History

This brings us back to the existential question that started this book. So what if Stella was the beer of Egypt? As I have argued, tracking its Egyptianization and the subsequent denial of this history allows us to view the astounding social, economic, and technological change that took place in Egypt in the period from 1880 to 2003.

This book showed how Stella, through social changes and clever advertising, became an important part of Egyptian culture. Only thirty years after Pyramid and Crown created the brand in the 1920s as a luxury offering, it became the dominant local brand. It reached such a level of cultural penetration that it achieved the goal of any brand, becoming synonymous with the product that it sold. It would not be an exaggeration to state that for a certain class of Egyptians, Stella *was* beer.

Its journey started when a set of Belgian entrepreneurs established Crown Brewery in Alexandria and Pyramid Brewery in Cairo in 1897 and 1898, respectively. Those early years before World War I were difficult, as the two breweries had to compete with a host of foreign beers and other local and foreign alcohols. Fortunately for the breweries, the sale of ice and malt proved profitable enough to make up for any lag in the sales of beer until the arrival of World War I. It was during this war that these two companies, freed by Egypt's disjuncture from the world market, established a profitable business selling beer. Linked to a parent company in Brussels, both companies found customers among the heterogeneous expatriate communities in Egypt: Greeks, Italians, Maltese, Britons, and others who had ventured to

Egypt in search of new economic opportunities following the opening of the Suez Canal in 1869. It soon became clear that the two Belgian beer companies had tapped into another significant pool of customers: native Egyptians.

Specifically, they targeted and were successful in selling to a developing class of Egyptians, the *effendiyya*. This group, like beer itself, went through a historical transformation. The first generation of *effendiyya* who had their origins in the Mehmet Ali era in 1840s Egypt were a small group of "new men," set apart from other Egyptians by their education, their Western manners and dress, and their worldviews. By the end of the century, the *effendiyya* came to represent a "new urban society, new social institutions, and new ways of life" and served as engineers, doctors, lawyers, journalists, and political activists. The *effendiyya* included in their ranks the sons of the provincial elite on their path to the honorific title of *pasha* or *bey* and their full inclusion into the national hierarchy. However, by Egypt's semi-independence in 1922, the *effendiyya*, the urban office class, came to represent, at least for the liberal nationalists, the perceived middle of Egyptian society. The *effendiyya* were the bearers of the national mission, and they were distinct from the *awlād al-balad* (native sons, "the good guys"), the fellahin, and the *awlād al-dhawāt* (Arabic: "sons of distinction," the "elite"). In practice, to be an effendi was to inhabit a liminal place between the lower and upper classes, to be a secular, modern, and liberally educated person who strove for the modern, secular, elite lifestyle but whose background and financial status kept one separate from that elite.[2]

Regardless of the era, the beer companies targeted the effendi in their sales strategy because they were the ideal consumer of their local product. On the one hand, for many of this group, alcohol served as the perfect commodity to perform modernity because its consumption achieved a double effect: while linking its Egyptian drinker to the "modern" European, who drank on social occasions, it separated him from both the nonelite and the religious Egyptian, who viewed alcohol as socially suspect at best or as religious anathema at worst. On the other hand, they did not have the financial wherewithal or the cultural prejudice of the Egyptian elite to strictly drink imported alcohol. Granted, the *effendiyya* were not a monolith. While there were those who found "modernity" at the bottom of a mug of beer, there were others who found it in total abstention from alcohol. For example, there were effendi teetotalers who were inspired by the indigenous tradition of temperance and by the international Christian temperance movement that entered Egypt in the 1880s in the form of the Woman's Christian Temperance Union.

But their calls for temperance did not present a serious challenge to the profitability or growth of the beer industry, or Stella, at the time. After 1933 Stella beer started to take off in Egypt. This ascendancy was the result of the continued growth of the effendi class that were consumers of the beer and the entry of one of the most successful brewers in the world, Heineken, into the Egyptian market. The Dutch brewers, who took control of Pyramid and bought a large number of Crown shares, did their best to take a rather successful brand in the 1920s and 1930s, Stella, and transform it into the beer of Egypt. As I have shown, they crafted a brand of beer that traded on its light golden color, its crisp taste, and its effervescence to make it synonymous with summertime refreshment. They also did their best to portray Stella as a drink of the young and the hip, an instant party starter and icebreaker. For a time, this characterization overrode any depiction of it as a harmful intoxicant.

Thus, when the Nasser regime cast its first look at the beer industry, they recognized the value of the product that Pyramid and Crown were selling. While the people selling the beer may have been obstacles to Egypt and its economy's progress, the beer was not. It had value to the regime as a drink that was both popular within Egypt and abroad. Unsurprisingly for a leader with an unquestioned effendi background, Nasser, an Egyptian beer was to be part of Egypt's push for economic independence and international respect. It was thus foolish speculation to imagine that Nasser would not nationalize the beer industry when he began his experiment in statism and transformed a large portion of the Egyptian economy from private to public.

The times of Nasser were good times for Stella. The social welfare policies that the Nasser government was instituting in the country—i.e., minimum wages, overtime bans to encourage new hires, and forced price cuts— all meant more disposable income for average workers to buy beer.[3] On a cultural level, Nasser's ascendance made the culture of the effendi the hegemonic cultural discourse in the country.[4] Both of these realities worked well with the fact that government ownership meant that the newly constituted al-Ahram Brewing Company had a monopoly on the market, with Stella making up the great majority of their sales. If Stella was not officially the beer of Egypt before nationalization, it was the de facto and de jure beer of Egypt afterward.

It would, for better or worse, maintain this status for more than thirty years. Fortunately for Egyptians, for the great majority of this time it was under the control of an executive who cared about delivering a quality product regardless of the difficulties that government ownership presented. Nevertheless, in those thirty years of government ownership, the Egypt surrounding Stella underwent massive cultural change. Most significantly for Stella, the Islamic Revival in Egypt created a public culture less likely to ignore Stella's intoxicating effects and thus condone its presence. It was no longer the effendi who were the dominant cultural force but the *Islami*. As a result, the antibeer rhetoric of the Egyptian Temperance Association and other Egyptian temperance advocates in the 1920s and 1930s found a new life in the 1980s. As they argued, and many more Egyptians came to believe, the benefits of beer, and Stella in particular, were far outweighed by the dangers of the alcohol contained within.

This new reality struck at Stella but did not push it from its perch as Egypt's beer. For example, Sakkara beer, the flagship offering of the upstart El-Gouna Brewery that debuted in 1999 as the first serious postnationalization challenger to Stella, was easily dispatched. Stella had a hundred-year head start, the support of the Egyptian government, and a newly empowered ownership, which enabled them to crush their only competition in roughly fifty years. A viable challenger has not appeared since.

And so it remains today. Stella is the king, but of a much smaller kingdom. Egyptian public culture remains hostile to its presence, and the company that sells it seems resigned to let it fade into the background as it focuses on its nonalcoholic ventures.

## An Economic History

On a purely financial level, Stella remains profitable to this day. In fact, the economic story of Stella is one of almost unimpeded success. Stella's story spans six Egyptian economic eras: the precolonial era (pre-1880); the colonial and semicolonial era (1880–1930), the economic nationalist era (1930–1960), the Arab socialist era (1960–1970), the era of Infitah (1970–1981), and the neoliberal era (1981–present). Across these eras, selling Stella in Egypt has consistently been a profitable venture. The real struggle for the companies or company who sold Stella was what it meant for an enterprise to be Egyptian.

The two companies that created Stella, the Crown and Pyramid Breweries, were founded when Cromer ruled Egypt and attempted to make the country attractive to foreign direct investment. At that time, nationality in the economy was viewed the same way Alexandrians at the turn of the century saw it: "Most Alexandrians paid little attention to foreignness, localness, or nationality, except on the rare occasions when they were called on to identify themselves in those terms."[5] The belief that Egyptians should run the Egyptian economy emerged between 1916 and 1922, with the establishment of the Sidqi Commission on Commerce and Industry, Bank Misr, and the Egyptian Federation of Industries. Bank Misr, which was founded and led by Egyptians, seemed to be the example par excellence of Egypt's new economic nationalism. However, these institutions were still tied intimately to non-Egyptian capital. In the 1920s, economic nationalism was a convenient way to support new ventures and garner public support for the multinational business groups that were forming around certain enterprising Egyptian individuals.[6] However, beginning in the 1930s and culminating with the Joint-Stock Company Law of 1947, the ideals of Egyptian economic nationalism became more of a reality.[7]

This legislation divided Pyramid and Crown, as well as the rest of the private sector, into four main identity groupings. The first group was those reasonably well-off foreigners who were secure both in Egypt and abroad. Next were those well-to-do or well-connected *mutamaṣṣirūn*, those "people of foreign origin who had become permanent residents" and in their language and habits had become "Egyptianized."[8] The third grouping included all those workers and laborers who the government classified as foreign. The final group contained those who did not have any foreign status.[9]

Although these divisions developed in the 1940s, they became much stronger under a Nasser-led government with legislation such as the 1955 modification of the Company Law of 1947. This legislation, which clearly favored the Muslim Egyptian, encouraged the removal of disadvantaged foreign workers through expulsion or transformation into Egyptians and altered the relationship between the well-off foreigners, like the Dutch technocrats who had been sent by Heineken to make sure the company ran "properly," and the Egyptian managers and executives. Emboldened by a government that supported the Muslim Egyptian over every other group, these managers and executives used their Egyptianness as a tool in their personal struggles for more control or more money with the Dutch representatives of Heineken. Thus, all business conflicts became struggles between the "foreign" and the "Egyptian."

These conflicts were settled only with the full nationalization of the private sector in 1963. Nationalization marked the full Egyptianization of the Crown and Pyramid Breweries. This "Egyptianization" went beyond ensuring that everyone who worked in the companies had an Egyptian passport. It entailed the excising of all "foreign" elements, many Coptic Christians included, and those Egyptians who, in the eyes of the government, had used their financial position to exploit the country. Tied to that, Egyptianizing also encompassed closing the power and wealth gap between the executive and the workers. Most important, it meant placing the entire industry under the control of the government. Ultimately, it had to do with the narrowing of the definition of Egyptian to exclude those elites who had money during the time before Nasser. When men like Farghali Pasha were no longer acceptable to the regime because of their exploitation of the people, men like Kettner and Wittert van Hoogland became doubly offensive as both foreigners and exploiters.

Between 1963 and 1997, there is simply no way to claim that the company that made Stella, al-Ahram Brewery—the conglomeration of Crown and Pyramid—was not Egyptian. It was owned by the Egyptian government, staffed only by those with Egyptian passports, and fully enmeshed in the Egyptian economy. It suffered and benefited from this reality. It was unable to import what it wanted and was generally hamstrung in its ability to make any change due to the red tape of Egyptian bureaucracy. It also saw an unprecedented period of stability and was the only show in town when it came to beer. Its only competitors, wine and liquor sellers, were also owned by the government. When these benefits were coupled with the powerful intellectual and technological legacy Heineken left behind, it made the period from 1963 to 1988 a profitable one of greater and greater Stella production.

Nevertheless, 1988 would be Stella's peak. After that point, external cultural and economic factors, Egypt's Islamic Revival, and the collapse of the Egyptian economy, as well as internal factors—loss of leadership and administrative and bureaucratic bloat—would start undercutting the sales of Stella and turn al-Ahram Brewing into a distressed asset. It is then that the Luxor Group stepped in. Interestingly, besides changing the fortunes of the company, they also brought back the ambiguity of al-Ahram's national identity.

Three members of their eight-member board were foreigners (Americans and a German), and the CEO, Ahmed Zayat, was an Egyptian American with a mysterious identity. In tandem with a new multinational board, the key technical positions were filled with Danish beer scientists associated with a foreign brewery. Not only was it a return to the transnational roots of the company, but it was also a return to its unquestioned profitability. The group even brought about the reentry of a foreign multinational. Heineken bought the company in 2002. They eventually replaced Zayat with a non-Egyptian, Marc Busain, in 2006, and though Busain has moved on, Heineken has kept a non-Egyptian in charge and maintained that reality to this day.

What does all of this mean for the nationality of al-Ahram Beverage Company? The same question could be asked of Anheuser-Busch, the quintessential American beer company, after it merged with InBev, which itself was a conglomeration of the Belgian Interbrew and Brazilian AmBev. The reality of beer making in the twenty-first century, like corporations in general, is that we have entered an era of transnational organizations that cannot be easily associated with a certain nationality.

Regardless, the story of Stella, and the companies that sold it, is the story of modern Egypt's economic evolution. Egypt's beer has been survivor and witness to a century of economic change in the country.

## A Technological History

The history of Stella in Egypt is also a history of the country's industrialization. As the technologies of beer allowed for greater transportability, the beer industry entered Egypt in the form of Crown Brewery in 1897. However, it would be too simplistic to attribute the arrival of the techniques and technologies for making modern beer to European entrepreneurs "enlightening" the Middle East. Although these Europeans had an integral role in bringing many of these technologies to Egypt, the beer industry succeeded only after it had adapted itself to the environment of Egypt.

The Europeans who tried to manufacture beer in Egypt had faith that "total-control brewing" would allow them to produce beer in Egypt. The Europeans assumed that through the assiduous application of the most current techniques and technologies, brewers could produce a standardized and durable product in a timely and cost-efficient manner. For the most part, they were right, but they also needed to adapt. It was simply not feasible to produce a beer in Egypt by importing all the materials and making no concessions to the environmental realities of the country. That is part of the reason that it took until World War I for the breweries to find a firm footing in Egypt. The breweries did eventually find a winning formula for the alcoholic beverage business in Egypt, using cutting-edge technological practices to exploit the local advantages of the Egyptian market: primarily cheap labor, plentiful water, a hot and dry climate, and a thirsty population who was eager for a refrigerated product. Stella beer was the product of this formula.

Although the Bomontis pioneered Stella and René Gaston-Dreyfus continued the tradition, it was Heineken who perfected it. Heineken was on the cutting edge of brewing techniques and technologies and did everything in its power to instill those principles in Egypt's breweries. Although the management on the ground was oftentimes imperious and adversarial, Heineken also worked to adapt as best it could to the workforce and the Egyptian market. One of the great innovations of Egyptian brewing—the adaptation of a strain of barley, beer's main ingredient, to the Egyptian climate—happened under the watch of a Heineken-trained brewmaster.

Heineken was so committed to producing the highest-quality beer that when Crown and Pyramid Breweries underwent the slow transformation from a completely private to a state-controlled enterprise, the Heineken representatives on the ground never forgot about the product. Private correspondence suggests that they may have disliked the working conditions and the fractiousness between the workers and the local members of the executive, but they never stopped caring about the beer they made until they were no longer welcome in Egypt. The Nasser-led government recognized that Heineken brought something special to the equation. When they negotiated with Heineken to hammer out the details of nationalization, the government fought hard to maintain the relationship with Heineken and hold on to their "secrets" for making great beer.

Because of the contentious political atmosphere, these hopes proved impossible. Nevertheless, the impact of Heineken would remain. The men who produced Stella beer in its most prosperous period, 1960–1990, all relied on the infrastructure and education the conglomerate had gifted Crown and Pyramid. In fact, part of the reason for Stella's swoon in the 1990s was the loss of any real connection to Heineken as those trained in their methods retired or left al-Ahram.

It is not coincidental that a significant part of Zayat's reshaping of al-Ahram was the reimportation of foreign brewing knowledge and technology. He recognized, as everyone who ran Crown and Pyramid did, that without the proper technological infrastructure, no beer company can survive in Egypt. That commitment to cutting-edge brewing is why the return of Heineken in 2002 can only be seen as a positive for the survival of Stella.

Stella remains the beer of Egypt and has few serious challengers to that claim. That title, however, means a great deal less now, with a stagnant market and no cultural presence. Birrell, the nonalcoholic descendant of Stella, with its growing sales and cultural footprint, has inherited some of the tradition of Stella. But as any beer drinker will tell you, nonalcoholic beer is just not the same.

Nevertheless, this book is not about Stella's uncertain future but about its magnificent past. By looking at Stella's story, we are able to grasp the fantastic social, economic, and technological change that has transpired in one hundred years of Egyptian history. In no uncertain terms, Stella's story is Egypt's story. Although he may have fallen short in his grand plans of making beer Egypt's national distraction, Isma'il Hafiz and all those who believed in Stella surely can savor this fact.

# NOTES

## Introduction

1 François Georgeon, "Ottomans and Drinkers: The Consumption of Alcohol in Istanbul in the Nineteenth Century," 18.

## Chapter 1: Grand Plans in Glass Bottles

1 P. J. Cain and A. G. Hopkins, *British Imperialism, 1688–2000*, 313.

2 Cynthia Myntti, *Paris along the Nile: Architecture in Cairo from the Belle Epoque*; Juan Cole, *Colonialism and Revolution in the Middle East: Social and Cultural Origins of Egypt's ʿUrabi Movement*.

3 David Landes, *Bankers and Pashas: International Finance and Economic Imperialism in Egypt*, 92–97.

4 Cole, *Colonialism and Revolution*.

5 E. R. J. Owen, "From Liberalism to Liberal Imperialism: Lord Cromer and the First Wave of Globalization in Egypt"; Robert Tignor, *Modernization and British Colonial Rule in Egypt, 1882–1914*, 59.

6 Owen, "From Liberalism to Liberal Imperialism, 101.

7 E. R. J. Owen, *Cotton and the Egyptian Economy, 1820–1914: A Study in Trade and Development*, 281.

8 Arthur E. Crouchley, *Investment of Foreign Capital in Egyptian Companies and Public Debt*, 117.

9 Mohammad A. Chaichian, "The Effects of World Capitalist Economy on Urbanization in Egypt, 1800–1970," 28.

10 On Barak, *On Time: Technology and Temporality in Modern Egypt*, 105, 298.

11 Ziad Fahmy, *Ordinary Egyptians: Creating the Modern Nation through Popular Culture*, 26–27.

12 Barak, *On Time*, 153–159. An example of this commitment to building infrastructure is that between the years 1880 and 1907, the amount of cargo transported on the Egyptian rail lines increased from 1.145 million to nearly 4.2 million tons (in Z. Fahmy, *Ordinary Egyptians*, 25).

13 R. G. Wilson and T. R. Gourvish, eds., *The Dynamics of the International Brewing Industry since 1800*, 4.

14 Syed Nomanul Haq, *Names, Natures, and Things: The Alchemist Jābir ibn Ḥayyān and His Kitāb al-Aḥjār*.

15 Louis Pasteur, "Memoir on the Alcoholic Fermentation," in *Milestones in Microbiology*, ed. and trans. Thomas D. Brock, 31–38; Ulf Lagerkvist, *The Enigma of Ferment: From the*

*Philosopher's Stone to the First Biochemical Nobel Prize*. See also Justis Liebig, "Concerning the Phenomena of Fermentation, Putrefaction, and Decay, and Their Causes," in *Milestones in Microbiology*, ed. and trans. Brock, 24–27; Anders Brinch Kissmeyer, "Emil Christen Hansen"; Louis Pasteur, "On the Organized Bodies Which Exist in the Atmosphere: Examination of the Doctrine of Spontaneous Generation," in *Milestones in Microbiology*, ed. and trans. Brock, 43–48.

16  Mikael Hård, *Machines Are Frozen Spirit: The Scientification of Refrigeration in the 19th Century, a Weberian Interpretation*, 181–192, 210–220.

17  Ibid., 6, 181–192.

18  Barak, *On Time*.

19  George Philliskirk, "Pasteurization."

20  Lucie Ryzova, "Egyptianizing Modernity through the 'New *Effendiyya*': Social and Cultural Constructions of the Middle Class in Egypt under the Monarchy," 127–128, 129.

21  Keith David Watenpaugh, *Being Modern in the Middle East: Revolution, Nationalism, Colonialism, and the Arab Middle Class*, 16.

22  Nancy Y. Reynolds, "Commodity Communities: Interweavings of Market Cultures, Consumption Practices, and Social Power in Egypt, 1907–1961," 16–28.

23  Ryzova, "Egyptianizing Modernity," 190n26.

24  Michael J. Reimer, "Colonial Bridgehead: Social and Spatial Change in Alexandria, 1850–1882," 533; Chaichian, "Effects of World Capitalist Economy," 26; Robert Ilbert, *Alexandrie, 1830–1930: Histoire d'une communauté citadine*, 2:758–759, cited in Nancy Y. Reynolds, *A City Consumed: Urban Commerce, the Cairo Fire, and the Politics of Decolonization in Egypt*, 24; Janet Abu-Lughod, *Cairo: 1001 Years of the City Victorious*, 119.

25  Reimer, "Colonial Bridgehead," 533; Chaichian, "Effects of World Capitalist Economy," 26.

26  Richard Pococke, *A Description of the East and Some Other Countries*, 1:182–183.

27  Chaichian, "Effects of World Capitalist Economy," 30.

28  Owen, *Cotton and the Egyptian Economy*, 237.

29  Mohammad A. Chaichian, *Town and Country in the Middle East: Iran and Egypt in the Transition to Globalization, 1800–1970*, 138.

30  Z. Fahmy, *Ordinary Egyptians*, 28, from Timothy Mitchell, *Rule of Experts: Egypt, Techno-politics, Modernity*, 60–62; Joel Beinin and Zachary Lockman, *Workers on the Nile: Nationalism, Communism, Islamism and the Egyptian Working Class, 1882–1954*, 12, 26.

31  Reynolds, *City Consumed*, 24–26.

32  Abu-Lughod, *Cairo*, 118–131; Ilbert, *Alexandrie*, 2:758–759, cited in Reynolds, *City Consumed*, 24.

33  Chaichian, "Effects of World Capitalist Economy," 32.

34  Z. Fahmy, *Ordinary Egyptians*, 28.

35  For a more in-depth look at these immigrants in Alexandria, see Will Hanley, *Identifying with Nationality: Europeans, Ottomans, and Egyptians in Alexandria*.

36  His Majesty's Agent and Consul General, *Report on the Finances, Administration, and Condition of Egypt and the Soudan, 1906*, 75.

37  2001-008151–2001-008159, "Wathaʾiq wa-Tasrihat bi-Fath Badʾ al-Hanat Rakhs Mahallat Khamur," DD, DWQ.

38  Alexander Kitroeff, *Greeks in Egypt, 1919–1937*, 73–124.

39  Relli Shechter, *Smoking, Culture and Economy in the Middle East: The Egyptian Tobacco Market, 1850–2000*, 32–34, 106–108.

40  His Majesty's Agent and Consul General, *Report on the Finances, Administration, and Condition of Egypt and the Soudan*, 1904, 54.

41  Gudrun Krämer, *The Jews in Modern Egypt, 1914–1952*, 88–89.

42  Maurice Mizrahi, "The Role of Jews in Economic Development," in *The Jews of Egypt: A Mediterranean Society in Modern Times*, ed. Simon Shamir, 87–88.

43  2001-008151–2001-008157, "Wathaʾiq wa-Tasrihat bi-Fath Badʾ al-Hanat," DWQ, DD.

44  Ibid.

45  Doris Behrens-Abouseif, *Azbakiyya and Its Environs: From Azbak to Ismail, 1476–1879*, 82.

46  Zachary Lockman, "Imagining the Working Class: Culture, Nationalism, and Class Formation in Egypt, 1899–1914," 164–168.

47  Muhammad ʿUmar, *Kitab Hadir al-Misriyyin aw Sirr Taʾakhkhurihim*, 61, 183–185, 250.

48  For discussion of this work, see Muhammad al-Muwaylihi, *Hadith ʿIsa ibn Hisham*, translated as *A Period of Time: A Study and Translation of Hadith ʿIsá ibn Hisham*, trans. Roger M. A. Allen, 72.

49  Ibid., 258, 307. For an in-depth discussion of ʿAtaba, see Reynolds, *City Consumed*, 31–36.

50  Allen, *Period of Time*, 316.

51  Ibid., 329.

52  Karin van Nieuwkerk, *"A Trade Like Any Other": Female Singers and Dancers in Egypt*, 182.

53  Wilson Chacko Jacob, *Working Out Egypt: Effendi Masculinity and Subject Formation in Colonial Modernity, 1870–1940*, 202.

54  Ibid.

55  See founding documents in 3019-005503-0009, Maslahat al-Sharikat, Department of Companies Archives, MS, DWQ.

56  Robert L. Tignor, "The Economic Activities of Foreigners in Egypt, 1920–1950: From Millet to Haute Bourgeoisie," 427.

57  Owen, *Cotton and the Egyptian Economy*, 6–7, 281.

58  Uri M. Kupferschmidt, *Henri Naus Bey: Retrieving the Biography of a Belgian Industrialist in Egypt*, 110.

59  Tignor, "Economic Activity of Foreigners," 428.

60  Henry de Saint-Omer, *Les enterprises Belges en Égypte: Rapport sur la situation économique des sociétés Belges et Belge-Égyptiennes fonctionnant en Égypte*, 153.

61  British Chamber of Commerce of Egypt, *List of Companies Established in Egypt*, 23, 27, 31, 40, 45, 50.

62  Athanasios G. Politis, *L'Hellénisme et l'Égypte moderne*, 360.

63  Stefano G. Poffandi, *Indicateur égyptien administratif et commercial* (1902), 236; Stefano G. Poffandi, *Indicateur égyptien administratif et commercial* (1904), 88.

64  Hård, *Machines Are Frozen Spirit*, 184.

65  Politis, *L'Hellénisme et l'Égypte moderne*, 362.

66  de Saint-Omer, *Les enterprises Belges en Égypte*, 112.

67  Ibid., 184, 362.

68  Charles W. Bamforth, "Top Fermentation."

69  Nick R. Jones, "Ale."

70  Hård, *Machines Are Frozen Spirit*, 184.

71  de Saint-Omer, *Les enterprises Belges en Égypte*, 153.

72  Ibid., 111.

73  Politis, *L'Hellénisme et l'Égypte moderne*, 360.

74  Owen, *Cotton and the Egyptian Economy*, 283–285.

75  Edouard Papasian, *L'Égypte economique et financiere*, 384.

76  "Rapport de Monsieur H. Faivre sur l'Egypte," June 4, 1935, typed, 14, 2.2.9.2.5-1053, AH, SAA.

77  Robert L. Tignor, *State, Private Enterprise, and Economic Change in Egypt, 1918-1952*, 41.

78  Politis, *L'Hellénisme et l'Égypte moderne*, 363.

79  Reynolds, *City Consumed*, 143; Hård, *Machines Are Frozen Spirit*, 200–201.

80  Chris Holliland, "Rice."

81  Politis, *L'Hellénisme et l'Égypte moderne*, 362.

### Chapter 2: A Star Rises

1  Tignor, *State, Private Enterprise, and Economic Change*, 49; G. H. Selous, *Report on Economic and Commercial Conditions in Egypt*, 94–95; M. G. P. A. Jacobs, W. H. G. Maas, and Mark Baker, *The Magic of Heineken*, 8.4.

2  8 League of Nations Treaty Series, "Convention Relating to Liquor Traffic in Africa and Protocol, Signed at Saint-Germain-En-Laye 1919," 1922, HeinOnline, proxy .library.upenn.edu:2445/HOL/Page?handle=hein.unl/lnts0008&div=3&collection= unl&set_as_cursor=7&men_tab=srchresults&terms=liquor&type=matchall#17, 17.

3  Justin Willis, *Potent Brews: A Social History of Alcohol in East Africa, 1850-1999*, 95–97.

4  8 League of Nations Treaty Series, "Convention Relating to Liquor Traffic in Africa," 17.

5  For a history of East African Brewing, see Willis, *Potent Brews*; for Nigeria, see Simon Heap, "Before 'Star': The Import Substitution of Western-Style Alcohol in Nigeria, 1870-1970."

6  Tignor, *State, Private Enterprise, and Economic Change*, 33.

7  The brewery was one of the first modern factories in Istanbul and became such a recognizable landmark that the neighborhood in which it was located, to this day, bears the name Bomonti.

8  Fredrick George Banbury, "Report from the Select Committee on Navy and Army Canteens Together with Minutes of Evidence and Appendices."

9  Papasian, *L'Égypte economique et financiere*, 384.

10  G. L. Mortera Firm, Brokers, *Handbook of Egyptian Securities*.

11 "Rapport de Monsieur H. Faivre sur l'Égypte," June 4, 1935, typed, 7, 2.2.9.2.5-1053, AH, SAA.

12 "Historical Background on the Activity of the René Gaston–Dreyfus Group in Egypt," typed and undated, 2.2.9.2.5-1080, AH, SAA.

13 Ibid.

14 Ibid.

15 "Rapport de Monsieur H. Faivre," 7, 116–120.

16 CB to Cobra, November 9, 1937, 4.1.2.4.2.2-1948, AH, SAA.

17 Shechter, *Smoking, Culture and Economy*, 99.

18 Robert L. Tignor, *Egyptian Textiles and British Capital, 1930–1956*, 13.

19 Ibid., 7, 90–91.

20 Ibid., 86.

21 Ibid., 86, 87.

22 Ibid., 50, 82.

23 Ibid., 5.

24 Relli Shechter, "Press Advertising in Egypt: Business Realities and Local Meaning, 1882–1956," 45–48, 49.

25 Edward Beatty, "Bottles for Beer: The Business of Technological Innovation in Mexico, 1800–1920," 322.

26 *al-Ahram*, August 10, 1928, 3.

27 Aristotle, *Aristotle's Meteorology in the Arabico-Latin Tradition: A Critical Edition of the Texts, with Introduction and Indices*.

28 Wladimir Köppen, *Die Klimate der Erde, Grundriss de Kilakunde*.

29 *al-Ahram*, July 15, 1938, 7.

30 *al-Ahram*, July 22, 1938, 4.

31 John Burnett, *Liquid Pleasures: A Social History of Drinks in Modern Britain*, 97, 98–99.

32 Nick R. Jones, "Counterpressure."

33 *al-Ahram*, July 29, 1938.

34 *al-Ahram*, July 15, 1938, 7.

35 "The vast inequalities of wealth in old-regime Egypt often led contemporaries to attribute consumption patterns to two primary but separate dynamics: a concern about price among the lower classes and a desire to emulate European cultural practices." See Nancy Y. Reynolds, "National Socks and the 'Nylon Woman': Materiality, Gender, and Nationalism in Textile Marketing in Semicolonial Egypt, 1930–56," 51.

36 Hanan Hammad, *Industrial Sexuality: Gender, Urbanization, and Social Transformation in Egypt*, 73–77.

37 Ryzova, "Egyptianizing Modernity," 127–128; Lockman, "Imagining the Working Class," 164–168; Jacob, *Working Out Egypt*.

38 "The crucial feature of effendi identity was not a desire to create a conceptual middle, but the desire to be upwardly mobile." Ryzova, "Egyptianizing Modernity," 133. See also Yoav Di-Capua, "The Professional Worldview of the Effendi Historian."

39 Eve Troutt Powell, *A Different Shade of Colonialism: Egypt, Great Britain, and the Mastery of the Sudan*.

40 *al-Ahram*, July 25, 1932, 11.

41 *al-Ahram*, February 16, 1931, 12.

42 *Al-Ahram*, February 23, 1931, 10.

43 Politis, *L'Hellénisme et l'Égypte moderne*, 363.

44 *al-Ahram*, February 16, 1931, 12.

45 *al-Ahram*, April 17, 1939, 4.

46 Shechter, "Press Advertising in Egypt," 56.

47 T. R. Gourvish and R. G. Wilson, *The British Brewing Industry*, 351.

48 Ibn Rushd, *The Distinguished Jurist's Primer*, 1:577.

49 Paulina B. Lewicka, *Food and Foodways of Medieval Cairenes: Aspects of Life in an Islamic Metropolis of the Eastern Mediterranean*, 500.

50 T. J. Jackson Lears, *Fables of Abundance: A Cultural History of Advertising in America*, 154–162 (quote 157–158).

51 Arthur Goldschmidt, *The Biographical Dictionary of Egypt*, 166–167.

52 ʿAbd Allah, ibn Muslim Ibn Qutayba, *Kitab al-Ashriba wa Dhakr Ikhtilaf al-Nas fiha*, 81.

53 Ahmad Ahmad Ghalwash, *Athar al-Khumur fi al-Hayya al-Ijtimaʿiyya*, 6.

54 Ibid., 15, 16.

55 Omar Foda, "Anna and Ahmad: Building Modern Temperance in Egypt (1884–1940)," 121, 149.

56 Ibid., 149.

57 Ibid., 140; James Jankowski, *Egypt's Young Rebels: "Young Egypt,"* 1933–1952, 38–41, 48.

58 Egyptian Temperance Association (ETA), \*4029-000365-Egyptian Temperance Association, "Taqrir al-Jam\iyya Marfuʿ ila al-Inzar al-Malakiyya al-Karima Yahya Mawlana al-Malak al-Muazzam al-Malak Ahmad Fuʾad al-Awil," Egyptian National Archives.

59 Foda, "Anna and Ahmad," 148.

60 "Rapport de Monsieur H. Faivre," 24, 25.

61 *al-Ahram*, August 31, 1928, 4.

62 "Rapport de Monsieur H. Faivre," 82.

63 Ibid., 23, 45.

64 Ibid., 5, 6.

65 Ibid., 52, 86–87, 89.

66 Selous, *Report on Economic and Commercial Conditions*, 42.

67 "Rapport de Monsieur H. Faivre," 94.

68 Ibid., 5.

69 Ibid., 5, 35.

70 Ibid., 10.

71 Ibid., 10, 11.

72 Ibid., 12, 15.

73 Ibid., 10, 12.

74 Ibid., 12.

75 Ibid.

76 Ibid., 39, 45.

77 Ibid., 40.

78 Ibid.

79 Ibid., 41.

80 Ibid., 11, 41, 48.

81 Ibid., 54.

82 Ibid., 3.

83 Joel Beinin, *The Dispersion of Egyptian Jewry: Culture, Politics, and the Formation of a Modern Diaspora*, 18–22.

84 Pierre Geisenberger, "Situation economique de l'Égypte au debut 1936," typed, produced in Alexandria 1938, 2.2.9.2.5-1053, AH, SAA.

85 Ibid., 48.

86 "Rapport de Monsieur H. Faivre," 82.

87 Ibid.

88 Tignor, *State, Private Enterprise, and Economic Change*, table A.10.

89 Ibid.

## Chapter 3: Crowning the Pyramid

1 Nieuwkerk, *"Trade Like Any Other,"* 43–45.

2 These actions reflected Heineken's attempt to transform these companies, in the words of Robert L. Tignor, from being loosely administered firms to tightly controlled firms. See Tignor, *Egyptian Textiles and British Capital*, 82–106.

3 Roy Armes, *African Filmmaking: North and South of the Sahara*, 22.

4 Jacques Aumont, "Lumière Revisited"; Georges Sadoul, *Louis Lumière, 1904–1967*.

5 Viola Shafik, *Popular Egyptian Cinema: Gender, Class, and Nation*, 18–19.

6 Ibid.

7 Walter Armbrust, "The Golden Age before the Golden Age," in *Mass Mediations*, ed. Armbrust (Berkeley: University of California Press, 2000), 312, cited in Reynolds, *City Consumed*, 147.

8 "Rapport du Conseil d'Administration," 4.1.2.4.2.2-1949, AH, SAA.

9 Ryzova, "Egyptianizing Modernity," 131, 133.

10 Ibid., 260.

11 Shechter, *Smoking, Culture and Economy*, 119–120.

12 Marilyn Booth, *Bayram al-Tunisi's Egypt: Social Criticism and Narrative Strategies*, 10, 178.

13 Ryzova, "Egyptianizing Modernity," 133.

14 Introduction, AH, SAA, stadsarchief.amsterdam.nl/archieven/archiefbank/overzicht/834.nl.html.

15 Jacobs, Maas, and Baker, *The Magic of Heineken*, 8.4.

16 Cobra to CB, October 28, 1937, 4.1.2.4.2.2-1948, AH, SAA.

17 HBM, annual report, Gevestigd Te Amsterdam Verslag Over Het BoekJaar 1936-7, 8, 15–26, stadsarchief.amsterdam.nl/archieven/archiefbank/overzicht/834.nl.html.

18  Ibid.

19  Société de Bière "Les Pyramides," "Summary of the Services Rendered by Heineken's Breweries Netherlands to Pyramids Brewery of Cairo," November 4, 1961, 4.1.2.4.2.6-1977, AH, SAA.

20  Ibid.

21  Ibid.

22  Ibid.

23  Cobra to CB titled "Fûts en fer Étamé," May 24, 1938, 4.1.2.4.2.2-1948, AH, SAA.

24  Ibid.

25  CB to HBM, June 8, 1938, 4.1.2.4.2.2-1948, AH, SAA.

26  Banque de La Société de Belgique to HBM, June 2, 1939, 4.1.2.4.2.2-1948, AH, SAA.

27  Cobra to the director of HBM, April 22, 1940, 4.1.2.4.2.2-1948, AH, SAA.

28  OTOC to CB, March 23, 1946, 4.1.2.4.2.2-1948, AH, SAA.

29  OTOC to the director of the CB, June 27, 1948, 4.1.2.4.2.2-1949, AH, SAA.

30  OTOC to CB, March 23, 1946.

31  OTOC to the director of the CB, June 27, 1948.

32  Ibid.

33  Cobra to H. J. G. Ivens, April 16, 1947, 4.1.2.4.2.2-1949, AH, SAA.

34  The placement of someone on the board was an attempt to transform Cobra's beer venture from a loosely controlled venture into a tightly controlled venture. In loosely controlled firms, "foreign investors had considerable foreign managerial and technical involvement," but were unable to translate this involvement into domination. Tightly controlled firms, on the other hand, were carefully linked to European corporate and individual investors and oftentimes served as subsidiaries and branches of the firms. Before World War II, Crown and Pyramid were undeniably loosely controlled, as the managers and executives on the ground in Egypt exerted the most influence. However, seeing the difficulties that Heineken experienced during the war, Cobra tried to change that practice. See Tignor, *Egyptian Textiles and British Capital*, 82–106.

35  Ivens to HBM, May 12, 1947, 4.1.2.4.2.2-1949, AH, SAA.

36  This point becomes even clearer when we consider the reaction of one H. G. Ivens, an employee of Pyramid who was representing Cobra at this Crown shareholder meeting. Ivens, reporting that Crown's president, Spiro Spiridis, had, in 1947, requested representation on the Pyramid board in exchange for Cobra representation (and for a second time no less), called the request "absurd."

37  "Procés-verbal de la réunion du Conseil d'Administration de la Société Anonyme des Bières Bomonti et Pyramides tenue à Alexandrie le 21 Mars 1952," 4.1.2.4.2.2-1949, AH, SAA.

38  "A Letter from the Board to Stockholders," May 6, 1957, 3019-5504-0009, *Sharikat Birat al-Ahram*, MS, DWQ.

39  WvH to P. R. Feith at HBM, May 2, 1952, 4.1.2.4.2.2-1949, AH, SAA.

40  Constantin Qasdagli to Monsieur Administrateur-Delegue of PB, February 28, 1953, 4.1.2.4.2.2-1950, AH, SAA.

41 Cobra, "Declaration of Proxy," April 20, 1953, 4.1.2.4.2.2-1950, AH, SAA.

42 Wittert van Hoogland would leave Pyramid Brewery to become the head of Heineken's international holding company, Cobra, in 1957.

43 WvH to Feith at HBM, May 2, 1952.

44 The advantages of those with foreign citizenship clearly grew out of the history of the Capitulations, which gave foreign residents extraterritorial rights in Egypt. The Capitulations had a massive effect on the legal history of the country. See Nathan J. Brown, "The Precarious Life and Slow Death of the Mixed Courts in Egypt."

45 Ibid.

46 Ibid., 33.

47 Reynolds, City Consumed, 151.

48 Robert Vitalis, When Capitalists Collide: Business Conflict and the End of Empire in Egypt, 49.

49 Brown, "Precarious Life and Slow Death," 45–46.

50 Tignor, State, Private Enterprise, and Economic Change, 184.

51 Vitalis, When Capitalists Collide, 19; Eric Davis, Challenging Colonialism, 195.

52 Tignor, State, Private Enterprise, and Economic Change, 220.

53 E. J. Blattner, ed., Who's Who in Egypt and the Middle East, 219.

54 "Kashf bi-aʿdaʾ Idarat al-Sharikat Birat al-Ahram fi 1956," 3019-5504, DWQ, MS.

55 "Kashf bi-aʿdaʾ Idarat al-Sharikat Karwon Brewery Tabiqan li-l-Madat 23 min al-Qanun Raqm 26 fi 1954," 3019-6808, MS, DWQ.

56 Tignor, "Economic Activities of Foreigners in Egypt," 434.

57 Kitroeff, Greeks in Egypt.

58 Beinin and Lockman, Workers on the Nile, 9.

59 Krämer, Jews in Modern Egypt, 31.

60 Tignor, "Economic Activities of Foreigners in Egypt," 427.

61 Beinin, Dispersion of Egyptian Jewry, 18–22.

62 Simon Shamir, "Nationality of the Jews in the Monarchy Period," in Jews of Egypt, ed. Shamir, 48–51, 52–59.

63 "Iqrar Hanna Yusuf Hanna," 3019-006808-0009, MS, DWQ.

## Chapter 4: Stella Is Always Delicious

1 Reynolds, City Consumed, 189.

2 Ibid., 185–189.

3 Robert L. Tignor, Capitalism and Nationalism at the End of Empire: State and Business in Decolonizing Egypt, Nigeria, and Kenya, 1945–1963, 63.

4 WvH to Cobra, May 7, 1954, 4.1.2.4.2.2-1950, AH, SAA.

5 "Extension of Stay for Mr. Ulenberg." PB to the Depart of Companies (l'Administration des Sociétés), 4.1.2.4.2.6, 1978, AH, SAA.

6 Keith Thomas, "Two-Row Malt"; Kevin Smith, "Six-Rowed Malt."

7 WvH to T. B. Bunting, April 22, 1958, 4.1.2.4.2.6, 1979, AH, SAA.

8 Ibid.

9  "Introduction Bouteilles Standard," Memo Société de Bière "Les Pyramides," 4.1.2. 4.2.6, 1978, AH, SAA.

10 Adel P. den Hartog, "Food Labeling and Packaging in the Dutch Food Industry: Persuading and Informing Consumers, 1870–1950s."

11 EK to WvH, April 10, 1957, 4.1.2.4.2.6-1978, AH, SAA. For more information on the power of J. Walter Thompson advertising, see Denise H. Sutton, *Globalizing Ideal Beauty: How Female Copyrighters of the J. Walter Thompson Advertising Agency Redefined Beauty for the Twentieth Century.*

12 Nicholas Mamatis to Direction Générale de la Amstel, 2.2.10.3-1187, AH, SAA.

13 WvH to EK, July 1, 1957, 4.1.2.4.2.6-1978, AH, SAA.

14 For example, see *al-Ahram,* July 15, 1938, 7; July 25, 1932, 11; and April 17, 1939, 4.

15 Lears, *Fables of Abundance,* 154–162.

16 *Akhir al-Saʿa,* May 8, 1957, 5.

17 *Akhir al-Saʿa,* May 15, 1957, 11.

18 *Akhir al-Saʿa,* September 25, 1957, 27.

19 *Akhir al-Saʿa,* November 20, 1957, 13.

20 *Akhir al-Saʿa,* May 29, 1957, 13.

21 *Akhir al-Saʿa,* May 29, 1958, 21.

22 *Akhir al-Saʿa,* June 18, 1958, 21.

23 For discussion of the extended Egyptianization saga, see HBM to PB, November 30, 1953, 4.1.2.4.2.2-1950, AH, SAA; WvH to HBM, July 14, 1955, 4.1.2.4.2.2-1950, AH, SAA; Cobra to CB, September 30, 1955, 4.1.2.4.2.2-1950, AH, SAA; CB to Cobra, October 13, 1955, 4.1.2.4.2.2-1950, AH, SAA; CB to PB, June 7, 1956, 4.1.2.4.2.2-1950, AH, SAA; and Cobra to PB titled "Votre ref.15234 du 7 crt," June 12, 1956, 4.1.2.4.2.2-1950, AH, SAA.

24 Leonard Binder, "Gamal ʿAbd al-Nasser: Iconology, Ideology, and Demonology," 46; Tignor, *Capitalism and Nationalism,* 83; Goldschmidt, *Biographical Dictionary of Egypt,* 150; Tignor, *Capitalism and Nationalism,* 84–85.

25 Tignor, *Capitalism and Nationalism,* 97.

26 Ibid., 123, 127, 133, 144, 166.

27 EK to WvH, December 4, 1959, 4.1.2.4.2.6, 1977, AH, SAA.

28 Tignor, *State, Private Enterprise, and Economic Change,* 184.

29 Tignor, *Capitalism and Nationalism,* 91.

30 Ibid.

31 Beinin, *Dispersion of Egyptian Jewry,* 18–22.

32 "Taqrir Taftish," 3019-5504, MS, DWQ; Reynolds, "Commodity Communities," 205; Floresca Karanasou, "Egyptianization, the 1947 Company Law and the Foreign Communities in Egypt," 118–121.

33 Jack Crabbs Jr., "Politics, History, and Culture in Nasser's Egypt."

34 Louis Awad, "Cultural and Intellectual Developments."

35 William Cleveland, *A History of the Modern Middle East,* 319, 321; Laura Bier, *Revolutionary Womenhood: Feminisms, Modernity, and the State in Nasser's Egypt.*

36 EK to WvH, July 9, 1957, 4.1.2.4.2.6-1978, AH, SAA.

37 Donald M. Reid, "Nationalizing the Pharaonic Past: Egyptology, Imperialism, and Egyptian Nationalism, 1922–1952," 141.

38 "A MM. Les actionnaires de la Société de la Bière 'Les Pyramides,' S.A.E. bureaux réunis à la réunion de la Société de Gizeh, Le 6 mai 1957," 3019-5504-0009, Sharikat Birat al-Ahram.

39 EK to WvH, July 18, 1957, 4.1.2.4.2.6-1978, AH, SAA.

40 "Some notes on WvH's visit Egypt, January 15 to February 11, 1957," 4.1.2.4.2.6-1977, AH, SAA.

41 WvH to EK, July 1, 1957, 4.1.2.4.2.6-1978, AH, SAA.

42 "Maandrapport no. 6; uw D-1064," September 18, 1957, 4.1.2.4.2.6-1978, AH, SAA.

43 "Hand Drawn Organizational Flow Chart", 4.1.2.4.2.6-1977, AH, SAA.

44 "Extension of Stay for Mr. Ulenberg." PB to the Department of Companies (l'Administration des Sociétés), 4.1.2.4.2.6-1978, SAA.

45 "Hand Drawn Organizational Flow Chart."

46 "Maandrapport no. 6; uw D-1064."

47 EK to WvH, July 9, 1957, 4.1.2.4.2.6-1978, AH, SAA.

48 EK to WvH, September 24, 1957, 4.1.2.4.2.6-1978, AH, SAA.

49 "Some Personal Impressions about the Société de Bière 'Les Pyramides' SAE, for Wittert," 8-4-1959, 4.1.2.4.2.6-1977, AH, SAA.

50 EK to WvH, July 9, 1957.

51 "Some Personal Impressions."

52 WvH to EK, July 17, 1957, 4.1.2.4.2.6-1978, AH, SAA.

53 WvH to EK, December 22, 1958, 4.1.2.4.2.6-1978, AH, SAA.

54 WvH to EK, July 17, 1957.

55 EK to WvH, December 13, 1958, 4.1.2.4.2.6-1978, AH, SAA.

56 EK to WvH, December 12, 1958, 4.1.2.4.2.6-1978, AH, SAA.

57 EK to WvH, September 29, 1958, 4.1.2.4.2.6-1978, AH, SAA.

58 EK to WvH, September 24, 1957, 4.1.2.4.2.6-1978, AH, SAA.

59 "Some Personal Impressions."

60 Jonkheer Pieter Feith, "Reisrapport," November–December 1949, 9, 2.2.9.2.7-1098, AH, SAA.

61 Elie Podeh and Onn Winckler, *Rethinking Nasserism: Revolution and Historical Memory in Modern Egypt*, 19–20.

62 Beinin, *Workers on the Nile*, 432.

63 Ibid., 433.

64 M. Riad El-Ghonemy, "An Assessment of Egypt's Development Strategy, 1952–1970," 255.

65 Podeh and Winckler, *Rethinking Nasserism*, 10.

66 EK to WvH, September 24, 1957, 4.1.2.4.2.6-1978, AH, SAA.

67 "Maandrapport no. 6; uw D-1064."

68 EK to WvH, October 11, 1957, 4.1.2.4.2.6-1978, AH, SAA.

69 "Maandrapport no. 6; uw D-1064."

70 EK to WvH, September 24, 1957; EK to WvH, October 11, 1957.

71 "Maandrapport no. 6; uw D-1064."

72 EK to WvH, December 31, 1957, 4.1.2.4.2.6-1978, AH, SAA.

73 Ibid.

74 In Kettner's eyes, the successful move against Eigenheer marked open season on one of the only remaining foreign workers, the head brewmaster, Gerardus Hubertus Ulenberg. EK to WvH, September 24, 1957.

75 Syndicat des Employés et Ouvriers de la Société de Bière "Les Pyramides" to EK, October 14, 1957, 4.1.2.4.2.6-1978, AH, SAA.

76 Ibid.

77 Ibid.

78 Ibid.

79 EK to WvH, December 31, 1957.

80 EK to WvH, September 24, 1957.

81 Robert Vitalis, *America's Kingdom: Mythmaking on the Saudi Oil Frontier*.

**Chapter 5: A Pan-Arab Brew**

1 Trevor Le Gassick, "Ihsan abd el-Qoddous," in *I Am Free, and Other Stories*, by Ihsan 'Abd al-Qaddus, 9.

2 Joel Gordon, *Revolutionary Melodrama: Popular Film and Civic Identity in Nasser's Egypt*, 134.

3 Ibid., 135.

4 Ihsan 'Abd al-Qaddus, *Al-Banat al-Sayf*, 97.

5 Gordon, *Revolutionary Melodrama*, 135.

6 'Abd al-Qaddus, *Al-Banat wa al-Sayf*, 149, 184.

7 Ibid., 12.

8 Ibid., 13, 20.

9 Gordon, *Revolutionary Melodrama*, 134.

10 "Report on the Actual Situation and Machinery Needed Urgently for the Production of Good Beer," 2.2.9.2.5-1086, AH, SAA.

11 Ibid.

12 John Waterbury, *The Egypt of Nasser and Sadat: The Political Economy of Two Regimes*, 42.

13 Relli Shechter, "The Cultural Economy of Development in Egypt: Economic Nationalism, Hidden Economy and the Emergence of Mass Consumer Society during Sadat's Infitah," 574.

14 "The Ten Commandments," typed, December 3, 1959, 4.1.2.4.2.6-1978, AH, SAA.

15 EK to WvH, December 4, 1959, 4.1.2.4.2.6-1978, AH, SAA.

16 "Report on the Crown Brewery at Alexandria Made during the Visit of Messrs. van Leeuwen and Ulenberg 8–13th March 1964," 6, 2.2.9.2.5-1086, AH, SAA.

17 EK to WvH, December 4, 1959.

18 Ibid.

19 EK to WvH (not written), July 9, 1957, 4.1.2.4.2.6-1978, AH, SAA.

20 EK to WvH, December 4, 1959.

21 Société de Bière "Les Pyramides," "Summary of the Services Rendered by Heineken's Breweries Netherlands to Pyramids Brewery of Cairo," November 4, 1961, 4.1.2.4.2.6-1978, AH, SAA.

22 Conrad Seidl and Horst Dornbusch, "Märzenbier."

23  "Minutes, Talks in Cairo, January 28–February 3, 1959."

24  WvH to EK, December 15, 1958, 4.1.2.4.2.6-1978, AH, SAA.

25  "Minutes, Talks in Cairo, January 28–February 3, 1959."

26  WvH to EK, December 15, 1958.

27  "Minutes, Talks in Cairo, January 28–February 3, 1959."

28  Ibid.

29  Ervand Abrahamian, "Khomeini: Fundamentalist or Populist?," *New Left Review*, no. 186 (1991), cited in Podeh and Winckler, *Rethinking Nasserism*, 7.

30  Podeh and Winckler, *Rethinking Nasserism*, 15, 14; Lucie Ryzova, *The Age of the Efendiyya: Passages to Modernity in National-Colonial Egypt*.

31  Elie Podeh, *The Decline of Arab Unity: The Rise and Fall of the United Arab Republic*, 68.

32  Ibid., 82.

33  "Rapport de Monsieur H. Faivre sur l'Égypte," June 4, 1935, typed, 7, 2.2.9.2.5-1053, AH, SAA.

34  "Rapport sur la politique d'Exportation soumis au Conseil d'Administration en sa réunion du Samedi 26 Novembre 1960 (crossed and replaced with 17 Decembre 1960)," 4.1.2.4.2.6-1977, AH, SAA.

35  WvH to T. B. Bunting, August 20, 1962, 4.1.2.4.2.6-1979, AH, SAA.

36  Troutt Powell, *Different Shade of Colonialism*.

37  WvH to Bunting, April 22, 1958, 4.1.2.4.2.6-1979, AH, SAA.

38  WvH to Bunting, January 14, 1959, 4.1.2.4.2.6-1979, AH, SAA.

39  WvH to EK, April 17, 1957, 4.1.2.4.2.6-1978, AH, SAA; Troutt Powell, *Different Shade of Colonialism*, 80.

40  WvH to EK, April 17, 1957; Prorogation Sejour M. Ulenberg Doss. No. 185-182/89/I, July 3, 1957, 4.1.2.4.2.6-1978, AH, SAA.

41  "Notulen besprekingen in Cairo," January 28–February 3, 1959, 4.1.2.4.2.6-1977, AH, SAA.

42  Ibid.

43  "Rapport sur la politique d'Exportation."

44  EK (administrateur-délégué) representing Société de Bière "Les Pyramides" to Spiro Spiridis (administrateur-délégué), February 19, 1957, 4.1.2.4.2.6-1978, AH, SAA; "Rapport sur la politique d'Exportation."

45  EK to WvH, December 4, 1959, 4.1.2.4.2.6-1978, AH, SAA.

46  EK to WvH, December 26, 1959, 4.1.2.4.2.6-1978, AH, SAA.

47  EK to WvH, December 4, 1959.

48  EK to WvH, September 29, 1958, 4.1.2.4.2.6-1978, AH, SAA.

49  Ibid.

50  Michel Mavroviti to EK, December 15, 1959, 4.1.2.4.2.6-1978, AH, SAA.

51  EK to WvH, December 4, 1959.

52  EK to WvH, December 26, 1959.

53  Unsigned and undated letter to EK, 4.1.2.4.2.6-1978, AH, SAA.

54  "Rapport sur la politique d'Exportation."

55  From Erick C. Kettner (administrateur-délégué) representing Société de Bière "Les Pyramides" to Spiridis, February 19, 1957.

56 "Rapport sur la politique d'Exportation."

57 Ibid.

58 EK to Spiridis, February 19, 1957.

59 Spiridis to EK, February 23, 1957, 4.1.2.4.2.6-1978, AH, SAA.

60 "Minutes of the meeting on Société de Bière 'Les Pyramides,' held in Amsterdam on August 18, 1959," 4.1.2.4.2.6-1977, AH, SAA.

61 EK to WvH, June 18, 1961, 4.1.2.4.2.6-1978, AH, SAA.

62 EK to WvH, December 29, 1960, 4.1.2.4.2.6-1978, AH, SAA.

63 Confidential letter from WvH to EK, May 19, 1961, 4.1.2.4.2.6-1978, AH, SAA.

64 EK to WvH, June 18, 1961.

65 "Private" letter from WvH to EK, April 7, 1961, 4.1.2.4.2.6-1978, AH, SAA.

66 "Rapport sur la visite de M. Le Président de la République Gamal Abdel Nasser au stand 'Stella' à la Foire de la Production Industrielle et Agricole, lors de son inauguration," January 3, 1960, 4.1.2.4.2.6-1978, AH, SAA.

67 Ibid.

68 Ibid.

69 Christopher Bird, "Lightstruck."

70 Horst Dornbusch and Garrett Oliver, "Bottles."

71 "Rapport sur la visite de M. Le Président."

72 Ibid.

73 Tignor, Capitalism and Nationalism, 179, 183.

74 "Rapport sur la visite de M. Le Président."

### Chapter 6: Getting the Dutch Out

1 Beinin and Lockman, Workers on the Nile, 9.

2 EK to WvH, May 29, 1960, 4.1.2.4.2.6-1978, AH, SAA.

3 Podeh and Winckler, introduction to Rethinking Nasserism, 19.

4 Ibid.

5 EK to WvH, December 29, 1960, 4.1.2.4.2.6-1978, AH, SAA.

6 Ibid.

7 Tignor, Capitalism and Nationalism, 165.

8 Waterbury, Egypt of Nasser and Sadat, 85.

9 Podeh, Decline of Arab Unity, 142.

10 Malak Zaalouk, Power, Class and Foreign Capital in Egypt: The Rise of the New Bourgeoisie, 33, 35. For a discussion of the term comprador, see Robert Vitalis, "On the Theory and Practice of Compradors: The Role of 'Abbud Pasha in the Egyptian Political Economy."

11 Vitalis, "Theory and Practice of Compradors," 291.

12 Vitalis, When Capitalists Collide.

13 Podeh, Decline of Arab Unity, 142.

14 Tignor, Capitalism and Nationalism, 165.

15 El-Ghonemy, "Assessment of Egypt's Development Strategy," 259.

16 "Telegram to HBM Amsterdam," 4.1.2.4.2.6, AH, SAA; Robert Mabro and Samir Radwan, *The Industrialization of Egypt, 1939–1973: Policy and Performance*, 135.

17 EK to WvH, July 29, 1961, 4.1.2.4.2.6-1978, AH, SAA.

18 EK to WvH, July 27, 1961, 4.1.2.4.2.6-1978, AH, SAA.

19 EK to WvH, August 3, 1961, 4.1.2.4.2.6-1978, AH, SAA.

20 EK to WvH, August 14, 1961, 4.1.2.4.2.6-1978, AH, SAA.

21 Ibid.

22 EK to WvH (Directie Heineken's Bierbrouwerij), September 1, 1961, 4.1.2.4.2.6-1978, AH, SAA.

23 Ibid.

24 EK to WvH, Directie HBM N.V., August 26, 1961, 4.1.2.4.2.6-1978, AH, SAA.

25 EK to WvH, August 14 1961.

26 EK to WvH, September 1, 1961.

27 "List of Shareholders in Pyramid and Crown Brewery Dated 1964," 3019-5506-0009, MS, DWQ.

28 Podeh, *Decline of Arab Unity*, 158.

29 EK to WvH, December 29, 1960, 4.1.2.4.2.6-1978, AH, SAA.

30 Tignor, *Capitalism and Nationalism*, 165.

31 EK to WvH, January 8, 1962, 1978, 4.1.2.4.2.6, AH, SAA; Yoav Di-Capua, "Sports, Society, and Revolution: Egypt in the Early Nasserite Period."

32 EK to WvH, January 30, 1962, 4.1.2.4.2.6-1978, AH, SAA.

33 This information comes from conversations with members of Ismail Omar Foda's family, including Hussein Foda (his son) and Joyce Foda (his wife), as well as from private papers in the family's possession.

34 EK to WvH, October 22–23, 1961, 4.1.2.4.2.6-1978, AH, SAA.

35 Ibid.

36 Ibid.

37 EK to WvH, November 24, 1961, 4.1.2.4.2.6-1978, AH, SAA.

38 EK to WvH, October 22–23, November 24, 1961.

39 EK to WvH, July 27, 1961, 4.1.2.4.2.6-1978, AH, SAA.

40 EK to Cobra, November 30, 1961, 2.2.10.3-1187, AH, SAA.

41 EK to WvH, November 24, 1961.

42 Ivan Sipkov, "Postwar Nationalizations and Alien Property in Bulgaria."

43 EK to WvH, November 24, 1961.

44 For discussion, see Angelo Dalanachis, *The Greek Exodus from Egypt: Diaspora Politics and Emigration, 1937–1962*.

45 Ibid., 204; EK to WvH, February 22, 1962, 4.1.2.4.2.6-1978, AH, SAA; "Egyptians Trying 15 as Spies," *New York Times*, July 16, 1962; "Cairo Arrests of 'French Spy Case Accomplices,'" *Times* (London), November 28, 1961, 9.

46 EK to WvH, February 22, 1962, 4.1.2.4.2.6-1978, AH, SAA.

47 EK to WvH, December 20, 1961, 4.1.2.4.2.6-1978, AH, SAA.

48 Waterbury, *Egypt of Nasser and Sadat*, 72, 79.

49 Ibid., 80.

50  Egyptian Minister of Trade, *Thawrat Misr al-sinaʿiyyah fi ʿishrin ʿam 1952–1972*, 30.

51  EK to WvH, April 26, 1962, 4.1.2.4.2.6-1978, AH, SAA.

52  "Signature d'un contrat pour l'exportation de la bière en Roumanie pour la valeur d'un million dollars," *Progres Egyptien*, January 31, 1968, 2.2.10.3-1187, AH, SAA.

53  EK to WvH, October 23, 1961, 4.1.2.4.2.6-1978, AH, SAA.

54  PB to al-Duktur Naʾib Raʾis al-Wuzaraʾli-l-Shuʾun al-Maliyya wa-l-Iqtisadiyya, 3019-0008, MS, DWQ.

55  WvH to EK, December 29, 1961, 4.1.2.4.2.6-1978, 834-AH, SAA.

56  EK to WvH, January 8, 1962, 4.1.2.4.2.6-1978, AH, SAA.

57  EK to Gerardus Hubertus Ulenberg, February 14, 1962, 4.1.2.4.2.6-1978, AH, SAA.

58  EK to WvH, April 26, 1962.

59  EK to WvH, May 10, 1962, 4.1.2.4.2.6-1978, AH, SAA.

60  Dr. L. Bels, Ir. E.h van Leeuwen, G. Ulenberg, "Visit to the Guinea Brewery at LAE (Australian New Guinea) 24th–26th April 1964," 2.2.9.2.7-1121, AH, SAA.

61  Albert Tager and Raymond Shumek to the General Director of the Department of Companies, 3019-5505, MS, DWQ; "Kairo wil economische samenwerking met Nederland uitbreiden," July 4, 1972, *NRC HandelsBlad*, 2.2.10.3-1187, AH, SAA.

62  HBM to Mr. D. J. Fontein (International Monetary Fund), April 26, 1967, 2.2.10.3-1187, AH, SAA.

63  Half of the sum was paid in exports to the Netherlands, and the remaining half was transferred between the central banks of each country. Royal Netherlands Embassy to Zakaria Tewfik, January 27, 1970, 2.2.10.3-1187, AH, SAA; "Heineken Interests in Egypt," February 24, 1975, 1187, 2.2.10.3, Afrika, AH, SAA.

64  Gordon, *Revolutionary Melodrama*, 146.

65  Deborah A. Starr, "Drinking, Gambling, and Making Merry: Waguih Ghali's Search for Cosmopolitan Agency," 271.

66  Waguih Ghali, *Beer in the Snooker Club*, 17.

67  Starr, "Drinking, Gambling, and Making Merry," 276.

68  Ghali, *Beer in the Snooker Club*, 55, 131, 141.

69  Starr, "Drinking, Gambling, and Making Merry," 271.

70  Gordon, *Revolutionary Melodrama*, 124.

## Chapter 7: Opening Up Stella

1  H. A. Meijer to E. J. de Vries, February 5, 1974, 2.2.10.3-1187, AH, SAA.

2  Waterbury, *Egypt of Nasser and Sadat*, 100.

3  Ibid., 129–130, 131.

4  Khalid Ikram, *The Egyptian Economy, 1952–2000: Performance, Policies, and Issues*, 22.

5  Ibid., 48.

6  Waterbury, *Egypt of Nasser and Sadat*, 171–187.

7  Ikram, *Egyptian Economy*, 50–53.

8  Joel Beinin, *Workers and Thieves: Labor Movements and Popular Uprisings in Tunisia and Egypt*, 40–41.

9  Ikram, *Egyptian Economy*, 48.

10  EK to WvH, November 21, 1961, 4.1.2.4.2.6-1978, AH, SAA; Mabro and Radwan, *Industrialization of Egypt*, 135–137.

11  EK to WvH, November 21, 1961.

12  EK to WvH, January 30, 1962, 4.1.2.4.2.6-1978, AH, SAA.

13  Mabro and Radwan, *Industrialization of Egypt*, 137.

14  Sharikat Birat al-Ahram, Farac al-Iskanderiyya, Mahdar Ijtimaʾ Lajnat Shuʾun al-Afrad bi-Masnac al-Iskanderiyya raqam 144, undated, IOF.

15  Joseph Treaster, "Inverting the Pyramid in Egypt: A Beer Maker Blossoms with Its Nonalcoholic Brew," *New York Times*, December 25, 1999, cited in Robert Green, "The ABC's of Privatization: A Case Study of the al-Ahram Beverage Company in Egypt."

16  Central Agency for Public Mobilisation and Statistics (CAMPAS), "Statistical Yearbook, Arab Republic of Egypt." (Cairo, 1991–1992); CAMPAS, "Statistical Handbook, Arab Republic of Egypt" (Cairo, 1980–1981); CAMPAS, "Statistical Handbook, Arab Republic of Egypt" (Cairo, 1976–1977).

17  Nicholas Mamatis to Direction Générale de la Amstel, 2.2.10.3-1187, AH, SAA.

18  Green, "ABC'S of Privatization," 44; Waterbury, *Egypt of Nasser and Sadat*, 93.

19  Sharikat Birat al-Ahram (Idarat al-Mabicat), Mabicat al-Makhazan wa Wukala al-Tawziac wa Muwazzacu al-Balad wa al-Aqalim, IOF.

20  Interview with Hussein Foda, June 23, 2017.

21  These plans were expanded when, at the advice of Erick Kettner, it became apparent that Pyramid needed even more expansion to meet demand. EK to WvH, December 4, 1959, June 18, 1961, 4.1.2.4.2.6-1978, AH, SAA.

22  "Report on the Visit to the Société de Bière 'Les Pyramides,' S.A.E. Cairo, by Drs. G. L. Rinkel from January 12th until 15th 1961," 2, 2.2.9.2.5-1086, AH, SAA.

23  Société de Bière "Les Pyramides," "Summary of the Services Rendered by Heineken's Breweries Netherlands to Pyramids Brewery of Cairo," November 4, 1961, 4.1.2.4.2.6-1978, AH, SAA.

24  "Minutes of the Meeting of the Board of Directors of the Company Bière 'Les Pyramids,' Held November 26, 1960, the Office of the Company," 4.1.2.4.2.6-1978, AH, SAA.

25  Ismail Omar Foda, "Studies on the Nutrition and Metabolism of *Acetobacter melanogenum* and Related Species."

26  Ismail Omar Foda and Reese H. Vaughn, "Oxidation of Maltose by *Acetobacter Melanogenum*," 236.

27  Fergus G. Priest, "Acetic Acid Bacteria."

28  Interview with Hussein Foda, June 23, 2017.

29  Omar Foda to Maslahat al-Sharikat, 1966, 3019-00506, MS, DWQ.

30  "Bayan Khasa bi-l-Sada Raʾis wa Acdaʾ Majlis Idara al-Sharikat" and Omar Foda to Maslahat al-Sharikat, 1967, 3019-005506, MS, DWQ.

31  Sharikat Birat al-Ahram, Mudhakkira l-il-ʿArd al-Sayyid al-Muhandis Wazir al-Sinaʿa wa al-Tharwa al-Maʿdniyya bi-Shaʾn al-Istifadu min Khidmat al-Sayyid al-Muhandis al-Ziraʿi Muḥammad Ramses ʿAwad, February 6, 1980, IOF.

32  Sharikat Birat al-Ahram, Farac al-Iskandariyya, Mahdar Ijtimac Lajnat Shuʾun al-Afrad bi-Masnac al-Iskandariyya Raqam 144, undated, IOF.

33  Omar Foda to al-Sayyid al-Muhandis Wazir al-Sinaʿa wa al-Tharwa al-Maʿdiniyya, February 4, 1980, IOF.

34  Sharikat Birat al-Ahram, Mudhakkira, li-l-ʿArd ʿala al-Sayyid al-Muhandis Wazir al-Sinaʿa wa al-Tharwa al-Maʿdiniyya bi-Shaʾin Shughl Wazifat Raʾis Qitaʿ Intaj al-Bira wa ʿudu Majlis Idarat al-Sharika, December 18, 1979, IOF.

35  EK to WvH, December 29, 1960, 4.1.2.4.2.6-1978, AH, SAA.

36  Muhammad ʿAbd al-Majed (legal adviser to the minister of industry and mineral resources in the Wazirat al-Sinaʿa wa al-Bitrol wa al-Taʿdin) to head of the executive of Sharikat Birat al-Ahram, January 1980, IOF.

37  Sharikat Birat al-Ahram, Mudhakkira l-il-ʿArd al-Sayyid al-Muhandis Wazir al-Sinaʿa wa Tharwa al-Maʿdniyya bi-Shaʾn al-Istifadu min Khidmat al-Sayyid al-Muhandis al-Ziraʿi Muhammad Ramses ʿAwad, February 6, 1980, IOF.

38  Artois Engineering to Dr. Omar Foda, January 17, 1980, IOF.

39  Untitled letter #2 from Ismail Omar Foda to al-Sayyid al-Muhandis Wazir al-Sinaʿa wa al-Tharwa al-Maʿdiniyya, February 4, 1980, IOF.

40  Interview with Hussein Foda, June 23, 2017.

41  Jens Erik Holmsgaard, "Brewing in Egypt: Bringing a 5,000-Year-Old Tradition Up to International Standards," 14.

42  Interview with Joyce Foda, November 15, 2015.

43  Ikram, *Egyptian Economy*, 24, 25–26.

44  Relli Shechter, "From Effendi to Infitāḥī? Consumerism and Its Malcontents in the Emergence of Egyptian Market Society," 27, 28.

45  Ibid., 28.

46  Husayn Kamal, *Arjuka Iʿtini Hadha Al-Dawa*.

47  Husayn Kamal, *Imbaraturiyyat Mim*.

48  Kamal, *Arjuka Iʿtini Hadha Al-Dawa*.

49  Watenpaugh, *Being Modern in the Middle East*, 16; Reynolds, *City Consumed*.

50  Barak, *On Time*.

51  Omar D. Foda, "The Pyramid and the Crown: The Egyptian Beer Industry, from 1897 to 1963."

52  Samira Haj, *Reconfiguring Islamic Tradition: Reform, Rationality, and Modernity*, 75–76.

53  Abdullah al-Arian, *Answering the Call: Popular Islamic Activism in Sadat's Egypt*, 23–24, 26, 28.

54  Ibid., 18.

55  Carrie Rosefsky Wickham, *Mobilizing Islam: Religion, Activism, and Political Change in Egypt*, 61.

56  al-Arian, *Answering the Call*, 43, 48.

57  EK to Dr. I. O. Foda, February 14, 1962, 4.1.2.4.2.6-1978, AH, SAA.

58  al-Arian, *Answering the Call*, 86.

59  Aaron Rock-Singer, "A Pious Public: Islamic Magazines and Revival in Egypt, 1976–1981," 437.

60  al-Arian, *Answering the Call*, 93–94.

61  Basil El-Dabh, "Alcohol Laws: Leaving Egyptians High and Dry," *Daily News Egypt*, September 5, 2012, dailynewsegypt.com/2012/09/05/alcohol-laws-leaving-egyptians -high-and-dry/.

62  al-Arian, *Answering the Call*, 93–94.

63  Wickham, *Mobilizing Islam*, 61.

64  Aaron Rock-Singer, "Prayer and the Islamic Revival: A Timely Challenge."

65  Saba Mahmood, *The Politics of Piety: The Islamic Revival and the Feminist Subject*, 3.

66  Ibid., 57.

67  ʿAbd al-Halim Mahmud, "Islam wa Tanzim al-Mujtamaʾ," *al-Azhar* 4 (1976): 403–413.

## Chapter 8: An American Pharaoh and the Egyptian Star

1  "Corporate Strategies: Egyptian Brewer Enters New Era," *Crossborder Monitor*, September 24, 1997, 1, 9, cited in Green, "ABC's of Privatization," 24.

2  Joseph Treaster, "Inverting the Pyramid in Egypt: A Beer Maker Blossoms with Its Nonalcoholic Brew," *New York Times*, December 25, 1999, cited in Green, "ABC's of Privatization," 24.

3  Holmsgaard, "Brewing in Egypt," 10.

4  Interview with Steve Keefer, June 5, 2016.

5  "Corporate Strategies," 1, 9, cited in Green, "ABC's of Privatization," 24.

6  Mark Huband, "Waste and Corruption 'Beyond Imagination,'" *Financial Times*, May 13, 1997, 10, cited in Green, "ABC's of Privatization," 24.

7  Holmsgaard, "Brewing in Egypt," 10.

8  Treaster, "Inverting the Pyramid in Egypt."

9  Interview with Keefer, June 5, 2016.

10  Interview with Hussein Foda, June 23, 2017.

11  Interview with Keefer, June 5, 2016.

12  Mona Eltahawy, "Make Mine . . . a Stella: In Egypt, What Beer Says about Faith," *U.S. News & World Report*, July 5, 1999.

13  Ikram, *Egyptian Economy*, 58.

14  Beinin, *Workers and Thieves*, 43.

15  Gregory Starrett, *Putting Islam to Work: Education, Politics, and Religious Transformation in Egypt*, 230.

16  Rock-Singer, "Prayer and the Islamic Revival."

17  Central Agency for Public Mobilisation and Statistics (CAMPAS), "Statistical Handbook, Arab Republic of Egypt" (Cairo, June 1999), 86.

18  Green, "ABC's of Privatization," 4.

19  Ibid., 4.

20  Ibid., 38.

21  Treaster, "Inverting the Pyramid in Egypt."

22  Green, "ABC's of Privatization," 38.

23  Treaster, "Inverting the Pyramid in Egypt."

24  Ibid.

25  Dorte Holm Rykaer and Jens Erik Holmsgaard, "Danbrew in Egypt: Al-Ahram Beverages Co.–El-Obour Brewery in Cairo," 31.

26  Green, "ABC's of Privatization", 38.

27  Treaster, "Inverting the Pyramid in Egypt."

28  Interview with Keefer, June 5, 2016.

29  Holmsgaard, "Brewing in Egypt," 10, 12.

30  Ibid., 10.

31  Rykaer and Holmsgaard, "Danbrew in Egypt," 31–32.

32  Holmsgaard, "Brewing in Egypt," 12.

33  Ibid., 14.

34  "Corporate Strategies," 9.

35  International Business & Technical Consultants, Inc. (IBTCI), "Special Study for the Privatization Program in Egypt — Privatization Case Study," 26, cited in Green, "ABC's of Privatization."

36  Holmsgaard, "Brewing in Egypt," 14.

37  Rykaer and Holmsgaard, "Danbrew in Egypt," 34.

38  IBTCI, "Special Study," 27.

39  Ibid., 26, 27.

40  Holmsgaard, "Brewing in Egypt," 12.

41  Ibid., 14.

42  Jens Holmsgaard, e-mail correspondence, July 16, 2017; Rykaer and Holmsgaard, "Danbrew in Egypt," 36.

43  Rykaer and Holmsgaard, "Danbrew in Egypt," 34, 39.

44  For reference on this process, see chapter 2.

45  Rykaer and Holmsgaard, "Danbrew in Egypt," 46.

46  Ibid., 50, 54, 56.

47  Interview with Keefer, June 5, 2016.

48  Treaster, "Inverting the Pyramid in Egypt."

49  Interview with Keefer, August 22, 2017.

50  "Corporate Strategies," 9.

51  Treaster, "Inverting the Pyramid in Egypt."

52  "Corporate Strategies," 9.

53  Interview with Keefer, June 5, 2016.

54  WvH to EK, July 1, 1957, 4.1.2.4.2.6-1977, AH, SAA.

55  EK to WvH, November 21, 1961, 4.1.2.4.2.6-1977, AH, SAA.

56  Interview with Joyce Foda, November 15, 2015.

57  Untitled letter from Omar Foda to Al-Sayyid al-Muhandis wazir al-sina'a wa al-tharwa al-ma'diniyya, February 4, 1980, IOF.

58  Ruz al-Yusuf, July 17, 1972.

59  Ibid.

60  Jonkheer Pieter Feith, "Reisrapport," November–December 1949, 11, 2.2.9.2.7-1098, AH, SAA; Galal Amin, Whatever Happened to the Egyptians? Changes in Egyptian Society from 1950 to the Present, 31–45.

61  David A. Thomas, "Non-alcoholic 'Beer.'"

62  *al-Manar* 30 (1929).

63  This jibes with my anecdotal experience where most nonalcoholic beer drinkers have some familiarity with beer culture.

64  "Jadal Hawla Fatwa li-l-Qaradawi Tabih al-Mashrubat bi-Nisbat Kahul Da'ila," *al-Arabiyya*, November 1, 2010, alarabiya.net/articles/2008/04/11/48148.html.

65  Holmsgaard, "Brewing in Egypt," 14.

66  Jens Holmsgaard, e-mail, July 16, 2017.

67  CAMPAS, "Statistical Yearbook, Arab Republic of Egypt" (Cairo, 1992).

68  Ibid.

69  al-Ahram Beverage Company (ABC), "al-Ahram Beverages Annual Report," 4.

70  Holmsgaard, "Brewing in Egypt," 14.

71  Rykaer and Holmsgaard, "Danbrew in Egypt," 48.

72  Holmsgaard, e-mail, July 16, 2017.

73  ABC, "al-Ahram Beverages Annual Report," 2, 13.

74  Treaster, "Inverting the Pyramid in Egypt."

75  de Saint-Omer, *Les enterprises belges en Égypte*, 153.

76  "Kashf bi-A'da' Idarat al-Sharikat Birat al-Ahram fi 1956," 3019-5504, MS, DWQ.

77  "Kashf bi-A'da' Idarat al-Sharikat Karwon Brewery Tabiqan li-l-Madat 23 min al-Qanun Raqm 26 fi 1954," 3019-6808, MS, DWQ.

78  ABC, "Al-Ahram Beverages Annual Report," 26.

79  Ibid., 27.

80  Ibid.

81  "About Tempo," tempo.co.il/about/about-tempo/.

82  Joe Drape, "Ahmed Zayat's Journey: Bankruptcy and Big Bets," *New York Times*, June 4, 2015, nytimes.com/2015/06/05/sports/american-pharoah-cant-erase-all-of-ahmed-zayats-missteps.html.

83  Interview with Keefer, June 5, 2016.

84  Foda, "Anna and Ahmad."

85  Holmsgaard, e-mail, July 16, 2017.

86  Cobra to the director of HBM, April 22, 1940, 4.1.2.4.2.2-1948, AH, SAA.

87  EK to WvH, January 21, 1958, 4.1.2.4.2.6-1978, AH, SAA.

88  EK to WvH, December 4, 1959, 4.1.2.4.2.6-1978, AH, SAA.

89  EK to WvH, November 26, 1961, 2.2.10.3-1187, AH, SAA.

90  Seidl and Dornbusch, "Märzenbier."

91  "Minutes, Talks in Cairo, January 28–February 3, 1959," 4.1.2.4.2.6-1977, AH, SAA.

92  "Kashf bi-asma' A'da' al-sada Majlis Idarat Sharika," January 3, 1954, 3019-011919 MS, DWQ; "Kashf bi-asma' Muwazzafin al-Misriyyin," January 3, 1955, 3019-011919 MS, DWQ; "Kashf bi-asma al-'Ummal al-Misriyyin fi yawm," December 29, 1954, 3019-011919 MS, DWQ.

93  Green, "ABC's of Privatization," 31.

94  Ibid., 12.

95  Ibid., 33.

96  Ibid., 47.

97  Waleed Khalil Rasromani, "Heineken Takes over Management of Al-Ahram Beverages Co.," *Daily News Egypt*, February 27, 2006.


**Conclusion**

1  "Rapport sur la visite de M. Le Président de la République Gamal Abdel Nasser au stand 'Stella' à la Foire de la Production Industrielle et Agricole, lors de son inauguration," January 3, 1960, 4.1.2.4.2.6-1978, AH, SAA.

2  Ryzova, "Egyptianizing Modernity," 27–28, 129, 131, 133.

3  Ibid., 133.

4  Shechter, "Cultural Economy of Development," 574.

5  Will Hanley, "Foreignness and Localness in Alexandria, 1880–1914," 228.

6  Vitalis, *When Capitalists Collide*, 49.

7  Tignor, *State, Private Enterprise, and Economic Change*, 184.

8  Beinin and Lockman, *Workers on the Nile*, 9.

9  Hanley, "Foreignness and Localness," 7–9.

# BIBLIOGRAPHY

## Archival Sources

### Egyptian National Archives (Dar al-Watha'iq al-Qaymiyya) (typed, unless otherwise noted)

ʿABDIN

- 0069–12634 "ʿAwraq Tafiyya Shakwa baʿd al-Sudaniyyat min Muhakimat al-Bulis al-Mahalat al-Buza illati Taʿish fiha"

DIWAN AL-DAKHILIYYA (DD)

- 2001-008151–2001-008159. "Watha'iq wa Tasrihat bi-Fath Bada' al-Hanat Rakhs Mahallat Khamur (Documents and Reports relating to the opening of some of the bars and alcohol distributors)

MAKTABAT AL-MUSTASHAR AL-MALI

- 0075–032992. Waqaʿha qanun al-mashrubat al-baladiyya 1913 wa mudhakira taghyiriyya.

MASLAHAT AL-SHARIKAT (DEPARTMENT OF COMPANIES ARCHIVES, MS)

- 3019–005501–3019–005506. *Sharikat Birat al-Ahram*
- 3019-007235. *Tawziʿa al-Bira*
- 3019-006807–3019-006810. *Sharikat Birat Crown Brewery*
- 3019-011917–3019-011918. *Sharikat Birat al-Nil*

WIZARAT AL-SHU'UN AL-IJTIMAʿIYYA

- 4029-000365. Egyptian Temperance Association, "Taqrir al-Jamʿiyya Marfuʿ ila al-Inzar al-Malakiyya al-Karima Yahya Mawlana al-Malak al-Muazzam al-Malak Ahmad Fu'ad al-Awil."

### Ismail Omar Foda Personal Collection (typed, unless otherwise noted)

### Presbyterian Historical Society (untyped, unless otherwise noted)

ANNA YOUNG THOMPSON PAPERS (1868–1931)

- RG-58-1-6
- RG-58-1-8

### Stadsarchief Amsterdam (typed, unless otherwise noted)

834-ARCHIVES OF HEINEKEN NV
*2.2.9.2.5-Afrika*

- 1053 — Reisrapporten inzake Egypte, Soedan, Palestina en Syrie
- 1080 — Nota houdende een overzicht van de lopende zaken, met een historisch overzicht van de contacten van R. Gaston-Dreyfus met Egypte
- 1086 — Reisrapporten inzake Noord-Afrika: Egypte en Soedan

*2.2.9.2.7-Azië en het Midden-Oosten*

- 1098 — Reisrapporten van Jhr. P. R. Feith inzake het Midden en Verre Oosten (Egypte, Singapore, Australië, Indonesië, Soedan, Papua Nieuw-Guinea en Italië)
- 1121 — Reisverslagen inzake het midden en verre oosten (Iran, Kuwait, Bahrein, Quatar, Jordanië, Libanon, Afghanistan, Cyprus, Singapore, Egypte, Australisch Nieuw-Guinea, Indonesië, Australië, Nieuw Zeeland, Hawaii)

*2.2.10.3*

- 1187 — Stukken betreffende de sequestratie en daarna nationalisatie van Les Pyramides door de Egyptische overheid, alsmede betreffende schadeloosstelling en de affaire Maitre Delenda

*4.1.2.4.2.2-Crown Brewery SA Alexandria*

- 1937–1948 Oktober 1946 Mei
- 1946–1949 Juni 1952
- 1950–1953–1960 Juli

*4.1.2.4.2.6 — Overige brouwerijen buiten Europa*

- 1977 — Verslagen van bezoeken en besprekingen inzake de Société de Bière Les Pyramides S.A.E.
- 1978 — Correspondentie tussen Wittert van Hoogland
- 1979 — Stukken betreffende het directorship van HBM in de Blue Nile Brewery te Khartoum

### United Presbyterian Church in the U.S.A. Commission on Ecumenical Mission and Relations, Records (1833–1966)

- John R. Alexander Papers
- RG 209-1-22

## Newspapers

| | |
|---|---|
| *al-Ahram* | *Majallat al-Azhar* |
| *Akhir al-Saʿa* | *al-Manar* |
| *al-Arabiyya* | *al-Monitor* |
| *Crossborder Monitor* | *New York Times* |
| *Daily News Egypt* | *Ruz al-Yusuf* |
| *Economist* | *al-Tankit wa-al-Tabith* |
| *Kan wa Yakun* | |

## Interviews

| | |
|---|---|
| Hussein Foda | Jens Holmsgaard |
| Joyce Foda | Steve Keefer |

## Films

*Abi Fawq al-Shajara.* Directed by Husayn Kamal. Cairo: Sawt al-Fann, 2004.

*Ana Hurra (Je Cherche La Liberté).* Directed by Najib Ramsis et al. al-Qahira: Sharikat Funun lil-Tawziʿ, 2004.

*Anf Wa Thalath ʿUyun.* Directed by Husayn Kamal. al-Qahira: Aflam Jamal al-Laythi lil-Sinima wa-al-Vidiyu, 1990s.

*Arjuka Iʿtini Hadha al-Dawa.* Directed by Husayn Kamal. al-Qahira: Fidiyu Film, 1980s.

*Al-ʿAzima.* Directed by Kamal Salim, Fatimah Rushdi, Husayn Sidqi, Anwar Wajdi, al-Sharika al-ʿAmmah li-Tawziʿ wa-ʿArd al-Aflam al-Sinimaiyya (Egypt), and Aflam Jamal al-Laythi lil-Sinima wa-al-Vidiyu. al-Qahira: Aflam Jamal al-Laythi, 1939.

*Al-Banat al-Sayf.* Directed by Izz al-Din Zuficar, Salah Abu Sayf, and Fatin ʿAbd al-Wahab. Cairo, 1960.

*Fi Baytina Rajul.* Directed by Ihsan ʿAbd al-Qaddus, Yusuf ʿIsa Barakat et al. Seattle: Arab Film Distribution, 2003.

*Ibn al-Haddad.* Directed by Yusuf Wahbi. Cairo: Sharikat al-Aflam al-Misriyya, 1944.

*Ibn al-Nil.* Directed by Mari Kwini et al. Giza: al-Subki Vidiyu Film, 1990s.

*Ihna Bituʾ al-Utubis.* Directed by Husayn Kamal. al-Qahira: Sahrikat Funun lil-Tawziʾ, 2000s.

*Imbaraturiyyat Mim.* Directed by Husayn Kamal. Cairo: Funun, 2000.

*La Anam.* Directed by Ihsan ʿAbd al-Qaddus et al. Cairo: Rutana, 2000.

*Al-Masatil.* Directed by Husayn Kamal. Cairo: Rotana, 2000s.

*Al-Nazzara al-Sawdaʾ.* Directed by Husam al-Din Mustaf al-Qahira: al-Subki lil-Intaj al-Sinima, 1980s.

*Al-Suq al-Sawda.* Directed by Kamil Tilimsani et al. al-Qahira: Aflam Jamal al-Laythi, 1945.

*Uhibbuka Anta.* Directed by Ahmad Badrakhan. Cairo: Aflam Fareed al-Atrash, 1949.

*Al-ʿUsta Hasan.* Directed by Salah Abu Sayf; Production, Huda Sultan and LC Purchase Collection (Library of Congress). Cairo: Markaz al-Sharq al-Awsat lil-Taswiq, 1980s.

## Secondary Sources

ʿAbd al-Qaddus, Ihsan. *Ana Hurra*. Cairo: Dar al-Hilal, 1967.

―――. *Al-Banat wa-al-Sayf*. Beirut: Manshurat Maktabat al-Maʿarif, 1959.

―――. *I Am Free, and Other Stories*. Translated by Trevor Le Gassick. Cairo: General Egyptian Book Organization, 1978.

―――. *Lan aʿisha Fijilbab Abi*. Cairo: Maktabat Gharīb, 1980.

―――. *al-Nisaʾ la-Hunna Asnan Baydaʾ*. Cairo: Muassasat Akhbar al-Yawm, 1969.

Abul-Magd, Zeinab. *Militarizing the Nation: The Army, Business, and Revolution in Egypt*. New York: Columbia University Press, 2017.

Abu-Lughod, Janet. *Cairo: 1001 Years of the City Victorious*. Princeton, NJ: Princeton University Press, 1971.

al-Ahram Beverage Company (ABC). "Al Ahram Beverages Annual Report." 1999.

Akyeampong, Emmanuel Kwaku. *Drink, Power, and Cultural Change: A Social History of Alcohol in Ghana, c. 1800 to Recent Times*. Portsmouth, NH: James Currey, 1996.

Alexander, Jeffrey W. *Brewed in Japan: The Evolution of the Japanese Beer Industry*. Vancouver: UBC Press, 2013.

Allen, Roger M. A., ed. *The Arabic Novel: An Historical and Critical Introduction*. Syracuse, NY: Syracuse University Press, 1982.

―――. *Critical Perspectives on Yusuf Idris*. Colorado Springs: Three Continents Press, 1994.

―――, trans. *A Period of Time: A Study and Translation of Hadith ʿIsá ibn Hisham*. London: Ithaca Press for the Middle East Centre, St. Anthony's College, Oxford, 1992.

Amin, Ahmad. *Qamus al-ʿadat wa-al-taqalid wa-al-taʿabir al-Misriyya*. 2nd ed. al-Qahira: Maktabat al-Nahda al-Misriyya, 1982.

Amin, Galal A. *Egypt's Economic Predicament: A Study in the Interaction of External Pressure, Political Folly and Social Tension in Egypt, 1960–1990*. Leiden: E. J. Brill, 1995.

―――. *Whatever Happened to the Egyptians? Changes in Egyptian Society from 1950 to the Present*. New York: American University in Cairo Press, 2000.

Appadurai, Arjun, ed. *The Social Life of Things: Commodities in Cultural Perspective*. Cambridge: Cambridge University Press, 1986.

al-Arian, Abdullah A. *Answering the Call: Popular Islamic Activism in Sadat's Egypt*. New York: Oxford University Press, 2014.

Aristotle. *Aristotle's Meteorology in the Arabico-Latin Tradition: A Critical Edition of the Texts, with Introduction and Indices*. Edited and translated by Pieter L. Schoonheim. Leiden: Brill, 2000.

Armbrust, Walter. "The Golden Age before the Golden Age: Commercial Egyptian Cinema before the 1960s." In *Mass Mediations: New Approaches to Popular Culture in the Middle East and Beyond*, edited by Walter Armbrust. Berkeley: University of California Press, 2000.

―――. *Mass Culture and Modernism in Egypt*. New York: Cambridge University Press, 1996.

Armes, Roy. *African Filmmaking: North and South of the Sahara*. Edinburgh: Edinburgh, 2006.

Aumont, Jacques. "Lumière Revisited." Translated by Ben Brewster. International Trends in Film Studies. *Film History* 8, no. 4 (1996): 416–430.

Awad, Louis. "Cultural and Intellectual Developments." In *Egypt since the Revolution*, edited by P. J. Vatikiotis, 143–162. New York: Praeger, 1968.

Aynur, Hatice, and Jan Schmidt. "A Debate between Opium, Berş Hashish, Boza, Wine and Coffee: The Use and Perception of Pleasurable Substances among Ottomans." *Journal of Turkish Studies* 31, no. 1 (2007): 51–117.

Badawi, Mahmud. *Al-Aʾraj fi al-Minaʾ, wa-Qisas Ukhra*. al-Qahira: al-Hayʾa al-Misriyya al-ʿAmma lil-Kitab, 1975.

Badran, Margot, and Miriam Cooke, eds. *Opening the Gates: A Century of Arab Feminist Writing*. Bloomington: Indiana University Press, 1990.

Baer, Gabriel. *Egyptian Guilds in Modern Times*. Jerusalem: Israel Oriental Society, 1964.

Bakhtin, M. M. *The Dialogic Imagination: Four Essays*. Austin: University of Texas Press, 1981.

Bamforth, Charles W. "Top Fermentation." In *The Oxford Companion to Beer*, edited by Garret Oliver. Oxford: Oxford University Press, 2011.

Banbury, Frederick George. "Report from the Select Committee on Navy and Army Canteens Together with Minutes of Evidence and Appendices." House of Commons Papers, Reports of Committees, 1924. ProQuest. gateway.aa1.proquest.com/open url?url_ver=Z39.88-2004&res_dat=xri:hcpp&rft_dat=xri:hcpp:rec:1923-025864.

Banna, Hasan. *Majmuʿat Rasaʾil al-Imam al-Shahid Hasan al-Banna*. Beirut: al-Muʾassasa al-Islamiyya lil-Tibaʿa wa-al-Sihafa wa-al-Nashr, 1981.

———. *Mudhakkiraat al-Daʾwa wa-al-Daʾiyya*. Cairo: Dār al-Shihab, 1978.

Barak, On. "Egyptian Times: Temporality, Personhood, and the Technopolitical Making of Modern Egypt, 1830–1930." PhD diss., New York University, 2009.

———. *On Time: Technology and Temporality in Modern Egypt*. Berkeley: University of California Press, 2013.

Baraka, Magda. *The Egyptian Upper Class between Revolutions, 1919–1952*. 1st ed. London: Ithaca Press for the Middle East Centre, St. Anthony's College, Oxford, 1998.

Baron, Beth. *Egypt as a Woman: Nationalism, Gender, and Politics*. Berkeley: University of California Press, 2005.

Baron, Stanley Wade. *Brewed in America: A History of Beer and Ale in the United States*. Boston: Little, Brown, 1962.

Barudi, Mahmud Sami. *Diwan*. Edited by ʾAli Jarim and Muhammad Shafiq Maʾruf. Cairo: Dar al-Maʾarif, 1971.

Beatty, Edward. "Bottles for Beer: The Business of Technological Innovation in Mexico, 1890–1920." Special issue. *Business History Review* 83, no. 2 (2009): 317–348.

Behrens-Abouseif, Doris. *Azbakiyya and Its Environs: From Azbak to Ismail, 1476–1879*. Cairo: Institut français archéologie Orientale, 1985.

Beinin, Joel. *The Dispersion of Egyptian Jewry: Culture, Politics, and the Formation of a Modern Diaspora*. Berkeley: University of California Press, 1998.

———. *Workers and Thieves: Labor Movements and Popular Uprisings in Tunisia and Egypt*. Stanford, CA: Stanford University Press, 2016. E-book.

Beinin, Joel, and Zachary Lockman. *Workers on the Nile: Nationalism, Communism, Islamism and the Egyptian Working Class, 1882–1954.* Princeton, NJ: Princeton University Press, 1987.

Berkey, Jonathan Porter. *The Formation of Islam: Religion and Society in the Near East, 600–1800.* Cambridge: Cambridge University Press, 2003.

Bier, Laura. *Revolutionary Womenhood: Feminisms, Modernity, and the State in Nasser's Egypt.* Stanford, CA: Stanford University Press, 2011.

Binder, Leonard. "Gamal 'Abd Al-Nasser: Iconology, Ideology, and Demonology." In *Rethinking Nasserism: Revolution and Historical Memory in Modern Egypt,* edited by Elie Podeh and Onn Winckler, 45–72. Gainesville: University Press of Florida, 2004.

Bird, Christopher. "Lightstruck." In *The Oxford Companion to Beer,* edited by Garrett Oliver. Oxford: Oxford University Press, 2011.

Blattner, E. J., ed. "Ahmed Farghaly: Who's Who in Egypt and the Middle East." In *Who's Who in U.A.R. and the Near East / Le Mondain égyptien et du Proche-Orient, Who's Who in Egypt and the Near East.* 1950.

———, ed. *Who's Who in Egypt and the Middle East.* Cairo: Imprimerie Francaise, 1950.

Blunt, Wilfrid Scawen. *Secret History of the English Occupation of Egypt Being a Personal Narrative of Events.* Farnborough, UK: Gregg International, 1969.

Bonanno, Alessandro, ed. *From Columbus to ConAgra: The Globalization of Agriculture and Food.* Lawrence: University Press of Kansas, 1994.

Booth, Marilyn. *Bayram Al-Tunisi's Egypt: Social Criticism and Narrative Strategies.* London: Ithaca Press for the Middle East Centre, St. Anthony's College, Oxford, 1990.

Bordin, Ruth Birgitta Anderson. *Woman and Temperance: The Quest for Power and Liberty, 1873–1900.* Philadelphia: Temple University Press, 1981.

Boullata, Issa J., ed. *Modern Arab Poets, 1950–1975.* Washington, DC: Three Continents Press, 1976.

Bowen, Donna Lee, Evelyn A. Early, and Becky Lyn Schulthies, eds. *Everyday Life in the Muslim Middle East.* 2nd ed. Bloomington: Indiana University Press, 2002.

British Chamber of Commerce of Egypt. *List of Companies Established in Egypt.* 4th ed. Alexandria: British Chamber of Commerce of Egypt, 1905.

———. *List of Financial, Manufacturing, Transport and Other Companies Established in Egypt.* Alexandria: A. Mourès & cie, 1900.

———. *List of Financial, Manufacturing, Transport and Other Companies Established in Egypt, etc.* 3rd ed. Alexandria, 1901.

Brock, Thomas D., ed. and trans. *Milestones in Microbiology.* Englewood Cliffs, NJ: Prentice Hall, 1961.

Brown, Nathan J. "The Precarious Life and Slow Death of the Mixed Courts of Egypt." *International Journal of Middle East Studies* 25, no. 1 (1993): 33–52.

Buisson-Fenet, Emmanuel. "Ivresse et rapport à l'occidentalisation au Maghreb." *Égypte/Monde arabe,* nos. 30–31 (September 30, 1997): 303–320.

Burke, Timothy. *Lifebuoy Men, Lux Women: Commodification, Consumption, and Cleanliness in Modern Zimbabwe.* Durham, NC: Duke University Press, 1996.

Burnett, John. *Liquid Pleasures: A Social History of Drinks in Modern Britain.* New York: Routledge, 1999.

Business Middle East. "Corporate Strategies: Egyptian Brewer Enters a New Era." *Cross-border Monitor* (September 24, 1997).

Buttrick, Paul A. "Hopback." In *The Oxford Companion to Beer*, edited by Garret Oliver. Oxford: Oxford University Press, 2011.

Cain, P. J., and A. G. Hopkins. *British Imperialism, 1688-2000*. 2nd ed. New York: Longman, 2002.

Central Agency for Public Mobilisation and Statistics (CAMPAS). "Statistical Handbook, Arab Republic of Egypt." Cairo, 1977.

———. "Statistical Handbook, Arab Republic of Egypt." Cairo, 1981.

———. "Statistical Yearbook, Arab Republic of Egypt." Cairo, 1992.

———. "Statistical Handbook, Arab Republic of Egypt." Cairo, June 1999.

Chaichian, Mohammad A. "The Effects of World Capitalist Economy on Urbanization in Egypt, 1800-1970." *International Journal of Middle East Studies* 20, no. 1 (1988): 23-43.

———. *Town and Country in the Middle East: Iran and Egypt in the Transition to Globalization, 1800-1970*. Lanham, MD: Lexington Books, 2009.

Chalcraft, John T. *The Striking Cabbies of Cairo and Other Stories: Crafts and Guilds in Egypt, 1863-1914*. Albany: State University of New York Press, 2004.

Cleveland, William. *A History of the Modern Middle East*. Edited by Martin Bunton. 4th ed. Boulder, CO: Westview Press, 2009.

Cohen, Lizabeth. *A Consumer's Republic: The Politics of Mass Consumption in Postwar America*. New York: Alfred A. Knopf, 2003.

Cole, Juan Ricardo. *Colonialism and Revolution in the Middle East: Social and Cultural Origins of Egypt's 'Urabi Movement*. Princeton, NJ: Princeton University Press, 1993.

Commission des sciences et arts d'Égypte. *Description de l'Égypte; ou, Recueil des observations et des recherches qui ont été faites en Égypte pendant l'expédition de l'armée française*. Paris: Impr. impériale, 1808-1828.

Cook, Michael. *Commanding Right and Forbidding Wrong in Islamic Thought*. Cambridge: Cambridge University Press, 2001.

Cozzika, M. P. "La distillerie de Tourah." *L'Égypte Contemporaine* (January 1917): 46-49.

Crabbs Jr., Jack A. "Politics, History, and Culture in Nasser's Egypt." *International Journal of Middle East Studies* 6, no. 4 (1975): 386-421.

———. *The Writing of History in Nineteenth-Century Egypt: A Study in National Transformation*. Detroit: Wayne State University Press, 1984.

Crawford, Dorothy J. "Food: Tradition and Change in Hellenistic Egypt." *Food and Nutrition. World Archaeology* 11, no. 2 (1979): 136-146.

Crecelius, Daniel, ed. *Eighteenth Century Egypt: The Arabic Manuscript Sources*. Claremont, CA: Regina Books, 1990.

Crouchley, Arthur Edwin. *The Economic Development of Modern Egypt*. London: Longmans, Green, 1938.

———. *Investment of Foreign Capital in Egyptian Companies and Public Debt*. New York: Arno Press, 1977.

Dalanachis, Angelo. *The Greek Exodus from Egypt: Diaspora Politics and Emigration, 1937-1962*. New York: Berghahn Books, 2017.

Damurdashi, Ahmad. *Al-Damurdashi's Chronicle of Egypt, 1688–1755: Al-Durra al-Musana fi Akhbar al-Kinana*. Edited by Daniel Crecelius. Leiden: Brill, 1991.

Dara, Rajendar. *The Real Pepsi, the Real Story*. New Delhi: R. Dara, 1991.

Davis, Eric. *Challenging Colonialism*. Princeton, NJ: Princeton University Press, 1983.

Davis, Pearce. *The Development of the American Glass Industry*. Cambridge, MA: Harvard University Press, 1949.

Deeb, Marius. *Party Politics in Egypt: The Wafd & Its Rivals, 1919–1939*. London: Ithaca Press for the Middle East Centre, St. Anthony's College, Oxford, 1979.

den Hartog, Adel P. "Food Labeling and Packaging in the Dutch Food Industry: Persuading and Informing Consumers, 1870–1950s." In *The Food Industries of Europe in the Nineteenth and Twentieth Centuries*, edited by Derek J. Oddy and Alain Drouard, 165–179. Burlington, VT: Ashgate, 2013.

de Saint-Omer, Henry. *Les entreprises Belges en Égypte: Rapport sur la situation économique des sociétés Belges et Belge-Égyptiennes fonctionnant en Égypte*. Bruxelles: Piquart, 1907.

Desmet-Grégoire, Hélène, and François Georgeon. *Cafés d'Orient revisités*. Paris: CNRS, 1997.

Di-Capua, Yoav. "The Professional Worldview of the Effendi Historian." *History Compass* 7, no. 1 (2009): 306–328.

———. "Sports, Society, and Revolution: Egypt in the Early Nasserite Period." In *Rethinking Nasserism: Revolution and Historical Memory in Modern Egypt*, edited by Elie Podeh and Onn Winckler, 144–162. Gainesville: University Press of Florida, 2004.

Dirar, Hamid A. *The Indigenous Fermented Foods of the Sudan: A Study in African Food and Nutrition*. Wallingford, Oxon: CAB International, 1993.

Dombusch, Horst. "Carl Von Linde." In *The Oxford Companion to Beer*, edited by Garret Oliver. Oxford: Oxford University Press, 2011.

Dornbusch, Horst, and Garrett Oliver. "Bottles." In *The Oxford Companion to Beer*, edited by Garret Oliver. Oxford: Oxford University Press, 2011.

Doumani, Beshara. *Rediscovering Palestine: Merchants and Peasants in Jabal Nablus, 1700–1900*. Berkeley: University of California Press, 1995.

Egyptian Minister of Trade. *Thawrat Misr al-sinaʿiyyah fi ʿishrin ʿam 1952–1972*. Cairo: n.p., 1973.

Eickelman, Dale F., and Jon W. Anderson, eds. *New Media in the Muslim World: The Emerging Public Sphere*. Bloomington: Indiana University Press, 1999.

Eldem, Edhem. *The Ottoman City between East and West: Aleppo, Izmir, and Istanbul*. Cambridge: Cambridge University Press, 1999.

El-Ghonemy, M. Riad. "An Assessment of Egypt's Development Strategy, 1952–1970." In *Rethinking Nasserism: Revolution and Historical Memory in Modern Egypt*, edited by Elie Podeh and Onn Winckler, 253–264. Gainesville: University Press of Florida, 2004.

El Shakry, Omnia S. *The Great Social Laboratory: Subjects of Knowledge in Colonial and Postcolonial Egypt*. Stanford, CA: Stanford University Press, 2007.

Evliya Çelebi. *An Ottoman Traveller: Selections from the Book of Travels of Evliya Çelebi*. London: Eland, 2010.

Fahmy, Khaled. *All the Pasha's Men: Mehmed Ali, His Army, and the Making of Modern Egypt*. New York: Cambridge University Press, 1997.

———. "Prostitution in Egypt in the Nineteenth Century." In *Outside In: On the Margins of the Modern Middle East,* edited by Eugene Rogan, 77–104. New York: I. B. Tauris, in association with the European Science Foundation, in the United States distributed by Palgrave, 2002.

Fahmy, Ziad Adel. *Ordinary Egyptians: Creating the Modern Nation through Popular Culture.* Stanford, CA: Stanford University Press, 2011.

Fawzi, Ibrahim. *The History of the Sudan between the Times of Gordon and Kitchener by Ibrahim Fawzi Pasha.* Translated and annotated by Khalid J. D. Deemer and Zohaa El Gamal. Mafraq, Hashemite Kingdom of Jordan: al-Bayt University, 1997.

Fay, Mary Ann, ed. *Auto/biography and the Construction of Identity and Community in the Middle East.* New York: Palgrave, 2002.

Flaubert, Gustave. *Flaubert in Egypt: A Sensibility on Tour, a Narrative Drawn from Gustave Flaubert's Travel Notes & Letters.* Chicago: Academy Chicago, 1979.

Foda, Ismail Omar. "Studies on the Nutrition and Metabolism of *Acetobacter Melanogenum* and Related Species." PhD diss, University of California–Berkeley, 1952.

Foda, Ismail Omar, and Reese H. Vaughan. "Oxidation of Maltose by *Acetobacter Melanogenum.*" *Journal of Bacteriology* 65 (1952): 233–237.

Foda, Omar. "Anna and Ahmad Building Modern Temperance in Egypt (1884–1940)." *Social Sciences and Missions* 28 (2015): 116–149.

———. "The Pyramid and the Crown: The Egyptian Beer Industry from 1897 to 1963." *International Journal of Middle East Studies* 46, no. 1 (2014): 139–158.

Fonder, Nathan. "Pleasure, Leisure, or Vice? Public Morality in Imperial Cairo, 1882–1949." PhD diss., Harvard University, 2013.

Fortna, Benjamin C. *Imperial Classroom: Islam, the State, and Education in the Late Ottoman Empire.* Oxford: Oxford University Press, 2002.

Freidberg, Susanne. *Fresh: A Perishable History.* Cambridge, MA: Belknap Press of Harvard University Press, 2009.

Fuhrmann, Malte. "Beer, the Drink of a Changing World: Beer Consumption and Production on the Shores of the Aegean in the 19th Century." *Turcica* 45 (2014): 79–123.

Gallagher, Nancy Elizabeth. *Egypt's Other Wars: Epidemics and the Politics of Public Health.* Syracuse, NY: Syracuse University Press, 1990.

Gately, Iain. *Drink: A Cultural History of Alcohol.* New York: Gotham Books, 2008.

Gaytán, Marie Sarita. *Tequila! Distilling the Spirit of Mexico.* Stanford, CA: Stanford University Press, 2014.

Gefou-Madianou, Dimitra, ed. *Alcohol, Gender, and Culture.* London: Routledge, 1992.

Georgeon, François. "Ottomans and Drinkers: The Consumption of Alcohol in Istanbul in the Nineteenth Century." In *Outside In: On the Margins of the Modern Middle East,* edited by Eugene Rogan. New York: I. B. Tauris, 2002.

Gershoni, I. *Confronting Fascism in Egypt: Dictatorship versus Democracy in the 1930s.* Stanford, CA: Stanford University Press, 2010.

———. *Egypt, Islam, and the Arabs: The Search for Egyptian Nationhood, 1900–1930.* New York: Oxford University Press, 1986.

———. *Redefining the Egyptian Nation, 1930–1945.* New York: Cambridge University Press, 1995.

Ghali, Waguih. *Beer in the Snooker Club*. 1st American ed. New York: Alfred A. Knopf, 1964.

Ghalwash, Ahmad Ahmad. *Athar al-Khumur fi al-Hayya al-Ijtimaʿiyya*. Cairo: al-Imana al-ʿAmma Idarat al-shuʾun al-Ijtimaʿiyya, al-Sihiyya Jamiyya al-Duwal al-ʿArabiyya, 1957.

———. *The Religion of Islam: A Standard Book*. 2nd ed. Cairo: al-Ettemad Press, 1945.

———. *Al-Tanzim al-Ijtimaʾi fi al-Shariʾa al-Islamiyya*. N.p., 1980.

Ghazaleh, Pascale. *Masters of the Trade: Crafts and Craftspeople in Cairo, 1750-1850*. Cairo: American University in Cairo Press, 1999.

Gingeras, Ryan. *Heroin, Organized Crime, and the Making of Modern Turkey*. Oxford: Oxford University Press, 2014.

Goldberg, Ellis. *Tinker, Tailor, and Textile Worker: Class and Politics in Egypt, 1930-1952*. Berkeley: University of California Press, 1986.

Goldschmidt, Arthur. *The Biographical Dictionary of Egypt*. Cairo: American University in Cairo Press, 2000.

Gordon, Joel. *Nasser's Blessed Movement: Egypt's Free Officers and the July Revolution*. New York: Oxford University Press, 1992.

———. *Revolutionary Melodrama: Popular Film and Civic Identity in Nasser's Egypt*. Chicago: Middle East Documentation Center, 2002.

Gourvish, T. R., and R. G. Wilson. *The British Brewing Industry*. Cambridge: Cambridge University Press, 1994.

Graham, Margaret B. W. *R&D for Industry: A Century of Technical Innovation at Alcoa*. Cambridge: Cambridge University Press, 1990.

Gran, Peter. *Islamic Roots of Capitalism: Egypt, 1760-1840*. Austin: University of Texas Press, 1979.

Grant, Marcus, ed. *Alcohol and Emerging Markets: Patterns, Problems, and Responses*. Philadelphia: Brunner/Mazel, 1998.

Green, Robert. "The ABC's of Privatization: A Case Study of the al-Ahram Beverage Company in Egypt." Master's thesis, University of Chicago, 2011.

Grehan, James. *Everyday Life & Consumer Culture in 18th-Century Damascus*. Seattle: University of Washington Press, 2007.

Haj, Samira. *Reconfiguring Islamic Tradition: Reform, Rationality, and Modernity*. Stanford, CA: Stanford University Press, 2009.

Hallaq, Wael B. *An Introduction to Islamic Law*. Cambridge: Cambridge University Press, 2009.

Hämeen-Anttila, Jaakko. *Maqama: A History of a Genre*. Wiesbaden: Harrassowitz, 2002.

Hamid, Raʾuf ʿAbbas. *The Large Landowning Class and the Peasantry in Egypt, 1837-1952*. Syracuse, NY: Syracuse University Press, 2011.

Hammad, Hanan. *Industrial Sexuality: Gender, Urbanization, and Social Transformation in Egypt*. Austin: University of Texas Press, 2016.

Hammud, Muhammad. *Mawsuʾat Asmaʾ al-atfal wa-Maʾaniha: Masʾuliyyat al-Ahl fi ikhtiyar Asmaʾ al-Atfal*. al-Tabʿa 1st ed. Bayrut: Dar al-Fikr al-Lubnani, 1995.

Hamouda, Sahar, and Colin Clement, eds. *Victoria College: A History Revealed*. New York: American University in Cairo Press, 2002.

Hamouda, Sahar, Yunan Labib Rizq, and Aliksandrina (Library). *Omar Toussoun: Prince of Alexandria*. Alexandria: Alexandria and Mediterranean Research Center Monographs, Bibliotheca Alexandria, 2005.

Hanioğlu, M. Şükrü. *A Brief History of the Late Ottoman Empire*. Princeton, NJ: Princeton University Press, 2008.

Hanley, Will. "Foreignness and Localness in Alexandria, 1880–1914." PhD diss., Princeton University, 2007.

———. "Grieving Cosmopolitanism in Middle East Studies." *History Compass* 6, no. 5 (2008): 1346–1367.

———. *Identifying with Nationality: Europeans, Ottomans, and Egyptians in Alexandria*. New York: Columbia University Press, 2017.

Hanna, Nelly. *Artisan Entrepreneurs in Cairo and Early-Modern Capitalism (1600–1800)*. Syracuse, NY: Syracuse University Press, 2011.

———. *In Praise of Books: A Cultural History of Cairo's Middle Class, Sixteenth to the Eighteenth Century*. Syracuse, NY: Syracuse University Press, 2003.

Hanna, Nelly, and Raʾūf ʾAbbās Ḥāmid, eds. *Society and Economy in Egypt and the Eastern Mediterranean, 1600–1900: Essays in Honor of André Raymond*. New York: American University in Cairo Press, 2005.

Haq, Syed Nomanul. *Names, Natures, and Things: The Alchemist Jābir ibn Ḥayyān and His Kitāb al-Aḥjār*. Dordrecht: Kluwer Academic, 1994.

Hård, Mikael. *Machines Are Frozen Spirit: The Scientification of Refrigeration and Brewing in the 19th Century, a Weberian Interpretation*. Boulder, CO: Westview Press, 1994.

Hård, Mikael, and Andrew Jamison. *The Intellectual Appropriation of Technology: Discourses on Modernity, 1900–1939*. Cambridge, MA: MIT Press, 1998.

Hård, Mikael, and Thomas J. Misa. *Urban Machinery: Inside Modern European Cities*. Cambridge, MA: MIT Press, 2010.

Ḥaritani, Sulayman. *Al-Mawqif min al-Khamra wa-Zahirat Intishar al-Hanat wa-Majalis al-Sharab fi al-Mujtamaʾ al-ʾArabi al-Islāmi*. al-Ṭabʾah 1st ed. Dimashq: Dar al-Hasad lil-Nashr wa-al-Tawziʾ, 1996.

Ḥasanayn, ʾIzzat. *Al-Muskirat wa-al-Mukhaddirat bayna al-Shariʾah wa-al-Qanun: Dirasa Muqarana*. al-Ṭabʾah 1st ed. Cairo: n.p., 1986.

Hathaway, Jane. *The Politics of Households in Ottoman Egypt: The Rise of the Qazdaglis*. Cambridge: Cambridge University Press, 1997.

Heap, Simon. "Before 'Star': The Import Substitution of Western-Style Alcohol in Nigeria, 1870–1970." *African Economic History* 24 (1996): 69–89.

Heath, Dwight B. *Alcohol Use and World Cultures: A Comprehensive Bibliography of Anthropological Sources*. Toronto: Addiction Research Foundation, 1981.

Heine, Peter. "Nadibh." In *Encyclopaedia of Islam*, edited by P. Bearman, Th. Bianquis, C. E. Bosworth, E. van Donzel, and W. P. Heinrichs. 2nd ed. Brill Online. University of Pennsylvania, January 20, 2014. referenceworks.brillonline.com/entries/encyclopaedia-of-islam-2/mashrubat-COM_0698.

Heyworth-Dunne, James. *An Introduction to the History of Education in Modern Egypt*. London: Luzac, 1939.

His Majesty's Agent and Consul General. *Report on the Finances, Administration, and Con-*

dition of Egypt and the Soudan, 1904. London: Harrison and Sons, His Majesty's Stationery Office, 1905.

———. Report on the Finances, Administration, and Condition of Egypt and the Soudan, 1906. London: Harrison and Sons, His Majesty's Stationery Office, 1907.

Hodgson, Marshall G. S. The Venture of Islam: Conscience and History in a World Civilization. Chicago: University of Chicago Press, 1977.

Hoexter, Miriam, Shmuel Noah Eisenstadt, and Nehemia Levtzion, eds. The Public Sphere in Muslim Societies. Albany: State University of New York Press, 2002.

Holliland, Chris. "Rice." In The Oxford Companion to Beer, edited by Garret Oliver. Oxford: Oxford University Press, 2011.

Holmsgaard, Jens Erik. "Brewing in Egypt: Bringing a 5,000-Year-Old Tradition Up to International Standards." Brygmesteren (Scandinavian Brewers' Review) 56, no. 6 (1999): 9–16.

Homan, Michael M. "Beer and Its Drinkers: An Ancient Near Eastern Love Story." Near Eastern Archaeology 67, no. 2 (2004): 84–95.

Homerin, Th. Emil. Passion before Me, My Fate Behind: Ibn Al-Farid and the Poetry of Recollection. Albany: State University of New York Press, 2011.

Hornsey, Ian S., and Royal Society of Chemistry (Great Britain). A History of Beer and Brewing. Cambridge: Royal Society of Chemistry, 2003.

Hunt, Brian. "Refrigeration." In The Oxford Companion to Beer, edited by Garrett Oliver. Oxford: Oxford University Press, 2011.

Hunter, John A. Alcohol and Life: A Manual of Scientific Temperance Teaching for Schools. London: Macmillan, 1918.

Hussein, Mahmoud. Class Conflict in Egypt, 1945–1970. New York: Monthly Review Press, 1973.

Ibn Abi al-Dunya, 'Abd Allah, ibn Muhammad. Kitab Dhamm al-Muskir. al-Tab'a 1st ed. Dimashq: Dar al-Basha'ir, 1992.

Ibn Hanbal, Ahmad, ibn Muh. Kitab al-Ashriba. al-Qahira: al-Markaz al-Salafi lil-Kitab, 1981.

Ibn Hayyan, Jabir. Names, Natures, and Things: The Alchemist Jabir Ibn Hayyan and His Kitab Al-Ahjar (Book of Stones). Edited and translated by Syed Nomanul Haq. Boston Studies in the Philosophy of Science. Boston: Kluwer Academic, 1994.

Ibn al-'Imad al-Aqfahsi, Ahmad. Ikram Man ya'ish Bi-tahrim al-Khamr wa-al-Hashish. al-Tab'a 1st ed. Tanta: Dar al-Sahabah lil-Turath, 1991.

Ibn Qutayba, 'Abd Allah, ibn Muslim. Kitab al-Ashriba: wa-Dhikr al-Ikhtilaf al-Nas fiha. al-Qahira: Maktabat Zahra' al-Sharq, 1998.

Ibn Rushd. The Distinguished Jurist's Primer. Translated by I. A. K. Nyazee. 2 vols. Reading: Garnet Press, 1994.

Ibn Sayyar al-Warraq, al-Muzaffar ibn Nasr. Annals of the Caliphs' Kitchens: Ibn Sayyar al-Warraq's Tenth-Century Baghdadi Cookbook. Edited and translated by Nawal Nasrallah, Kaj Öhrnberg, and Sahban Muruwah. Islamic History and Civilization, vol. 70. Boston: Brill, 2007.

Ibn al-Wakil, Yusuf, ibn Muh. Tuhfat al-Ahbab bi-Man Malaka Misr min al-Muluk wa-al-nuwab. Cairo: Dar al-Kitab al-Jami'i, 1998.

Ikram, Khalid. *The Egyptian Economy, 1952–2000: Performance, Policies, and Issues.* London: Routledge, 2006.

Ilbert, Robert. *Alexandrie, 1830–1930: Histoire d'Une Communauté Citadine.* 2 vols. Cairo: Institut Français d'Archéologie Orientale, 1996.

Ilbert, Robert, Ilios Yannakakis, and Jacques Hassoun, eds. *Alexandria, 1860–1960: The Brief Life of a Cosmopolitan Community.* Alexandria: Harpocrates, 1997.

International Business and Technical Consultants, Inc. (IBTCI). "Special Study for the Privatization Program in Egypt—Privatization Case Study." USAID, 1998. dec.usaid.gov.

Issawi, Charles Philip. *An Economic History of the Middle East and North Africa.* New York: Columbia University Press, 1982.

———. *Egypt at Mid-Century: An Economic Survey.* Rev. ed. London: Oxford University Press, 1954.

Jabarti, ʿAbd al-Rahman. *Napoleon in Egypt: Al-Jabartī's Chronicle of the French Occupation, 1798.* Translated by Shmuel Moreh. Expanded ed. in honor of al-Jabartī's 250th birthday. Princeton, NJ: Markus Wiener, 2004.

Jacob, Wilson Chacko. *Working Out Egypt: Effendi Masculinity and Subject Formation in Colonial Modernity, 1870–1940.* Durham, NC: Duke University Press, 2011.

Jacobs, M. G. P. A., W. H. G. Maas, and Mark Baker. *The Magic of Heineken.* Amsterdam: Heineken, 2001.

Jacquemin, Alex. *L'évolution de la concentration dans l'industrie de la brasserie et des boissons en Belgique.* Brussels: Commission des Communauteˊs européennes, 1976.

Jaḥiz. *The Life and Works of Jāḥiz.* Translated by Charles Pellat. Berkeley: University of California Press, 1969.

Jankowski, James P. *Egypt's Young Rebels: "Young Egypt," 1933–1952.* Stanford, CA: Hoover Institution Press, 1975.

Jhally, Sut. *The Codes of Advertising: Fetishism and the Political Economy of Meaning in the Consumer Society.* New York: St. Martin's Press, 1987.

Johnson, Amy J. *Reconstructing Rural Egypt: Ahmed Hussein and the History of Egyptian Development.* Syracuse, NY: Syracuse University Press, 2004.

Johnson-Davies, Denys, ed. *Arabic Short Stories.* London: Quartet Books, 1983.

Jones, Nick R. "Ale." In *The Oxford Companion to Beer,* edited by Garret Oliver. Oxford: Oxford University Press, online version, 2013.

———. "Counterpressure." In *The Oxford Companion to Beer,* edited by Garret Oliver. Oxford: Oxford University Press, 2011.

Junker, Wilhelm. *Travels in Africa during the Years 1875 . . . 1886.* London: Chapman and Hall, 1892.

Kamal, Husayn. *Arjuka Iʿtini Hadha Al-Dawa.* Aflam Nasr, 1984.

———. *Imbaraturiyyat Mim.* Murad Film, Wakalat al-Jawuni, 1972.

Kamil, Mahmud. *Baʾi al-Ahlam.* Cairo: Kitab al-Yawm, 1974.

———. *Hayat al-Zalam wa-Qisas Ukhra.* Cairo: al-Hayʾa al-Miṣriyya al-ʿAmma lil-Kitab, 1975.

———. *Sheikh Mursi Marries the Land: A Collection of Egyptian Short Stories.* Cairo: General Egyptian Book Organization, 1984.

Karanasou, Floresca. "Egyptianization, the 1947 Company Law and the Foreign Communities in Egypt." PhD diss., Oxford University, 1992.

Karl Baedeker (Firm). *Egypt: Handbook for Travellers.* 5th ed. Leipsic: K. Baedeker, 1902.

Kennedy, Philip F. *Abu Nuwas: A Genius of Poetry.* Oxford: OneWorld, 2005.

Kerr, Malcolm H. *Egypt under Nasser.* New York: Foreign Policy Association, 1963.

Kharraṭ, Idwar. *Rama and the Dragon.* Cairo: American University in Cairo Press, 2002.

Khashshab, Isma'il, ibn Sa. *Khulaṣat ma Yurad min Akhbar al-Amir Murad.* al-Qahira: al-'Arabī, 1992.

Kinnear, Elizabeth Kelsey. *She Sat Where They Sat: A Memoir of Anna Young Thompson of Egypt.* Christian World Mission Books. Grand Rapids, MI: Eerdmans, 1971.

Kissmeyer, Anders Brinch. "Cleaning in Place (CIP)." In *The Oxford Companion to Beer,* edited by Garret Oliver. Oxford: Oxford University Press, 2011.

———. "Emil Christen Hansen." In *The Oxford Companion to Beer,* edited by Garret Oliver. Oxford: Oxford University Press, 2011.

Kitroeff, Alexander. *The Greeks in Egypt, 1919–1937.* London: Ithaca Press for the Middle East Centre, St. Anthony's College, Oxford, 1989.

Köppen, Wladimir. *Die Klimate der Erde, Grundriss de Kilakunde.* Berlin: Walter de Gruyter, 1923.

Kozma, Liat. *Policing Egyptian Women: Sex, Law, and Medicine in Khedival Egypt.* Syracuse, NY: Syracuse University Press, 2011.

Krämer, Gudrun. *The Jews in Modern Egypt, 1914–1952.* Publications on the Near East, no. 4. Seattle: University of Washington Press, 1989.

Kueny, Kathryn. *The Rhetoric of Sobriety: Wine in Early Islam.* Albany: State University of New York Press, 2001.

Kunz, Diane B. *The Economic Diplomacy of the Suez Crisis.* Chapel Hill: University of North Carolina Press, 1991.

Kupferschmidt, Uri M. *Henri Naus Bey: Retrieving the Biography of a Belgian Industrialist in Egypt.* Brussels: Académie royale des sciences d'outre-mer, 1999.

Kurpershoek, P. M. *The Short Stories of Yusuf Idris: A Modern Egyptian Author.* Leiden: E. J. Brill, 1981.

Lagerkvist, Ulf. *The Enigma of Ferment: From the Philosopher's Stone to the First Biochemical Nobel Prize.* Hackensack, NJ: World Scientific, 2005.

Landau, Jacob M. *Jews in Nineteenth-Century Egypt Uniform / Yehudim be-Mitsrayim Ba-Meah Ha-Tesha'-'esreh.* New York University Studies in Near Eastern Civilization, no. 2. New York: New York University Press, 1969.

Landes, David S. *Bankers and Pashas: International Finance and Economic Imperialism in Egypt.* New York: Harper and Row, 1969.

Lane, Edward William. *An Account of the Manners and Customs of the Modern Egyptians: The Definitive 1860 Edition.* New York: American University in Cairo Press, 2003.

Lawson, Fred Haley. *The Social Origins of Egyptian Expansionism during the Muhammad 'Ali Period.* New York: Columbia University Press, 1992.

Lears, T. J. Jackson. *Fables of Abundance: A Cultural History of Advertising in America.* New York: Basic Books, 1994.

Leavitt, Mary G. C., and World's Woman's Christian Temperance Union. "Report of the …

Convention of the World's Woman's Christian Temperance Union." N.p. aspresolver
.com/aspresolver.asp?WASI;1597293; Materials specified: Alexander Street Press
aspresolver.com/aspresolver.asp?WASI;1597293.

Le Gassick, Trevor. Introduction to *I Am Free, and Other Stories*. Translated by Trevor Le
Gassick. Cairo: General Egyptian Book Organization, 1978.

Lewicka, Paulina B. "Alcohol and Its Consumption in Medieval Cairo: The Story of a
Habit." *Studia Arabistyczne i Islamistyczne* 12, no. 2004 (2006): 55–97.

———. *Food and Foodways of Medieval Cairenes: Aspects of Life in an Islamic Metropolis of
the Eastern Mediterranean*. Leiden: Brill, 2011.

———. "Restaurants, Inns and Taverns That Never Were: Some Reflections on Public
Consumption in Medieval Cairo." *Journal of the Economic and Social History of the Orient* 48, no. 1 (2005): 40–91.

Lindell, Wolfgang David. "Spent Grain." In *The Oxford Companion to Beer*, edited by Garret
Oliver. Oxford: Oxford University Press, 2011.

Lockman, Zachary. *Contending Visions of the Middle East: The History and Politics of Orien-
talism*. 2nd ed. Cambridge: Cambridge University Press, 2010.

———. "Imagining the Working Class: Culture, Nationalism, and Class Formation in
Egypt, 1899–1914." *Poetics Today* 15, no. 2 (1994): 157–190.

Loomba, Ania. *Colonialism/Postcolonialism*. 2nd ed. London: Routledge, 2005.

Louis, J. C. *The Cola Wars*. New York: Everest House, 1980.

Lucas, A., and J. R. Harris. *Ancient Egyptian Materials and Industries*. 4th ed. London: Histories & Mysteries of Man, 1989.

Mabro, Robert, and Samir Radwan. *The Industrialization of Egypt, 1939–1973: Policy and Performance*. Oxford: Clarendon Press, 1976.

Mahfuz, Najib. *Palace of Desire: The Cairo Trilogy*. Vol. 2. New York: Doubleday, 1991.

———. *Sugar Street*. 1st American ed. New York: Doubleday, 1992.

Mahmood, Saba. *The Politics of Piety: The Islamic Revival and the Feminist Subject*. Princeton, NJ: Princeton University Press, 2005.

Mahmoud, Abd al-Halim. "Islam wa Tanzim al-Mujtamaʾ." *al-Azhar* 4 (1976): 403–413.

Makkawi, Saʿd. *Al-Qamar al-Mashwi: Shahira wa-Qisas Ukhra*. Cairo: al-Hayʾa al-Misriyya
al-ʿAmma lil-Kitab, 1990.

Mappen, Marc. *Prohibition Gangsters: The Rise and Fall of a Bad Generation*. New Bruns-
wick, NJ: Rutgers University Press, 2013.

Marsafi, Husayn. *Al-Wasila al-Adabiyya ila al-ʿUlum al-ʿArabiyya*. al-Qahira: al-Hayʾa al-
Misriyya al-ʿAmma lil-Kitab, 1981.

Masters, Bruce Alan. *The Origins of Western Economic Dominance in the Middle East: Mer-
cantilism and the Islamic Economy in Aleppo, 1600–1750*. New York: New York University
Press, 1988.

Matthee, Rudolph P. "Alcohol in the Islamic Middle East: Ambivalence and Ambiguity."
*Past & Present* (2014): 100–125.

———. *The Politics of Trade in Safavid Iran: Silk for Silver, 1600–1730*. New York: Cambridge University Press, 1999.

———. *The Pursuit of Pleasure: Drugs and Stimulants in Iranian History, 1500–1900*. Princeton, NJ: Princeton University Press, 2005.

McPherson, J. W. *The Moulids of Egypt: Egyptian Saints-Days*. Cairo: N. M. Press, 1941.

Messiri, Sawsan. *Ibn al-Balad: A Concept of Egyptian Identity*. Leiden: Brill, 1978.

Miller, Ruth Austin. *Legislating Authority: Sin and Crime in the Ottoman Empire and Turkey*. New York: Routledge, 2005.

Mintz, Sidney Wilfred. *Sweetness and Power: The Place of Sugar in Modern History*. New York: Penguin Books, 1986.

Mitchell, Timothy. *Colonising Egypt*. Cambridge Middle East Library 17. New York: Cambridge University Press, 1988.

———. *Rule of Experts: Egypt, Techno-politics, Modernity*. Berkeley: University of California Press, 2002.

Mitchell, W. J. T. *Iconology: Image, Text, Ideology*. Chicago: University of Chicago Press, 1986.

Moffitt, Louisa Bond. "Anna Young Thompson: American Missionary, Cultural Ambassador, and Reluctant Feminist in Egypt, 1872–1932." PhD diss., Georgia State University, 2003.

Morcos, Sabry R., S. M. Hegazi, and Soraya T. El-Damhougy. "Fermented Foods in Common Use in Egypt: I. The Nutritive Value of Kishk." *Journal of the Science of Food and Agriculture* 24, no. 10 (1973): 1153–1156.

———. "Fermented Foods of Common Use in Egypt: II. The Chemical Composition of Bouza and Its Ingredients." *Journal of the Science of Food and Agriculture* 24, no. 10 (1973): 1157–1161.

Mortera, G. L., Firm, Brokers. *Handbook of Egyptian Securities*. Alexandria: Mortera, G. L. Firm, Brokers, 1900s–.

Mubarak, ʿAli. *Al-Khitat al-Tawfiqiyya 1*. al-Qahira: n.p., 2007.

———. *Al-Khitat al-Tawfiqiyya 2*. al-Qahira: n.p., 2007.

———. *Al-Khitat al-Tawfiqiyya 3*. al-Qahira: n.p., 2007.

———. *Al-Khitat al-Tawfiqiyya 4*. al-Qahira: n.p., 2007.

———. *Al-Khitat al-Tawfiqiyya 5*. al-Qahira: n.p., 2007.

———. *Al-Khitat al-Tawfiqiyya 6*. al-Qahira: n.p., 2007.

Muhammad, ʿAbd al-Wahhab Bakr. *Mujtamaʿ al-Qahira al-Sirri (1900–1951)*. al-Tabʿa 1st ed. al-Qahira: al-ʿArabi lil-Nashr wa-al-Tawziʿ, 2001.

———. *Al-Wujud al-Biritani fi al-Jaysh al-Misri, 1936–1947*. al-Qahira: Dar al-Maʿarif, 1982.

Muhammad, Muhsin. *Al-Shaytan: Tarikh Misr bi-al-Wathaʾiq al-Sirriyya al-Biritaniyya wa-al-Amrikiya*. al-Qahira: Dar al-Maʿarif, 1982.

Mutawalli, Ahmad Fuʾad. *Al-Alfaz al-Turkiyya fi al-Lahajat al-ʿArabiyya wa fi Lughyat al-kitabay*. al-Qahira: Dar al-Zahraʾ lil-Nashr, 1991.

Muwaylihi, Muhammad. *Hadith ʿIsa Ibn Hisham*. al-Qahira: al-Dar al-Qawmiyya lil-Tibʿa wa-al-Nashr, 1964.

Myntti, C. *Paris along the Nile: Architecture in Cairo from the Belle Epoque*. Cairo: American University in Cairo Press, 1999.

Nabarawi, Muhammad Sami. *Ahkam Tashriʿat al-Hudud: Al-Zina, al-Qadhf, al-Khamr*. Cairo: Maktabat Gharib, 1976.

Nadim, ʿAbd Allah. *Kana—wa-Yakun*. Cairo: al-Hayʾa al-ʿAmma li-Dar al-Kutub wa-al-Wathaʾiq al-Qawmiyya, Markaz Wathaʾiq wa-Tarikh Misr al-Muʿasir, 1995.

————. *Al-Tankit wa-al-Tabkit*. Cairo: al-Hay'a al-Misriyya al-ʿAmma lil-Kitab, Markaz Watha'iq wa-Tarikh Misr al-Muʿasir, 1994.

Nashat, Mustafa. *Jawanib min Tarikh al-Mashrubat al-Muskira bi-al-Maghrib al-Wasit*. al-Rabat: al-Zaman, 2006.

Nickel, Jeffery S. "Filtration." In *The Oxford Companion to Beer*, edited by Garret Oliver. Oxford: Oxford University Press, 2011.

Nieuwkerk, Karin van. *"A Trade Like Any Other": Female Singers and Dancers in Egypt*. Austin: University of Texas Press, 1995.

Norton, Marcy. *Sacred Gifts, Profane Pleasures: A History of Tobacco and Chocolate in the Atlantic World*. Ithaca, NY: Cornell University Press, 2008.

Oliver, Garret. "Kettle." In *The Oxford Companion to Beer*, edited by Garret Oliver. Oxford: Oxford University Press, 2011.

Owen, Edward Roger John. *Cotton and the Egyptian Economy, 1820–1914: A Study in Trade and Development*. Oxford: Clarendon Press, 1969.

————. "From Liberalism to Liberal Imperialism: Lord Cromer and the First Wave of Globalization in Egypt." In *Histories of the Modern Middle East: New Directions*, edited by I. Gershoni, Hakan Erdem, and Ursula Wokock, 95–112. Boulder, CO: Lynne Rienner, 2002.

————. *A History of Middle East Economies in the Twentieth Century*. Cambridge, MA: Harvard University Press, 1998.

————. *The Middle East in the World Economy, 1800–1914*. New York: Methuen, 1981.

Pallme, Ignatius. *Travels in Kordofan: Embracing a Description of That Province of Egypt, and of Some of the Bordering Countries, with a Review of the Present State of the Commerce in Those Countries, of the Habits and Customs of the Inhabitants, and Also an Account of the Slave Hunts Taking Place under the Government of Mehemed Ali*. London: J. Madden, 1844.

Pamuk, Sevket. *A Monetary History of the Ottoman Empire*. Cambridge: Cambridge University Press, 2000.

Papasian, Ed. *L'Égypte économique et financiere. Etudes financieres, 1924–1925*. 2nd ed. Cairo: Misr, 1926.

Peterson, Mark Allen. *Connected in Cairo: Growing Up Cosmopolitan in the Modern Middle East*. Bloomington: Indiana University Press, 2011.

Philipp, Thomas. *The Syrians in Egypt, 1725–1975*. Wiesbaden: F. Steiner, 1985.

Phillips, Charles John. *Glass: The Miracle Maker: Its History, Technology and Applications*. New York: Pitman, 1941.

Phillips, Phoebe, ed. *The Encyclopedia of Glass*. New York: Crown, 1981.

Philliskirk, George. "Pasteurization." In *Oxford Companion to Beer*, edited by Garret Oliver. Oxford: Oxford University Press, online version, 2013.

Pococke, Richard. *A Description of the East and Some Other Countries*. London: printed for the author, 1743.

Podeh, Elie. *The Decline of Arab Unity: The Rise and Fall of the United Arab Republic*. Portland, OR: Sussex Academic Press, 1999.

Podeh, Elie, and Onn Winckler, eds. *Rethinking Nasserism: Revolution and Historical Memory in Modern Egypt*. Gainesville: University Press of Florida, 2004.

Poffandi, Stefano G. *Indicateur égyptien administratif et commercial*. Alexandria: Imprimerie Générale, 1902.

———. *Indicateur égyptien administratif et commercial*. Alexandria: Imprimerie Générale, 1904.

Politis, Athanasios G. *L'hellenisme et l'Égypte moderne*. Paris: F. Alcan, 1929.

Priest, Fergus G. "Acectic Acid Bacteria." In *The Oxford Companion to Beer*, edited by Garret Oliver. Oxford: Oxford University Press, 2011.

*Proceedings of the International Conference on Egypt during the Ottoman Era, 26–30 November 2007, Cairo*. Istanbul: Research Centre for Islamic History, Art, and Culture, 2010.

Qasim, ʿAwn al-Sharif. *Qamus al-Lahja Al-ʿammiyya fi al-Sudan*. al-Tabʿa 2nd ed. al-Qahira: al-Maktab al-Misri al-Hadith, 1985.

Quataert, Donald, ed. *Consumption Studies and the History of the Ottoman Empire, 1550–1922: An Introduction*. Albany: State University of New York Press, 2000.

Rafeq, Abdul-Karim. "The Socioeconomic and Political Implications of the Introduction of Coffee into Syria: 16th–18th Centuries." In *Le commerce du café avant l'ère des plantations coloniales: Espaces, réseaux, Sociétés (XVe–XIXe ciècle)*, edited by M. Tuchscherer, 127–142. Cairo: Institut Français d'Archéologie Orientale, 2001.

Ramzi, Ibrahim. *Masrah Ibrahim Ramzi*. al-Qahira: Dar al-Hilal, 1982.

Raqiq al-Qayrawani, Ibrahim, ibn al, ed. *Qutb al-Surur fi Awsaf al-Khumur*. Edited by Ahmad Jund. Damascus: al-Muqaddima, 1969.

Raymond, André. *Artisans et commerçants au Caire au XVIIIe siècle*. Damas: Institut français de Damas, 1973.

Rayyan, Ahmad ʿAli Taha. *Al-Muskirat: Atharuha wa-ʿIlajuha fi al-Shariʿa al-Islamiyya*. al-Qahira: Dar al-Iʿtisam, 1984.

Redding, Sean. "Beer Brewing in Umtata: Women, Migrant Labor, and Social Control in a Rural Town." In *Liquor and Labor in Southern Africa*, edited by Jonathan Crush, and Charles Ambler, 235–252. Athens: Ohio University Press / Pietermaritzburg, S. Africa: University of Natal Press, 1992.

Reeves-Ellington, Barbara, Kathryn Kish Sklar, and Connie Anne Shemo, eds. *Competing Kingdoms: Women, Mission, Nation, and the American Protestant Empire, 1812–1960*. Durham, NC: Duke University Press, 2010.

Reid, Donald M. *Cairo University and the Making of a Modern Egypt*. New York: Cambridge University Press, 1990.

———. "Nationalizing the Pharaonic Past: Egyptology, Imperialism, and Egyptian Nationalism, 1922–1952." In *Rethinking Nationalism in the Arab Middle East*, edited by James Jankowski and Israel Gershoni, 127–150. New York: Columbia University Press, 1997.

———. *Whose Pharaohs? Archaeology, Museums, and Egyptian National Identity from Napoleon to World War I*. Berkeley: University of California Press, 2002.

Reimer, Michael J. *Colonial Bridgehead: Government and Society in Alexandria, 1807–1882*. Boulder, CO: Westview Press, 1997.

———. "Colonial Bridgehead: Social and Spatial Change in Alexandria, 1850–1882." *International Journal of Middle East Studies* 20, no. 4 (1988): 531–553.

Reynolds, Nancy Y. *A City Consumed: Urban Commerce, the Cairo Fire, and the Politics of Decolonization in Egypt*. Stanford, CA: Stanford University Press, 2012.

———. "Commodity Communities: Interweavings of Market Cultures, Consumption Practices, and Social Power in Egypt, 1907–1961." PhD diss, Stanford University, 2003.

———. "National Socks and the 'Nylon Woman': Materiality, Gender, and Nationalism in Textile Marketing in Semicolonial Egypt, 1930–56." *International Journal of Middle East Studies* 43, no. 1 (2011): 49–74.

Richards, Alan. *A Political Economy of the Middle East*. 2nd ed. Boulder, CO: Westview Press, 1996.

Richmond, Lesley, and Alison Turton, eds. *The Brewing Industry: A Guide to Historical Records*. Manchester: Manchester University Press, distributed by St. Martin's Press, 1990.

Rock-Singer, Aaron. "A Pious Public: Islamic Magazines and Revival in Egypt, 1976–1981." *British Journal of Middle Eastern Studies* 4, no. 42 (2015): 427–446.

———. "Prayer and the Islamic Revival: A Timely Challenge." *International Journal of Middle East Studies* 48, no. 2 (2016): 293–312.

———. "The Salafi Mystique: The Rise of Gender Segregation in 1970s Egypt." *Islamic Law and Society* 3, no. 23 (2016): 279–305.

———. "Scholarly Authority and Lay Mobilization: Yusuf Al-Qaradawi's Vision of Da'wa, 1976–1984." *Muslim World*, 3, no. 106 (2016): 588–604.

Ruska, Julius. "Alkohol und Al-kohl: Zur Geschichte der Entdeckung und des Namens." In *Chemistry and Alchemy: Texts and Studies*, vol. 8, *Studies Collected and Reprinted by Fuat Sezgin, in Collaboration with Carl Ehrig-Eggert, Eckhard Neubauer, Farid Benfeghoul*, 203–217. Frankfurt: Institute for the History of Arabic-Islamic Science at the Johann Wolfgang Goethe University, 2002. search.proquest.com.proxy.brynmawr.edu/index islamicus/docview/43513117/B0FCC8D38C634B95PQ/2.

Russell, Mona L. *Creating the New Egyptian Woman: Consumerism, Education, and National Identity, 1863–1922*. New York: Palgrave Macmillan, 2004.

Russell, Thomas Wentworth, Sir. *Egyptian Service, 1902–1946*. London: Murray, 1949.

Ryad, Omar. *Islamic Reformism and Christianity: A Critical Reading of the Works of Muḥammad Rashīd Riḍā and His Associates (1898–1935)*. Boston: Brill, 2009.

Rykaer, Dorte Holm, and Jens Erik Holmsgaard. "Danbrew in Egypt: Al-Ahram Beverages Co.- El-Obour Brewery in Cairo." *Brygmesteren (Scandinavian Brewers' Review)* 58, no. 2 (2001): 31–57.

Ryzova, Lucie. *The Age of the Efendiyya: Passages to Modernity in National-Colonial Egypt*. Oxford: Oxford University Press, 2014.

———. "Egyptianizing Modernity through the 'New *Effendiya*': Social and Cultural Constructions of the Middle Class in Egypt under the Monarchy." In *Re-envisioning Egypt, 1919–1952*, edited by Arthur Goldschmidt, Barak Salmoni, and Amy J. Johnson, 124–163. New York: American University in Cairo Press, 2005.

Sadan, Joseph. "Mashrubat." In *Encyclopaedia of Islam*, edited by P. Bearman, Th. Bianquis, C. E. Bosworth, E. van Donzel, and W. P. Heinrichs. 2nd ed. Brill Online. University of Pennsylvania, July 1, 2017. referenceworks.brillonline.com/entries/encyclopaedia-of-islam-2/mashrubat-COM_0698.

Sadeque, Syedah Fatima ed. *Baybars I of Egypt*. New York: AMS Press, 1980.

Sadoul, Georges. *Louis Lumière, 1904–1967*. Paris: Seghers, 1964.

Sadowski, Yahya M. *Political Vegetables? Businessman and Bureaucrat in the Development of Egyptian Agriculture*. Washington, DC: Brookings Institution, 1991.

Salih, al-Tayyib. *ʾUrs al-Zayn: Riwaya*. Bayrut: Dar al-ʾAwda, 1986.

Sanhuri, Muhammad Ahmad Faraj. *Muskirat*. al-Qahira: Dar al-Nahda al-ʿArabiyya, 1978.

Sannuʾ, Yaʿqub, ibn Raʾ. *Al-Luʿbat al-Tiyatriyya*. Cairo: al-Hayʾa al-Misriyya al-ʿAmma lil-Kitab, 1987.

Sarhan, Jamal. *Al-Musamara wa-al-Munadama ʾinda al-ʾArab hatta al-Qarn al-Rabiʾ al-Hijri*. al-Tabʾa 1 ed. Bayrut: Dar al-Wahda, 1981.

al-Sayyid-Marsot, Afaf Lutfi. *Egypt's Liberal Experiment, 1922–1936*. Berkeley: University of California Press, 1977.

Schoeler, Gregor. "Kita." In *Encyclopaedia of Islam*, edited by P. Bearman, Th. Bianquis, C. E. Bosworth, E. van Donzel, and W. P. Heinrichs. 2nd ed. Brill Online. University of Pennsylvania, January 2, 2014. referenceworks.brillonline.com/entries/encyclo paedia-of-islam-2/mashrubat-COM_0698.

Schweinfurth, Georg August. *The Heart of Africa: Three Years' Travels and Adventures in the Unexplored Regions of Central Africa, from 1868 to 1871*. New York: Harper, 1874.

Scoville, Warren Candler. *Revolution in Glassmaking; Entrepreneurship and Technological Change in the American Industry, 1880–1920*. Cambridge, MA: Harvard University Press, 1948.

Sedra, Paul. "Modernity's Mission: Evangelical Efforts to Discipline the Nineteenth-Century Coptic Community." In *Altruism and Imperialism: Western Cultural and Religious Missions in the Middle East*, edited by Reeva S. Simon and Eleanor Harvey Tejirian, 208–236. Occasional papers, no. 4. New York: Middle East Institute, Columbia University, 2002.

Segrave, Kerry. *Product Placement in Hollywood Films: A History*. Jefferson, NC: McFarland, 2004.

Seidl, Conrad, and Horst Dornbusch. "Märzenbier." In *The Oxford Companion to Beer*, edited by Garret Oliver. Oxford: Oxford University Press, 2011.

Seikaly, Sherene. *Men of Capital: Scarcity and Economy in Mandate Palestine*. Stanford, CA: Stanford University, 2016.

Selous, George H. *Report on Economic and Commercial Conditions in Egypt*. London: His Majesty's Stationery Office, 1935.

Semah, David. *Four Egyptian Literary Critics*. Leiden: Brill, 1974.

Shafik, Viola. *Popular Egyptian Cinema: Gender, Class, and Nation*. New York: American University in Cairo Press, 2007.

Shamir, Shimon, ed. *The Jews of Egypt: A Mediterranean Society in Modern Times*. Boulder, CO: Westview Press, 1987.

Sharkey, Heather J. *American Evangelicals in Egypt: Missionary Encounters in an Age of Empire*. Princeton, NJ: Princeton University Press, 2008.

———. "Domestic Slavery in the Nineteenth- and Early Twentieth-Century Northern Sudan." Master's thesis, University of Durham, 1992.

———. *Living with Colonialism: Nationalism and Culture in the Anglo-Egyptian Sudan.* Berkeley: University of California Press, 2003.

Sharubim, Mikhaʾil. *Al-Kafi fi Tarikh Misr al-Qadim wa-al-Hadith. al-Juzʾ 5.* al-Qahira: Matbaʿat Dar al-Kutub al-Misriyya bi-al-Qahira, 1998.

Shaw, Stanford J. *The Financial and Administrative Organization and Development of Ottoman Egypt, 1517-1798.* Princeton, NJ: Princeton University Press, 1962.

Shechter, Relli. "The Cultural Economy of Development in Egypt: Economic Nationalism, Hidden Economy and the Emergence of Mass Consumer Society during Sadat's Infitah." *Middle Eastern Studies* 44, no. 4 (2008): 571–583.

———. "From Effendi to Infitāḥī? Consumerism and Its Malcontents in the Emergence of Egyptian Market Society." *British Journal of Middle Eastern Studies* 36, no. 1 (2009): 21–35.

———. "Glocal Conservatism: How Marketing Articulated a Neotraditional Saudi Arabian Society during the First Oil Boom, c. 1974–1984." *Journal of Macromarketing* 31, no. 4 (2011): 376–386.

———. "Press Advertising in Egypt: Business Realities and Local Meaning, 1882–1956." *Arab Studies Journal* 10–11, nos. 1–2 (2002–2003): 44–66.

———. "Reading Advertisements in a Colonial/Development Context: Cigarette Advertising and Identity Politics in Egypt, c. 1919–1939." *Journal of Social History* 39, no. 2 (2005): 483–503.

———. *Smoking, Culture and Economy in the Middle East: The Egyptian Tobacco Market, 1850–2000.* New York: I. B. Tauris, 2006.

———, ed. *Transitions in Domestic Consumption and Family Life in the Modern Middle East: Houses in Motion.* New York: Palgrave Macmillan, 2003.

Shirbini, Yusuf, ibn Muh. *Yusuf al-Shirbini's Kitab Hazz al-Quhūf bi-Sharh Qasid Abi Shaduf = Brains Confounded by the Ode of Abu Shaduf Expounded.* Leuven, Belgium: Peeters, 2005.

Sikainga, Ahmad Alawad. "Slavery and Social Life in Turco-Egyptian Khartoum." In *Race and Slavery in the Middle East: Histories of Trans-Saharan Africans in Nineteenth-Century Egypt, Sudan, and the Ottoman Mediterranean*, edited by Kenneth Cuno and Terence Walz, 147–170. Cairo: American University in Cairo Press, 2010.

Singerman, Diane. *Avenues of Participation: Family, Politics, and Networks in Urban Quarters of Cairo.* Princeton, NJ: Princeton University Press, 1995.

Singerman, Diane, and Paul Amar, eds. *Cairo Cosmopolitan: Politics, Culture, and Urban Space in the Globalized Middle East.* New York: American University in Cairo Press, 2006.

Sipkov, Ivan. "Postwar Nationalizations and Alien Property in Bulgaria." *American Journal of International Law* 52, no. 3 (1958): 469–494.

Skovgaard-Petersen, Jakob. *Defining Islam for the Egyptian State: Muftis and Fatwas of the Dar al-Ifta.* New York: Brill, 1997.

Sladen, Douglas Brooke Wheelton. *Oriental Cairo: The City of the "Arabian Nights."* Philadelphia: Lippincott, 1911.

Smith, Harvey Henry. *Area Handbook for the United Arab Republic (Egypt).* Washington, DC: US Government Printing Office, 1970.

Smith, Kevin. "Six-Rowed Malt." In *The Oxford Companion to Beer*, edited by Garret Oliver. Oxford: Oxford University Press, 2011.

Smith, Norman. *Intoxicating Manchuria: Alcohol, Opium, and Culture in China's Northeast.* Vancouver: UBC Press, 2012.

Sonbol, Amira El Azhary. *The New Mamluks: Egyptian Society and Modern Feudalism.* Syracuse, NY: Syracuse University Press, 2000.

Starr, Deborah A. "Drinking, Gambling, and Making Merry: Waguih Ghali's Search for Cosmopolitan Agency." *Middle Eastern Literatures* 9, no. 3 (2006): 271–285.

Starrett, Gregory. "The Political Economy of Religious Commodities in Cairo." *American Anthropologist* 97, no. 1 (1995): 51–68.

———. *Putting Islam to Work: Education, Politics, and Religious Transformation in Egypt.* Berkeley: University of California Press, 1998.

Sutton, Denise H. *Globalizing Ideal Beauty: How Female Copywriters of the J. Walter Thompson Advertising Agency Redefined Beauty for the Twentieth Century.* New York: Palgrave Macmillan, 2009.

Swinnen, Johan F. M., ed. *The Economics of Beer.* New York: Oxford University Press, 2011.

Tahtawi, Rifaʿ Rafiʿ. *An Imam in Paris: Account of a Stay in France by an Egyptian Cleric (1826–1831) = (Takhlis al-Ibriz fi Talkhis Bariz aw al-Diwan al-Nafis bi-Iwan Baris).* Translated by Daniel Newman. London: Saqi, 2004.

Tawila, ʿAbd al-Wahhāb. *Fiqh al-Ashriba wa-Hadduha, aw, Hukm al-Islam fi al-Muskirat wa-al-Mukhaddirat wa-al-Tadkhin wa-Turuq muʾalajatiha.* al-Qahira: Dar al-Salam, 1986.

Taymur, Mahmud. *Firʿawn al-Saghir.* al-Qahira: Dar al-Qalam, 1963.

———. *Al-Hajj Shalabi.* Cairo: Ettimad Press, 1930–1939.

———. *Ihsan lillah—, wa-Qisas Ukhra.* Cairo: Maktabat al-Adab, 1983.

Taymur, Muhammad. *Muʾallafat Muhammad Taymur.* al-Qahira: al-Hayʾa al-Misriyya al-ʿAmma lil-Taʾlif wa-al-Nashr, 1971.

Tezcan, Baki, and Karl K. Barbir, eds. *Identity and Identity Formation in the Ottoman World: A Volume of Essays in Honor of Norman Itzkowitz.* Madison: Center for Turkish Studies, University of Wisconsin Press, 2007.

Thomas, Keith. "Hydrometer." In *The Oxford Companion to Beer*, edited by Garret Oliver. Oxford: Oxford University Press, 2011.

———. "Non-alcoholic 'Beer.'" In *The Oxford Companion to Beer*, edited by Garret Oliver. Oxford: Oxford University Press, 2011.

———. "Two-Row Malt." In *The Oxford Companion to Beer*, edited by Garret Oliver. Oxford: Oxford University Press, 2011.

Tignor, Robert L. *Capitalism and Nationalism at the End of Empire: State and Business in Decolonizing Egypt, Nigeria, and Kenya, 1945–1963.* Princeton, NJ: Princeton University Press, 1998.

———. *The Colonial Transformation of Kenya: The Kamba, Kikuyu, and Maasai from 1900 to 1939.* Princeton, NJ: Princeton University Press, 1976.

———. "The Economic Activities of Foreigners in Egypt, 1920–1950: From Millet to Haute Bourgeoisie." *Comparative Studies in Society and History* 22, no. 3 (1980): 416–449.

———. *Egyptian Textiles and British Capital, 1930–1956.* Cairo: American University in Cairo Press, 1989.

————. *Modernization and British Colonial Rule in Egypt, 1882–1914.* Princeton, NJ: Princeton University Press, 1966.

————. *State, Private Enterprise, and Economic Change in Egypt, 1918–1952.* Princeton, NJ: Princeton University Press, 1984.

Tignor, Robert L., and Gouda Abdel-Kahlek, eds. *The Political Economy of Income Distribution in Egypt.* New York: Holmes and Meier, 1982.

Toledano, Ehud R. *State and Society in Mid-Nineteenth-Century Egypt.* New York: Cambridge University Press, 1990.

Troutt Powell, Eve. *A Different Shade of Colonialism: Egypt, Great Britain, and the Mastery of the Sudan.* Berkeley: University of California Press, 2003.

Tuchscherer, Michel. "Les cafès dans l'Égypte Ottomane (XVIe–XVIIIe siècles)." In *Cafès d'Orient revisités,* edited by Hélène Desmet-Grégoire and François Georgeon. Paris: CNRS, 1997.

Tucker, Judith E. *Women in Nineteenth-Century Egypt.* New York: Cambridge University Press, 1985.

Tunisi, Muhammad Ibn 'Omar, and Halil Mahmud 'Asakir. *Tashid al-Adhan bi-Sirat Bilad al-'Arab wa-as-Sudan.* al-Qahira: al-Mu'assasa al-Misriyya al-'Amma, 1965.

Tyrrell, Ian R. *Woman's World/Woman's Empire: The Woman's Christian Temperance Union in International Perspective, 1800–1930.* Chapel Hill: University of North Carolina Press, 1991.

'Ukkaz, Fikri Ahmad. *Khamr fi al-Fiqh al-Islami.* al-Qahira: al-Mukhtar al-Islami, 1977.

'Umar, Muhammad, and Majdi 'Abd al-Hafiz. *Kitab Hadir al-Misriyyin aw Sirr Ta'akhkhurihim.* Edited by Majdi 'Abd al-Hafiz. Cairo: al-Maktab al-Misri, 1998.

Unger, Richard W. *A History of Brewing in Holland, 900–1900: Economy, Technology, and the State.* Boston: Brill, 2001.

Unrau, William E. *White Man's Wicked Water: The Alcohol Trade and Prohibition in Indian Country, 1802–1892.* Lawrence: University Press of Kansas, 1996.

Vitalis, Robert. *America's Kingdom: Mythmaking on the Saudi Oil Frontier.* Stanford, CA: Stanford University Press, 2007.

————. "On the Theory and Practice of Compradors: The Role of 'Abbud Pasha in the Egyptian Political Economy." *International Journal of Middle East Studies* 22, no. 3 (1990): 291–315.

————. *When Capitalists Collide: Business Conflict and the End of Empire in Egypt.* Berkeley: University of California Press, 1995.

Wakin, Edward. *A Lonely Minority: The Modern Story of Egypt's Copts.* New York: Morrow, 1963.

Walz, Terence. "Sudanese, Habasha, Takarna, and Barabira: Trans-Saharan Africans in Cairo as Shown in the 1848 Census." In *Race and Slavery in the Middle East: Histories of Trans-Saharan Africans in Nineteenth-Century Egypt, Sudan, and the Ottoman Mediterranean,* edited by Kenneth Cuno and Terence Walz, 43–77. Cairo: American University in Cairo Press, 2010.

Walz, Terence, and Kenneth Cuno. "Introduction: The Study of Slavery in Nineteenth-Century Egypt, Sudan and the Ottoman Mediterranean." In *Race and Slavery in the Middle East: Histories of Trans-Saharan Africans in Nineteenth-Century Egypt, Sudan, and the Ottoman Mediterranean*, edited by Kenneth Cuno and Terence Walz, 147–170. Cairo: American University in Cairo Press, 2010.

Watenpaugh, Keith David. *Being Modern in the Middle East: Revolution, Nationalism, Colonialism, and the Arab Middle Class*. Princeton, NJ: Princeton University Press, 2006.

Waterbury, John. *The Egypt of Nasser and Sadat: The Political Economy of Two Regimes*. Princeton Studies on the Near East. Princeton, NJ: Princeton University Press, 1983.

Weir, Ronald B. *The History of the Distillers Company, 1877–1939: Diversification and Growth in Whiskey and Chemicals*. New York: Clarendon Press / Oxford University Press, 1995.

Wendell, Charles. *The Evolution of the Egyptian National Image from Its Origins to Aḥmad Luṭfi Al-Sayyid*. Berkeley: University of California Press, 1972.

Wensinck, Arent J., and Joseph Sadan. "Khamr." In *Encyclopaedia of Islam*, edited by P. Bearman, Th. Bianquis, C. E. Bosworth, E. van Donzel, and W. P. Heinrichs. 2nd ed. Brill Online. University of Pennsylvania, January 12, 2014. referenceworks.brill online.com/entries/encyclopaedia-of-islam-2/mashrubat-COM_0698.

West, Colin J. "Saladin Box." In *The Oxford Companion to Beer*, edited by Garret Oliver. Oxford: Oxford University Press, 2011.

Wickham, Carrie Rosefsky. *Mobilizing Islam: Religion, Activism, and Political Change in Egypt*. New York: Columbia University Press, 2002.

Williams, Brian Glyn. *The Crimean Tatars: The Diaspora Experience and the Forging of a Nation*. Brill's Inner Asian Library, vol. 2. Boston: Brill, 2001.

Williamson, Judith. *Decoding Advertisements: Ideology and Meaning in Advertising*. London: Boyars, 1978.

Willis, Justin. *Potent Brews: A Social History of Alcohol in East Africa, 1850–1999*. London: British Institute in Eastern Africa in association with James Currey/Athens: Ohio University Press, 2002.

Wilson, R. G., and T. R. Gourvish. *The Dynamics of the Modern Brewing Industry since 1800*. London: Routledge, 1998.

World League against Alcoholism. *Report of the Activities of the World League against Alcoholism, 1919–1927*. Westerville, OH: WLAA, 1927.

Zaalouk, Malak. *Power, Class, and Foreign Capital in Egypt: The Rise of the New Bourgeoisie*. Atlantic Highlands, NJ: Zed Books, 1989.

Zahran, Faraj. *Al-Muskirat, Adraruha wa-Ahkamuha: Dirasa muqarana fi al-Shariʿah al-Islamiyya*. Cairo: Dar Misr lil-Tibaʿah, 1983.

Zarinebaf, Fariba. *Crime and Punishment in Istanbul, 1700–1800*. Berkeley: University of California Press, 2010.

# INDEX

Note: Page numbers in *italics* indicate photographs and illustrations.